AGING IN EARLY INDUSTRIAL SOCIETY

Work, Family, and Social Policy
in Nineteenth-Century England

STUDIES IN SOCIAL DISCONTINUITY

Under the Consulting Editorship of:

CHARLES TILLY
University of Michigan

EDWARD SHORTER
University of Toronto

The list of titles in this series continues on the last page of this volume

AGING IN EARLY INDUSTRIAL SOCIETY

Work, Family, and Social Policy
in Nineteenth-Century England

Jill S. Quadagno

Department of Sociology
University of Kansas
Lawrence, Kansas

ACADEMIC PRESS
A Subsidiary of Harcourt Brace Jovanovich, Publishers
New York   London
Paris   San Diego   San Francisco   São Paulo   Sydney   Tokyo   Toronto

ACADEMIC PRESS, INC.
111 Fifth Avenue, New York, New York 10003

United Kingdom Edition published by
ACADEMIC PRESS, INC. (LONDON) LTD.
24/28 Oval Road, London NW1   7DX

Library of Congress Cataloging in Publication Data

Quadagno, Jill S.
    Aging in early industrial society.

    (Studies in social discontinuity)
    Includes index.
    1. Aged--Great Britain--Social conditions--19th
century. 2. Aged--Great Britain--Family relationships.
3. Aged--Government policy--Great Britain. 4. Rural
poor--Great Britain--History--19th century. 5. Rural
aged--Great Britain--History--19th century. I. Title.
II. Series.
HQ1064.G7Q33 1982   305.2'6'0942   82-11621
ISBN 0-12-569450-4

PRINTED IN THE UNITED STATES OF AMERICA

82 83 84 85   9 8 7 6 5 4 3 2 1

To David

Contents

Contents

———— 3 ————
Household and Kin

———— 4 ————
Poor Law Policy and Old Age Pauperism

———— 5 ————
The Impact of Government Growth

———— 6 ————
Work and Retirement

Contents

7

The Degradation of Age

8

Lessons from the Past

Preface

One of the major theoretical issues in the study of aging concerns the impact of industrialization or modernization on the status of the aged. According to the model initially proposed by Ernest Burgess in *Aging in Western Society,* many of the changes that accompanied the transition from an agricultural to an industrial economy contributed in one way or another to a decline in the function and status of the aged. A variety of recent studies by sociologists and historians have pursued this theme, examining precisely how social change has affected life for older people. In this book, the issue of the impact of social change on the aged is explored through an analysis of historical records from nineteenth-century England.

One aspect of industrialization that has been extensively studied is the relationship between the mode of production and family structure. Specifically, researchers have been interested in determining if industrial change undermined the economic basis of the extended family household. Research on household composition has destroyed many of the myths surrounding the extended family. We now know that there is great diversity in family types around the world and that extended family households were probably never typical of Western European countries or the United States. Rural–urban comparisons of mid-nineteenth-century households have indicated that industrialization might have increased rather than decreased both household complexity and the number of older people living with children. However, there still remain many unanswered questions about how the decline of the household as a productive unit affects work opportunities and living arrangements for older people. This is one issue that this book addresses.

A second issue has arisen from concern about the impact of the transfer of economic support for the aged from the family to the state. There is no doubt that there has been an expansion of state support for old age in many Western and non-Western countries in the last century. However, the common position that a need for state support arose because of the breakdown of the family has not been adequately explored. More research is needed in the area of social policy in terms of the history of old age dependency and the impact of state support on the family relationships of the aged. This is another issue addressed in this volume.

There is considerable evidence to indicate that retirement is not exclusively a modern phenomenon, but little is known about what factors contributed to the rise of formal retirement in postindustrial society. Was it due to technological change, as some writers have suggested? Did increased competition among workers for jobs push the aged out of the labor force? This book contains extensive research on the specific technological, social, and political factors that affected the labor force position of the aged in industrializing England.

The first chapter traces the development of the major issues regarding societal development and aging and summarizes what is known about the history of old age. Chapter 2 describes English society in the nineteenth century and helps to place the issue of aging in a particular economic, social, and political context. Chapter 3 examines the effects of the demise of domestic production on work, household composition, and kinship relations. In Chapter 4, the history of old-age dependency within the framework of the poor law is discussed, and life for older people faced with the choice of outrelief or the workhouse is described. Chapter 5 examines the impact of government growth and changes in policies of income maintenance on the family relationships of the aged. Using workhouse censuses, records from the Cambridgeshire Board of Guardians, and testimony presented to the Royal Commission on the Aged poor, this chapter demonstrates that a nonbureaucratically administered, paternalistic system of income maintenance was more disruptive to family relationships than was impersonal bureaucratic administration. Given the present concern with budget cuts and changes in policies of income maintenance for the aged, the findings in this chapter are particularly relevant and timely. Chapter 6 analyzes changing patterns of work and retirement for older men and women. Among the conclusions are that many of the problems presently attributed to retirement, such as reduced income and lower status, were problems of old age and independent of work status. Chapter 7 evaluates the utility of the concept of veneration and suggests an alternative way of looking at attitudes toward the aged. In the late nineteenth century, opponents of the pension used beliefs about the aged to impede change, and working-class advocates used them to facilitate social reform. Finally, in Chapter 8 the findings of the preceding chapters are used to reevaluate modernization theory as an approach to the study of social change and to suggest alternative directions for future research.

Recognizing that bridging disciplines is a risky venture, I have nonetheless attempted to satisfy two masters, using a sociologist's eye to analyze historical data. In so doing, I hope this book will help to fill the need for detailed studies on the history of aging. In addition to the obvious relevance this book has for those involved in the study of aging, it also deals with broader issues of interest to those concerned with studies of the life cycle, family history, British history, and social policy.

Acknowledgments

This study was supported by a National Science Foundation National Needs Postdoctoral Fellowship, Grant No. SP179-14887. A University of Kansas General Research Fund, Grant No. 3170-0038 provided additional support. The research was conducted at the Cambridge Group for the History of Population and Social Structure, Cambridge University. I am most indebted to Peter Laslett, who served as my sponsor on my fellowship. He was a most gracious host and supplied guidance throughout the study. Richard Wall provided consistently helpful advice throughout my stay in Cambridge and commented on earlier drafts of portions of this book. Jill Russell, the Cambridge Group librarian, guided me in my search for sources of material, and I appreciate her friendship and neighborliness. I am grateful to the archivists at Shire Hall who spent many hours helping me locate the poor law records that form the basis of Chapter 5.
Others who have read and commented on various portions of the manuscript include Elizabeth Kuznesof, Ann Schofield, Alan Sica,

Acknowledgments

Janet Barber, Robert John, John Knodel, Howard Newbly, Sid Stahl, Brian Gratton, John Gilles, and Stan Engerman. Steve Brennan provided help with the computer analysis of the Chilvers Coton data, and Allan Long of the University of Kansas Cartographic Service did the graphics. Robert Antonio took the time to read the entire manuscript in its earliest stages and made detailed and insightful comments. Lew Mennerick read portions of the manuscript and spent many hours listening to my various strategies for revision. I am appreciative of the opportunity provided by Warren Peterson and the Midwest Council for Social Research in Aging to present various chapters of this volume to an informed audience. James Hilyer of the Spencer Research Library was helpful in locating the illustrations of nineteenth-century life. Sharon Cox typed numerous drafts of this book, not only correcting typographical errors but also pointing out such oddities of phrasing as ''scavenging for men.'' Finally, Charles Tilly read at least three entire drafts, making suggestions ranging from such major issues as the most coherent theoretical approach, to such minor corrections as the choice of a proper synonym. Both were done with wit and style. Throughout the entire process, my husband, David, to whom this book is dedicated, and my children, Jennifer and Bryan, helped me keep my priorities in perspective.

AGING IN EARLY INDUSTRIAL SOCIETY

Work, Family, and Social Policy
in Nineteenth-Century England

"The London Boardmen"

From John Thompson and Adolphe Smith, *Street Life in London.* New York and London: Benjamin Blom, Inc. First published 1877, reissued 1969.

1

The Golden Age of Aging

Gone are those days, and gone are the ties that then
Bound peers and gentry to their fellow men.
Now, in their place, behold the modern slave,
Doomed, from the very cradle to the grave,
To tread his lonely path of care and toil;
Bound, in sad truth, and bowed down to the soil,
He dies, and leaves his sons their heritage—
Work for their prime, and workhouse for their age.
(Lord John Manners, "England's Trust", p. 16,
quoted in Beer, 1953:179).

Lord John Manner's lament for the plight of the aged in industrializing England was a familiar nineteenth-century romantic theme, as poets, novelists, and artists joined together to decry the forces of change that had wrought such harm on traditional English society. The belching smokestacks that blackened the sky, the driving machines that tore relentlessly through the peaceful countryside, had disrupted the arcadian bliss of rural England, destroying not only the landscape but also a way of life.[1]

In traditional English society, according to the romantic view, each individual from the highest to the lowest had a position in the social order and an accompanying set of responsibilities. As Lord John Manners continued:

> Each knew his place—king, peasant, peer, or priest,
> The greatest owned connection with the least;
> From rank to rank the generous feeling ran,
> And linked society as man to man.
> [England's Trust, quoted in Beer, 1953:179].

Among the responsibilities of the upper classes was the care in old age of those below them in the social hierarchy. As the demands of industrial capitalism for free labor in an open market made market values the sole criteria of worth, older workers lost their guarantee of protection in their final years.

The theme of a golden age of aging was not unique to the romantic movement, for both earlier and subsequent writers noticed variations in the treatment of the aged in "primitive" as opposed to "civilized" societies. At least as early as the eighteenth century, social philosophers believed that the extent of societal development was the key determinant of the status of the aged. In 1776, Adam Smith (1937) wrote that among the hunting peoples of North America age was the sole foundation of rank and precedence, whereas in "opulent and civilized nations" its role was merely residual, regulating rank "among those who are in every other respect equal and among whom, therefore, there is nothing else to regulate it [p. 671]."

More than a century later, Emile Durkheim noted the great importance of the aged in traditional society. Durkheim viewed the old as the living expression of tradition, unique intermediaries between past

[1] The romantics reacted against the emphasis on materialism and rationalism that was linked to the new industrial order and sought to replace the emphasis on rational self-interest with a recognition of social obligations and responsibilities. Among those who pursued the rejection of reason and rationality were Thomas Carlyle, Charles Dickens, John Ruskin, and William Morris. For a more extended discussion of the themes of the romantic writers, see Sussman (1968) and Thompson (1955).

and present. Social solidarity was maintained, according to Durkheim (1964), by the "authority of age which gives tradition its authority [p. 293]." In contrast, in civilized society, old men are pitied more than feared, as ancestral customs lose their predominance and the worship of age is steadily weakened (Durkheim, 1964:294).

Max Weber (1968), too, discussed domination by *honoratoires* whose authority in olden times was based on age: "In all communities which orient their social conduct toward tradition, i.e., toward convention, customary law or sacred law, the elders are, so to speak, the natural *honoratiores* not only because of their prestige of wider experience, but also because they know the traditions [p. 950]." However, Weber (1968:950–951) also recognized that even in traditional society the power and prestige of the aged was subject to change under certain conditions, such as a food shortage when those who could no longer work became burdensome or under conditions of warfare when the prestige of older men was likely to sink below that of warriors. Inevitably, the status of the aged was lower in mass society, "as the growing complexity of administrative tasks and the complexity of their scope leads to the rise of technical superiority among those with training and experience [p. 951]."

Aging and Modernization

Many of these same issues have intrigued contemporary writers who have attempted to identify precisely how the changes wrought by industrialization or, in a broader sense, modernization affected older people. In examining changes in the status of the aged under the modernization rubric, scholars have used two different approaches. The first approach is analytic and most directly derived from the sociological perspective called structural functionalism. In this approach, societies are arranged on a continuum, and those that exhibit certain qualities of social structure are termed "modern" (Smith, 1973:61).

The second sense of modernization is historical. Particular periods of time are marked off from their predecessors by unique characteristics, such as the rise of capitalism, the French Revolution, or the Industrial Revolution. In this sense, modernization denotes a transition between tradition and modernity.[2] Let us examine each approach in turn and see how it has been applied to the issue of the status of the aged.

The Structural-Functional Approach

The precursor of this perspective was Burgess, who argued that industrialization had contributed to a decline in the status of the aged. According to Burgess (1960), urbanization and the mass production of commodities had undermined the economic basis of the extended family and decreased the number of self-employed entrepreneurs. The loss of extended family support isolated the aged, and the loss of decision-making power in the workplace created pressures for retirement. Paradoxically, as the quality of life for older people declined, improvements in life expectancy increased their proportion in society. Burgess's thesis was implicitly comparative and historical. However, the past was assumed, not examined, and discussion was limited to the position of the aged in contemporary Western society.

Burgess's theme was placed squarely within the structural-functional paradigm by Cowgill (1974a, 1974b), who expanded the analysis to include societies at different stages of development. The societies ranged from preliterate to modern, with preliterate societies now equated with preindustrial Western societies. As Cowgill and his coauthor Holmes concluded in *Aging and Modernization* (1972), "the status of the aged is high in preliterate societies and is lower and more ambiguous in modern societies [p. 310]." Thus, the lack of accurate, factual historical knowledge was satisfied by the assumption of linear development. In the shift that took place in the argument, the term

[2] There is a third view, in which modernization denotes a set of policies pursued by leaders or elites of developing countries. In this context, modernization is a conscious set of plans for changing a particular society in the direction of other contemporary societies defined as more "modern" (Smith, 1973:62). This definition has generally not been considered in the research on aging and modernization, with the exception of a study by Cherry and Magnuson-Martin (1979), who compared the status of the aged in prerevolutionary and postrevolutionary China.

modernization was substituted for *industrialization* where it became the permanent reference point.

A further transformation occurred in the terminology, as aspects of industrialization became quantifiable variables associated with modernization. This made it possible to array societies on a continuum according to the degree of modernization. In subsequent works, Cowgill (1974a, 1974b) focused specifically on the ways in which four variables—health technology, economic technology, urbanization, and mass education—contributed to a loss of status for the aged. According to Cowgill, modern health technology multiplies the numbers of elderly and contributes to the aging of the population and its work force. As the lives of workers are prolonged, death no longer creates openings in the labor force as rapidly as it did in the past, and competitive pressures are generated between generations. Eventually, retirement is initiated as a social substitute for death (Cowgill, 1974a:12). In a society that highly values a work ethic and allocates material and nonmaterial rewards accordingly, "retirement from this most valued and status-giving role is accompanied by a reduction in rewards, including monetary income and psychologically satisfying status." Modern economic technology also "creates new occupations and transforms most of the old ones," which means loss of jobs, income, and status by the aged. At the same time, urbanization attracts the young to the cities, breaking up the extended family as a household unit (Cowgill, 1974b:133). Finally, the growth of mass education and literacy means there can be no "mystique of age" based on the superior knowledge and wisdom of older people.

Following a similar model, others have since attempted various ways of measuring changes in the status of the aged through comparative research. Palmore and Manton (1974) elaborated the cross-cultural implications of the modernization thesis, narrowing the definition of status to the relative socioeconomic position of the aged. Palmore and Manton were concerned with three questions. First, does the status of the aged decline with modernization? Second, if the status of the aged does decline with modernization, which aspects of modernization best account for this decline? Third, is this decline linear, or is a point reached when the decline stops and status increases? To answer these questions, 31 societies were placed on a continuum according to degree of modernization, and comparisons between them were made in the socioeconomic status of the aged. Three measures of socioeconomic status were used: employment status (whether or not the aged were economically active), the prestige of the occupation of those economically active, and education. Using an Equality Index to compare the status of the aged with the nonaged, Palmore and Manton drew two conclusions from their comparison.[3] First, they determined that the two most important factors in reducing the status of the aged were the shift from agriculture to manufacturing and increased education. Second, they found that the relationship between modernization and the status of the aged was not linear but J-shaped. In the early stages of modernization, the status of the aged was reduced. However, as societies matured, the differences between the aged and nonaged in education and occupation tended to level off, and discrepancies in status decreased.[4]

Employing a similar approach, Cohn (1980) compared 30 countries exhibiting varying levels of economic development and rates of economic growth. He hypothesized that the demands of increased technology associated with societal development as well as cohort differences in education in a rapidly growing society would create age differences in occupational distribution. Relating the rate of economic growth and the extent of development to the proportion of older workers in prestigious occupations, Cohn concluded that the greater the development and the faster the rate of growth, the fewer older workers are found in higher-status occupations. Thus, economic growth and development led to a loss of occupational status for older workers.

Finally, Bengtson, Dowd, Smith, and Inkeles (1975) compared the attitudes of respondents from six developing nations, three with more European-oriented cultures and moderately high rates of per capita industrial output, and three more traditional, less Westernized

[3] The Equality Index is a way of measuring the status of the aged relative to that of the nonaged. "It is the proportion of two groups' percentage distributions (on a given variable) which overlap each other [Palmore and Manton, 1974:206]."
[4] This study has been heavily criticized on the grounds that the authors omitted deviant cases and used education as both the dependent and independent variable (Fischer, 1978:24).

societies with lower levels of per capita output. They asked males between the ages of 18 and 32 three attitude questions regarding aging and old age and found that individuals in the less modern countries looked forward more to old age and were more likely to respond positively to the statement "a boy learns most from the old." These findings, they concluded, indicated that positive attitudes toward the aged were inversely related to the degree of societal modernization.

There is now an immense body of literature that exists for the sole purpose of debunking modernization theory. It would be a rather tedious exercise to repeat all those arguments here. However, two criticisms—that modernization theory is ahistorical and that it idealizes the past—are of particular relevance to the structural-functional approach to aging and modernization. Let us see just how they apply.

In a direct sense, the problem of ahistoricity leads naturally to the second problem, the idealization of the past. As I noted earlier, those pursuing the structural-functional approach compensated for a lack of historical knowledge about the status of the aged in the past in Western countries by extrapolating from less developed nations today. However, we must recognize that what we have when we arrange societies on a continuum is merely a taxonomy—a system for classifying and ordering societies in a logical fashion from simple to complex. There are two major flaws in this method. First, the criteria for the classification of the peoples and cultures of the world become the qualities of Western society (Nisbet, 1969:191). Any different or unique qualities of non-Western societies are simply ignored. What we end up with is a museum exhibit of cultural artifacts arranged in sequence, representing some constructed history of development with no corresponding entity in real life. For what, we may ask, is this the history of? Certainly not the United States, nor China, nor Tasmania either for that matter. There is no evidence that would allow us to assume that it is historically natural and inevitable for cultures to move from a tribal society to a feudal peasantry to a modern industrial nation. The second flaw in this method is that even societies that seem superficially similar on some "variable," such as proportion of the population engaged in farming, may exhibit different demographic, economic, and social patterns (Macfarlane,

1978:13). To link such diverse nation–states as nineteenth-century Russia, India, and China in the present day and western Europe in the Middle Ages because they fit into the same slot on the continuum ignores the immense differences between them. Yet this is precisely what the structural-functional approach to modernization does.

If linear development is assumed, then it is easy to see how evidence from studies of less developed countries that indicate high status for the aged could lead to an idealization of the past in the Western world.[5] Certainly, evidence does exist that the aged hold power and prestige in some cultures. Among the Igbo, the Bantu, and the Samoans, older people act as political, judicial, and civic leaders, and children have a strong obligation to care for aged and infirm parents (Cowgill and Holmes, 1972:307). However, extensive variations in the treatment of the aged in even the least developed societies have been documented, so that it is false to conclude that veneration is ever universal in any societal type (Foner and Kertzer, 1978; Amoss and Harrell, 1981). That discrepant evidence is sometimes ignored by modernization theorists is part of what Laslett (1976) refers to as the ''world we have lost syndrome [p. 91],'' and as we shall see, the idea of a golden age of aging is not incompatible with those who pursue the historical approach either.

[5] This is not to suggest that the idealization of the past is unique to modernization theory. Rather, this portrait of aging and modernization is derived from a long-standing sociological tradition. The tradition originated in the concepts of *Gemeinschaft* ('community') and *Gesellschaft* (variously translated as 'society,' 'organization,' or 'association'), first coined by Ferdinand Tonnies. Tonnies's original concepts referred to forms of association, not types of communities (Tonnies, 1957). *Gemeinschaft* extended beyond a purely local community to include any set of relationships characterized by emotional cohesion, depth, continuity, and fulfillment. In contrast, *Gesellschaft* referred to the impersonal, the contractual, and the rational aspects of human association. What can be seen retrospectively as the major flaw in Tonnies's concepts was grounding these types of relationships in particular patterns of settlement and in particular geographical locales. Adopting the prevailing idealized views of traditional, rural society, Tonnies believed the rural village to represent *Gemeinschaft*, and modern urban communities, *Gesellschaft*. From a typology of social relationships, Tonnies's concepts became a taxonomy of settlement patterns, fitting with prevailing cultural views of urban and rural ways of life (Newby, 1977:95).

Without always recognizing the origins of their argument, those investigating the changes associated with a movement from traditional to modern society have

The Historical Approach

The primary exemplar of this approach is Fischer (1978), who used historical evidence to examine the relationship between the prestige of the aged and modernization. Fischer selected the modernization theme as a specific attack on the sociological literature that argued that industrialization and the changes that accompanied it contributed to a decline in the status of the aged. In a critique of this theory, Fischer (1978) found that the aged were venerated in the past and that veneration did decline. However, the decline occurred much earlier, before industrialization or modernization (in the sociological sense) had any impact. Using literature, style of dress, and iconography as indicators of prestige, as well as using more calculable measures such as assignment of meetinghouse seats, age of clergymen and political leaders, age of property ownership and household composition, Fischer (1978:231) concluded that a "cult of age" existed in early America but disappeared between 1770 and 1820 due to the influence of the ideals of equality and liberty perpetuated by the French Revolution. The ideal of equality destroyed the hierarchical conception of the world on which the authority of age had rested, and the growth of the ideal of liberty dissolved the communal base of power. Since the power of elders had depended upon the submergence of individuality, the growth of social atomism dissolved the ties of obligation between generations as well as those between classes (Fischer, 1978:109).

Throughout the nineteenth and into the twentieth century, attitudes toward the aged became increasingly negative. The effects of increased gerontophobia permeated nearly every aspect of American

---

perpetuated the belief that modern, urban society represents relationships characterized as *Gesellschaft*, which are simultaneously bad, alienating, and unnatural, whereas traditional society is the *Gemeinschaft* society of intimacy, the natural and healthy "community."

The idealized view of traditional, rural "peasant" communities came under increasing attack in the 1960s, as more and more social scientists began to recognize the tensions and schisms in both contemporary village life and traditional peasant societies of the past as well as the inadequacy of dichotomizing these complex concepts into two ideal types (Hauser, 1965; Gusfield, 1967). However, the concept still appears from time to time, most notably in the modernization literature.

life. Social commentators began to speak of the uselessness of old men, and the widespread belief that men made their greatest contributions to society while still young was promulgated (Fischer, 1978:138). It was this attitude combined with a rise in the median age of the work force that led to the growth of retirement (Fischer, 1978:143). Increased retirement, in turn, brought about a rapid increase in poverty among the aged (Fischer, 1978:144). Clearly, changes in attitudes toward the aged could not have been caused by industrialization, urbanization, demography, bureaucratization, or rationalization. All of these trends occurred after the demise of the exhaltation of age and were secondary in importance to the ideals of equality and liberty (Fischer, 1978:231). Thus, changes in ideals rather than in material life caused the decline in the status of the aged.

Andrew Achenbaum (1978) also explored the history of aging in the United States. Like Fischer, Achenbaum found a historical dichotomy in views of old age, but according to Achenbaum's evidence, the shift from veneration to degradation occurred much later, after the Civil War. Between 1790 and 1860, according to Achenbaum, the elderly were perceived as indispensable, providing valuable insights about healthful longevity and serving as ideally qualified moral exemplars. Although most Americans in this era were also cognizant of the difficulties that accompanied aging, these difficulties enhanced rather than diminished the elderly's social usefulness. After the Civil War, asserts Achenbaum (1978), "Americans began to challenge nearly every favorable belief about the usefulness and merits of age that had been set forth. . . . By the outbreak of World War I, if not before, most Americans were affirming the obsolescence of old age [p. 39]."

Achenbaum (1978:57) identified three possible relationships between the rhetoric and reality of age. First, changes in the position of the aged associated with industrialization and urbanization could have precipitated unfavorable evaluations about the usefulness of the elderly. Thus, significant increases in the numbers of older persons in the population, reductions in employment opportunities, and changes in the plight of dependents may have made Americans revise their opinions about growing old. This is essentially the sociological model. A second possibility is that changes in conceptions of the aged and changes in their actual position in society occurred simultaneously. If this were the case, then most changes in the position of the aged would have occurred after 1865. Finally, Achenbaum conceives of a third relationship—that Americans may have perceived of the aged as obsolete burdens before their position in society warranted such a verdict.

Achenbaum examines each of these hypotheses in regard to demographic change, work opportunities, and old age dependency. He eliminates demographic change as a causal factor on the grounds that the growth of the aged population was slow and undetectable until after 1920, when ideas about the aged had already become negative. The relationship between work opportunities and ideas about old age is somewhat more complex. Achenbaum (1978:48) argues that in the late nineteenth century the denigration of the value of older workers was used with increasing frequency by employers as a rationale to discharge older employees. Thus, negative ideas about the aged became a source of age discrimination in the marketplace. However, the greatest withdrawal of the aged from the labor force has occurred since 1930, long after unfavorable notions about the aged were already commonplace. In neither case did increased retirement cause a loss of prestige.

Achenbaum also asks whether developments in the history of old age dependency before 1914 could have caused a dramatic reevaluation of the elderly's status. Achenbaum (1978:82) notes that there was an increase in the number and variety of private institutions for the aged in the late nineteenth century and that retirement programs and insurance schemes proliferated. However, these innovations were piecemeal and had a negligible effect. Up until 1914, the family and the almshouse were still the main source of support for the aged. There was a tendency for older people to become more dependent on society in the late nineteenth century, but radical changes did not occur until after 1914.

Achenbaum (1978) concludes that changes in popular conceptions of the aged between 1790 and 1914 were unrelated to observable shifts in older Americans' actual position in society and that the intellectual history of old age is not identical to the social history of the aged. Rather, ideas about the worth and funtions of the elderly have a life of their own, the effect of "the interplay of broad intellectual trends and pervasive structural changes in society at large [p. 86]."

Although the turning point for Achenbaum is later, his basic theme is similar to Fischer's: The aged were venerated in the past, and their status declined in modern society. Yet we need not look too far to find contrary evidence. In direct contradiction, Stearns (1977:11) debunks the golden age mythos, arguing that older people were not better off in the past and that the golden age approach makes its modern subjects seem like helpless pawns. In exploring views about the aged in France, Stearns (1977:18) found not traditional veneration but rather unmitigated disdain, a disdain that has persisted well into the contemporary era. From the eighteenth century to the interwar periods, the outlook toward old age has remained unchanged (Stearns 1977:24).

Thomas (1976), in a discussion of old age in early modern England, also rejects the idea that there was once a golden age of aging. Thomas suggests that although a considerable body of literature venerates a gerontocratic ideal, rulers in the past were middle-aged, not old. Most seventeenth- and eighteenth-century writers took it for granted that "old age was a wretched time of physical deterioration" and portrayed the aged as peevish, forgetful, covetous, garrulous, and dirty (Thomas, 1976:244). Thomas concludes that there is no reason to look back wistfully to this period, for once health and mind had started to decay, wealth was the only source of respect.

Overall, we can conclude that any theory that postulates a simple causal relationship between the status of the aged and societal development should be abandoned. Although at least two historical studies have documented a "before" and "after" in age relations, others have suggested that the prestige of the aged was never universally high. It seems more likely that veneration in old age in preindustrial Western culture was reserved for a wealthy elite.

Old Age in History

Although the broad issue of status has been intriguing to many historians and sociologists, other researchers have turned to more specific issues and questions about work, retirement, family life, and old age dependency. Precise studies using historical data allow us to discard some of the myths about the past.

The Family and Old Age Dependency

According to modernization theory, industrialization destroyed the economic basis of the extended family by removing production from the home. Family members no longer worked together farming or in some household endeavor, and the nuclear family unit composed solely of parents and children replaced the extended family. Factory production accelerated the process of urbanization, and younger family members moved to cities, diminishing the likelihood that an aged parent would be taken into a child's home. The high proportion of older people living alone or solely with a spouse in modern society is often cited as evidence of the breakdown of extended family ties. The loss of support for the family forced the aged to rely increasingly upon the state.

This argument contains many misconceptions about family life in the past, for there is no single household type that characterizes traditional society (Shorter, 1975:29). Rather, research indicates tremendous diversity in typical patterns of household composition, ranging from simple, nuclear family types in England, the Low Countries, and northern France to complex stem households in Austria, Germany, and Japan (Wrigley, 1977:78).

The explanation for this diversity rests partly on different demographic conditions and partly on different cultural traditions. For example, Laslett (1976:110) has shown that older people in preindustrial England were not much more likely than they are today to be living in the homes of married children. Under the demographic conditions that existed in preindustrial England, typical family size was larger, and offspring continued to be born late in the life span of their mothers. Child rearing was extended over a longer portion of the life cycle. This factor combined with lower life expectancy meant that the aged in the past were living in a family situation in greater proportions than they are today simply because they were still living with their own unmarried children.

This does not mean, however, that the ideal–typical extended family household, consisting of two married couples, is a myth.

Rather, coresidence between parents and married children was likely to occur only during a limited phase of the family life cycle when the parents wished to retire or when one became widowed. From the Middle Ages to the nineteenth century, wills and retirement contracts between peasant farmers and their children indicate that property rights and ownership were exchanged for care and provisions in old age (Homans, 1940; Braun, 1966; Drake, 1969; Demos, 1970: Greven, 1970; Berkner, 1972; Howell, 1976; Sabean, 1976; Thomas, 1976; Stearns, 1977). Often these contracts were highly detailed, specifying the amount of food and other goods to be provided to the parents as well as what portion of the house they would occupy. For example, in one contract from Denmark in 1785 the retiring parents suggested that:

> Our son-in-law Peder will pay to us for the farm Gentofte once and for all 100 rigsdaler. We reserve the use of the old large house and Peder will build a new one for himself.
> In addition he will yearly pay us a pension of 20 rigsdaler, 3 barrels of good rye flour, 3 barrels of malt brewed into good quality beer, 1 barrel of unmilled rye, 1 barrel of barley, 1 barrel of oats. 4 geese with their goslings well fatted, 4 sheep with their lambs fed winter and summer, 2 fresh swine yearly and 1 barrel of good butter. 2 pots of milk daily when the cows are milking and 8 loads of peat-turf. Care and maintenance with wollens, linens and cleanliness [quoted in Gaunt, 1979].

Control of property gave the aged a good deal of power over their children. For example, among Austrian peasants a son could not marry until his father died or retired and gave him control of the farm. Then the son and his bride would live with his retired parents until their death. Although this custom provided security for the aged, the disadvantage was that it created tensions between generations. There are many folktales describing fighting and even murder between parents and children. An anonymous writer in the Westfalisches Anzieger in 1798 proposed the establishment of a Court for Morality to decide in conflicts between peasant parents and children (Gaunt, 1979:13). In Sweden and Germany and elsewhere in the Low Countries, there were recorded many cases of abuse of older people by their children after they retired and turned over their property. This conflict is expressed in an Austrian folk song from the early twentieth century:

> Father, when ya gonna gimme the farm,
> Father, when ya gonna sign it away?
> My girl's been growin' every day,
> And Single no longer wants to stay.
>
> Father, when ya gonna gimme the farm,
> Father, when ya gonna gimme the house?
> When ya gonna retire to your room out of the way,
> And dig up your potatoes all day?
> [quoted in Berkner, 1972:403]

The increase in wage labor has been associated with both the disappearance of retirement contracts and the rise of the nuclear family household. As children gained the freedom to take industrial employment, they were no longer dependent on their inheritance for the right to marry. Braun (1966:61) found that in late eighteenth-century Switzerland, landless cottage laborers no longer received allowances from children, whereas those with property still practiced *Rastgaben*. Similarly, in Austria the nuclear family predominated among the poor and landless (Berkner, 1972:408). Thus, extended family households were maintained in preindustrial Western societies not because parents and married children worked together as an economic unit, but rather because children had to care for retired parents in order to gain the right to marry and take over the farm. When other work opportunities became available, children chose other options.

In seventeenth-century New England, where land was abundant, sons also waited to marry until their fathers made them economically independent. Sometimes sons were deeded land outright; in other instances they were forced to wait for full ownership until the father died (Greven, 1970). Deeds of gift were often used like retirement contracts, specifying obligations owed to parents. Sometimes these obligations included money payments, and both deeds and wills carefully provided for widows, obligating children to give their mother lodging, as well as food and income.

In colonial New England, older couples enjoyed proximity to

children but preferred to look after themselves (Demos, 1978:268). Under some circumstances they did require assistance, in widowhood or when in failing health, and then children were often a resource. However, older people were cautious about placing too much trust in the goodwill or natural affections of children. In many instances, a husband would spell out in his will with extraordinary precision arrangements for his widow. Often the widow herself was empowered to see that these duties were fulfilled, with a penalty to be extracted from the child if they were not. Widowed men, too, sometimes made formal arrangements for their own care following the death of their wives, promising bequests on their deaths in exchange for care and maintenance in old age. Although pure familial affection was also the basis of care for the old and infirm, sometimes children challenged probate proceedings, arguing for charges for food and care rendered parents earlier. Nonfamilial support was a last resort, and those with no kin to rely upon had to appeal to the public authorities for charity. Thus, in preindustrial times coresidence of married parents and children in much of Europe and the United States was predicated on retirement and widowhood.

How, then, did industrialization affect family life? Some of the misconceptions about old age and family life arising from a broad modernization schema have been corrected by more precise studies investigating how industrialization affected household composition. Anderson (1972:225) compared rural and urban regions of Lancashire, England, in 1851. Contrary to expectations, he found that few old people lived apart from a relative in either region but that more older people were living with married children in urban Preston than in the rural portions of the county.

Anderson's findings contradict the hypothesis that industrialization destroyed the economic basis of the extended family household—an hypothesis that would predict low rates of coresidence in urban areas. Several factors explain the lower rates of coresidence between older parents and married children in rural areas. First, in rural farm families the family plot of land was often small, incapable of supporting several generations. Thus, even though children might not go far from home, the household generally separated both residentially and economically as children became independent

(Anderson, 1971:82). Second, in urban, industrial areas wives of factory workers often worked outside the home, and older parents were a helpful resource in caring for young children (Litchfield, 1978:192). Third, housing shortages in urban areas may have contributed to increased rates of coresidence.

Chudacoff and Hareven (1978:217) also studied the impact of urbanization and economic change on the household and family structure of the aged. They used data from four communities in Essex County, Massachusetts, in 1860 and 1880 to examine the functions of old people in the family. Confirming Anderson's research, they also found that aged men and women in urban areas were more likely to be living with children, in this instance as a result of housing shortages and economic strains caused by a recession. Chudacoff and Hareven (1978) concluded that "conditions of late nineteenth century urbanization moved aging parents closer to their progeny rather than isolating them. Further, the aged were not burdens on their children. Rather they entered into interdependent relationships with them, sharing housing in exchange for other resources [p. 239]." Thus, it appears that urban, industrial life temporarily increased the likelihood of an aged parent being taken into the household. However, it should be emphasized that this was apparently a transitional phase, since rates of coresidence did decline in the twentieth century.

Demographic change has also affected household structure and partially explains why rates of coresidence declined in the twentieth century. Uhlenberg (1978:65) analyzed the life course patterns of successive birth cohorts in the nineteenth and twentieth centuries to explicate how societal trends in demographic behavior produce specific types of change in family structure. He found that declining mortality between 1830 and 1920 increased the proportion of women surviving to age 60, so that the likelihood of a female reaching the empty-nest phase of the life cycle increased over time. Mortality declines also increased the duration of the empty nest, as did decreases in the age at birth of the last child (Uhlenberg, 1978:90). In addition, expectancy of life for women at age 60 increased more than the expectation of the duration of marriage. The higher proportion of older people, and particularly older women, living alone in modern society is at least partially attributable to significant demographic changes.

Reliance on kin continued to be the primary source of assistance for the aged in the United States until at least 1914 (Achenbaum, 1978:75). In Massachusetts as late as 1895, for example, few older people lived alone or with strangers. As in earlier times, the local community assumed responsibility for relieving the needy only if family members did not live in the area or had defaulted on their obligations. In many places, this aid took the form of care in an almshouse, where unfortunate and feeble old people could go to die. Throughout the nineteenth century, the proportion of almshouse residents who were old increased sharply, and after 1860 the number and variety of private institutions for the aged increased rapidly as well.

As part of the golden age mythos, it has been argued that state support of the aged became necessary because of a decline in familial support. The increase in institutions and the increase in the proportion of older people living alone have been cited as evidence. For example, Paillat (1977) views the demographic increase in the proportion of the aged as problematic, in that "the family network, which offered help and assistance during many centuries, does not—or cannot—play its role as completely and efficiently as before [p. 64]." This he attributes to the fact that the solidarity between generations has passed from the family network to society, with traditional family support replaced by bureaucratic structures (Paillat, 1977:66, 69). Halper (1978) ties this loss specifically to the pension system:

> The adoption of Social Security, for instance, was greeted as a great boon to the elderly, and yet it is obvious by now that its blessings have been very mixed. For the assertion of a governmental responsibility to provide for the aged would seem to have permitted the loosening of the bonds of family responsibility thereby making it easier for persons to neglect their debts to their elderly relatives. It is not quite so hard to shunt them aside, after all, when one believes that the government will take care of them [p. 324].

Finally, Stannard (1978) sees families as unable to absorb without trauma "the tedium of demographically unprecedented decades of isolated companionship with one or two others," which makes us "more and more dependent on large, impersonal, bureaucratic institutions for even minimal amounts of that needed support [p. 12]." In all of these arguments, a common theme is that large-scale, bureaucratically organized support of the aged is the enemy, either necessarily taking over familial tasks due to the breakdown of the family or actually causing this breakdown to occur.

Anderson (1977) examined changes in governmental policies in income maintenance in Great Britain in the nineteenth century to determine their effect on family relationships. In the prepension period in Britain before 1908, the main source of financial aid for the destitute aged was the poor law. Poor law policy toward the aged was comparatively lenient until 1871, when new policies were implemented that reduced payments to the aged and forced children to maintain their aged parents. The threat of the workhouse loomed for those older people whose children refused to help maintain them. Anderson found that reductions in support to the aged coupled with the threat of the workhouse increased the number of institutionalized aged and that forcing kin to contribute to the support of an aged parent increased family tensions. When the Old Age Pensions Act was passed, it reduced interfamilial tension by allowing the generations to function on the basis of mutual interdependency rather than one-sided dependency. Anderson (1977:57) concluded that the view that state-provided income maintenance undermines family relationships is false and that defining strong family relationships in terms of financial assistance demonstrates a lack of understanding of the basis of harmonious interaction.

The belief that the aged are neglected or repudiated by their children in modern industrial society is no longer an issue. Study after study has shown that this view of modern society is inaccurate, that children perform a variety of personal and protective services for their aged parents and that these relationships tend to be reciprocal (Townsend, 1957; Streib and Thompson, 1960; Shanas, 1962; Shanas, Townsend, Wedderburn, Friis, Milhoj, and Stehouwer, 1968). There is no doubt that there has been an increased reliance on governments for support in old age in many Western and non-Western nations (Munnichs, 1977:102). However, this does not mean that increased bureaucratization of support for the aged has intruded into family relationships in a negative way. Rather, it may be, as Kreps (1977:24) has suggested, that there is now a new role for children in modern–industrial society, as they provide a means of entry into the social order and act as a buffer against the pressures of bureaucracy.

Work in Old Age

The question of how industrialization affected work for the aged is perhaps the most complex. Modernization theory suggests that a variety of factors reduced work for the aged, leading to increased rates of retirement. One factor was the decline in domestic production that did away with the jobs that older workers typically performed. The shift from the home to the factory also eliminated autonomy in the workplace, so that older workers could no longer decide for themselves how long to continue working. Further, increases in life expectancy accompanying modernization led to increased intergenerational competition for jobs, with technological changes making the skills of the aged less valuable. Modernization theory also predicts that a decline in agriculture, which represents a predominant form of domestic production, should be accompanied by higher rates of retirement.

One of the difficulties in responding to these issues is that there is a paucity of information about the organization, nature, and quantity of work for the aged under preindustrial modes of production. One comparative study of 31 countries found a clear relationship between the percentage employed in agriculture and rates of retirement, "the less in agriculture, the more retirement and unemployment among the aged [Palmore and Manton, 1974:208]." Yet the evidence of the retirement contracts cited earlier certainly indicates that retirement is not a modern phenomenon and that peasants did retire in the past.

There is a sparse but intriguing literature describing patterns of work among older people who had no property to use in retirement. In England the gangs of migrant-type labor, the least desirable employment, that were commonly found in agricultural districts often included old men and women (Kitteringham, 1975:91). Old women also sometimes took care of young children and infants whose mothers had gone to work in the fields, reportedly caring for as many as 35 suckling infants in some districts (Heath, 1893:119). Generally, the work of the aged was marginal and sporadic, as in the following account:

> An old lady still living in the village used to scare crows for the whole of the harvest holidays: she was paid six shillings. She was given a wooden clapper and had to keep making noise with it: if she once stopped and the clapper was silent, the man who hired her would look out of his house to see what she was doing [Evans, 1957:175].

Demos (1978:271) has described a pattern of partial or gradual retirement that appeared to predominate in preindustrial New England, as old people worked at a variety of jobs, mowing grass, hauling grist to the local mill, acting as midwives, and performing other assorted occupations. Demos (1978:273, 275) also notes that withdrawal from office because of age was not uncommon and that some people were dismissed from positions for the same reason. Data from late nineteenth-century Massachusetts indicates high levels of employment, over 90%, for males over 55.[6] Their patterns of work differed from younger men in that they were less likely to be employed in manufacturing and more likely to be involved in building, retailing, service, and general labor (Chudacoff and Hareven, 1978:228). It may be that they drifted into menial service and labor jobs as they grew older, or they may have had fewer opportunities to acquire industrial employment as young men because they entered the labor force before factory employment was widely available.

Women in the nineteenth century tended to work when their children were young, leaving the labor force when children were old enough to contribute to the support of the family. They would sometimes return to work in old age when they became widowed or when their husbands were ailing or unemployed, although their "low levels of skill and sporadic employment experience restricted them to

[6] Chudacoff and Hareven (1978:228) assume that if an occupation was listed for an individual, it meant that that person was presently employed and that the reference was not to a previous occupation. This may not be true, in which case 90% employed would be an overestimation of the labor-force participation of the aged.

unskilled, irregular, and low-paying jobs [Tilly and Scott, 1978:128].'' In general, rates of employment for aged women were low, and when older women did work, they held jobs as domestics and washerwomen (Chudacoff and Hareven, 1978:230).

In summary, it appears that people in the past retired when they had the resources, either land or wealth, to do so. Those who continued to work did so out of financial necessity rather than out of desire. This does not mean that industrialization had no impact on retirement, for the modern form of retirement involving a formal system of income transfer administered through a large-scale bureaucracy appears to be historically unique.

Modernization Theory and Historical Knowledge

Modernization is an abstract category, summarizing a series of changes that took place over a span of more than 150 years in Western societies and that may never be replicated precisely in other societies just now developing. Thus, modernization ''theory'' is not really a theory of social change at all. Rather, it is a summarized description of contempory change that attempts to chart the interrelationship between the various processes into which recent trends may be grouped. The pattern that emerges is ''modernization,'' a concept that subsumes all of the features of contemporary life, that is, urbanization, secularization, mass education, factory production, mass media, and political participation. Insofar as it is complete, it provides a description rather than an explanation of social change.

There is an abundance of evidence that contradicts many of the assumptions of modernization theory. The prestige of the aged is not universally high in tribal societies and low in developed nations. Beliefs about the aged do not conform to their position in society. The extended family household of traditional society is not universal but varies significantly over time and space. Retirement is not solely a phenomenon of modern society. Increased reliance on large-scale organizations is not necessarily a symbol of the breakdown of the family network. Further, some of the changes that did occur may have been operating in different directions at different times. Thus, it is important to distinguish the effects of early industrialization from those associated with the development of postindustrial society.

This does not mean that the investigation of age relations in history should be abandoned, for it is apparent that some distinct effects of social change can be identified. There has been increased reliance on large-scale organizations for support in old age. Modern economic technology has transformed the labor force in terms of the numbers of older workers employed and the age distribution of occupations. Industrialization initially increased the number of extended family households. Older people are more likely to be living alone today than they were in the past.

Undoubtedly, the aged have felt the impact of industrialization. Some historical research has explained how industrialization affected older people, yet many intriguing questions remain unanswered. What is the real impact of the decline of the household as a unit of production on the work status and household position of the aged? Does increased reliance on the government for economic support undermine family relationships? Why has there been such a dramatic increase in state support of the aged? Can the factors associated with increased rates of retirement be identified? What is the source of changes in beliefs about the aged?

In ensuing chapters, I will explore the issue of aging and social change, examining those areas identified by modernization theorists as theoretically relevant—work and retirement, family relationships, old age dependency, the rhetoric of age. The book will deviate from traditional sociological analysis in the sense that broader political issues not typically considered relevant to the theme of aging and modernization will be included, for my immediate sense when I began my initial explorations into this topic was that a single list of measurable variables painted too narrow a picture of social change. However, my lack of focus on the analysis of variables and my inclusion of a broader historical orientation does not place this work squarely within a traditional historical framework either. I will not begin at one point in time—say, early industrialization—and end with analysis of postindustrial society, proceeding in a manner that is chronologically accurate. Rather, I have chosen the method of a series of historical case studies, with each chapter dealing in detail with specific issues regarding aging and social change. Certain issues, like retirement trends, lend themselves readily to analysis on a national scale, whereas others, such as the impact of household production on the lives of the aged, can be understood only on a more microscopic level. Thus, the book moves from regional-level case studies to analyses of broad national trends according to the type of issue under consideration. This somewhat hybrid approach allows me the advantage of a very detailed analysis of particular topics but, of course, carries with it the accompanying disadvantage of a lack of broad historical accuracy and thus generalizability.

I begin, then, in England, the first country to industrialize, and in the nineteenth century, which was, according to Wrigley (1977:82), a transition period in the history of old age. Echoing the Weberian theme that rapid social change creates insecurity for the aged, Wrigley argues that both the peasant in traditional society and the pensioner in the twentieth century have security in old age. The source of the peasant's security was land, which he could sell, rent, or give to his son in exchange for food and shelter. A wage earner in a welfare state also has no reason to fear old age, because a pension provides security even when there are no personal savings. Even a wage earner in a traditional village had claim to the resources of the parish. In the final analysis, the most vulnerable older people in history were those in communities that felt most distinctly the impact of the Industrial Revolution, who were displaced by the shifting demands of industrial capitalism. As Laslett (1976) notes:

> We simply do not know what happened to the old people living in a society undergoing industrialization but not themselves directly caught up in the process. This is a matter of capital importance because our immediate past, in high industrial society, is not that of traditional times at all, but that of the industrializing nineteenth century [p. 115].

In the ensuing chapters, I will explore the effect of rapid social change on the aged in nineteenth-century England, both for what it tells us about aging and for the light it sheds on the nature of industrial capitalism.

Although rural England may never have been so peaceful as

romantic writers wistfully recalled, Britain did experience substantial change in the nineteenth century. The forces of industrial capitalism not only disrupted the arcadian bliss of the countryside with the intrusion of belching smokestacks and clanging railroads but also permanently altered British political, economic, and social structure. Chapter 2 will explore the nature of those changes, focusing specifically on those most likely to have affected older people. It will examine population growth and demographic change, the changing role of domestic production during the growth of industrial capitalism, the expansion of factory production and accompanying technological change in textiles and heavy industry, the causes of rapid urbanization, and the changing political philosophy that gradually led to the acceptance of a welfare state.

2

England in Transition

The myth of a golden age of aging is derived from a linear model of societal development that presumes a distinct transition from domestic production to disciplined factory production in machine-based spatially concentrated units. This view of industrialization accepts the current convention of dating the first industrial revolution from the 1780s, when the statistics of British international trade showed a significant upward movement (Rostow, 1960). This watershed approach to history has been questioned by others who have challenged the historical boundary implied in the concept of a "takeoff" period (Nef, 1954). Those who view history as a continuous process emphasize that the beginnings of large-scale industry and technological change can be traced back to the sixteenth and seventeenth centuries in Great Britain.

Particular aspects of societal development have been stressed by those linking industrialization or modernization to a decline in the status of the aged. These include demographic change in terms of both urbanization and societal aging, a change in the mode of production including both the organization of work and the nature of work, and, finally, the usurpation of familial functions by the state. In subsequent chapters, each of these issues will be analyzed in terms of their impact on the aged. This chapter will describe the economic, social, and political changes that occurred in nineteenth-century England in terms of the general accuracy of a linear model of societal development.

Demographic Change

The relationship between population and industrialization is complex and has generated debate about the origins and significance of demographic change. These issues will be briefly discussed here, as the major trends are documented.

Although truly reliable figures of the British population are unavailable prior to 1840, when the public registration of births and deaths was introduced, there is general agreement that population began to rise around 1740, with the rate of growth accelerating after 1770. Between 1780 and 1840, the British population doubled and then doubled again from 1840 to 1900. A major factor that contributed to population growth was a drop in the death rate.

Mortality

Several explanations have been postulated for the declines in mortality. One important factor was the almost complete elimination of crises such as harvest failure or epidemic disease that in the past had occurred periodically and caused fluctuations in the crude mortality rate.[1] Although substantial declines in the mortality rate did not occur until late in the nineteenth century, the mortality peaks that characterized earlier periods disappeared, and the low level was consistently held (Wrigley, 1969:165).

[1] There were exceptions where crises did occur, such as the great cholera outbreaks or the Irish famine of 1845, but these did not cause the major fluctuations in the crude death rate that earlier disasters had (Wrigley, 1969:165).

A second major feature of mortality was the change in age-specific death rates. In general, death rates fell much more rapidly among children and teenagers than among adults, with the exception of infant mortality, which remained high until after 1900.[2] Death rates for those over 55 also remained stable until 1900. In fact, the impression of the time was that life expectancy for older people had actually declined with industrialization. It was stated in the 1901 census that "there is a general impression reasonably grounded on census returns and on official Death-rates and Life Tables, that as a consequence of recent changes in the general conditions of life, fewer people now live to old age, although more arrive at maturity and middle age than in former years [vol. 44:56]." Thus, mortality for the aged either remained stable or increased slightly until 1900, when it began a slight and very gradual decline (Wrigley, 1969:167).

The main factor in life expectancy improvements was not modern health technology, for it is generally agreed that the medical contribution to the reduction in mortality did not become influential until the last years of the nineteenth century, when a fuller understanding of the nature and means of the transmission of infectious disease was gained (Wrigley, 1969:169). More important factors include a general improvement in social and economic conditions—specifically, better diet and public sanitation inspired by the public health movement—some effect of vaccination from smallpox for youths, and a reduction in the virulence of disease itself (Greenwood, 1936:684; McKeown and Record, 1962:118).

A third feature of mortality during the period of the Industrial Revolution was the great variation found in different social and economic environments. In 1898, infant mortality among the poor was two and a half times the level among those wealthy enough to employ servants (Wrigley, 1969:173). One contemporary attempt to

[2] Child mortality was reduced because of better control over infectious diseases with improvements in sanitation and diet. However, in the early weeks of life, a baby is dependent on his or her mother for food, so that the type and quality of food does not alter much over a wide range of environmental conditions. Only at the end of the century was the necessary knowledge available to help reduce the infectious diseases of the chest and stomach to which infants were highly susceptible (Wrigley, 1969:170).

2. England in Transition

assess this difference systematically demonstrated major differences
in death rates between workers and employers in the same industry.
As Table 2.1 shows, builders between the ages of 35 and 45 had a
death rate per 1000 of 8 for employers and 16 for workers. Among
those 55–65 the rates were 28 per 1000 for employers and 49 for
workers. The same pattern held in all of the occupations analyzed
(March, 1912:525).

Life expectancy in the industrial slums of cities like Liverpool,
Manchester, and Glasgow was only half that of calculations for England as a whole. For example, at mid-century life expectancy at
birth was 40.2 for England but only 24.2 in Manchester (Wrigley,
1969:173). Although it seems logical to attribute these variations to
industrialization, studies have shown no clear relationship between
life expectancy and degree of industrialization. Rather high mortality
in the nineteenth century can more accurately be attributed to urbanization. Mortality was density dependent, and wherever there was
severe overcrowding, diseases spread rapidly. Yet in the strictly in-

TABLE 2.1. *Male Deaths per One Thousand by Age, Occupation, and Job Classification*

	Age			
	35–45		55–65	
Occupation	Employer	Worker	Employer	Worker
Farming class	7	8	21	30
Carpenters or joiners	7	10	30	43
Bakers	11	18	37	58
Printers	8	22	26	56
Textile industries	4	11	13	41
Butchers	17	29	41	86
Builders	8	16	28	49

Source: March, 1912:525.

dustrial areas, although large populations grew around the factories, mills, and pitheads, the people still lived in comparatively small towns and villages (Wrigley, 1969:175).

Fertility

During the early phases of industrialization, the birth rate remained high, reaching a peak in 1862–1878 of 35 births per thousand. It did not begin to decline until after 1879, and from 1896 on, the average birth rate was below 30 per thousand (Tilly and Scott, 1978:91). Any previous population in history characterized by such low levels would have disappeared from the face of the earth, but the associated decline in mortality meant that fertility could also fall without causing numbers to shrink.[3] Let us now examine the conditions created by the Industrial Revolution that were conducive to the adoption of family limitation on such an unprecedented scale.

High fertility combined with declining mortality produced the legendary Victorian family. It was not so much that the number of children born was greater than in the past but rather that with fewer children dying and fewer marriages broken by the early death of a parent, there were more children living with their parents in a family unit and more children raised in large sibling groups (Wrigley, 1969:184).

Family limitation occurred first among the upper class and then spread gradually to the lower echelons of society. For example, in 1890 professionals had the smallest family size, with an average of 2.80 children; salaried employees averaged 3.53 children and laborers 5.11 (Wrigley, 1969:186). Social class differentials were maintained for a comparatively long time, but the overall change was

[3] This does not mean that communities in the past had never attempted family limitation, for there was documentation of family limitation in seventeenth-century England and eighteenth- and nineteenth-century France in regions that had experienced little social change (Wrigley, 1969:181). Further, there is no simple relationship between fertility declines and industrialization. Knodel and van de Walle (1979) present evidence that the fertility transition in Europe took place under remarkably diverse socioeconomic conditions.

still revolutionary, for within two generations average family size fell by roughly two-thirds.

The cause of the fertility decline is still a subject of much scholarly debate. One factor was an increase in the age at marriage, which began to climb in the 1880s (Mitchison, 1977:74). Some researchers have suggested that modern methods of birth control played a role, but the evidence seems to indicate that most couples used traditional methods like coitus interruptus and abortion rather than newer methods like rubber sheaths. Thus, the growth of the use of contraception to limit family size that began in the late nineteenth century was due to the wider employment of means long known to European communities (Wrigley, 1969:190).

Although one of the results of declines in mortality and fertility in Western countries has been societal aging—that is, a higher proportion of the population over age 65—noticeable changes in population structure did not occur in England in the nineteenth century. In 1850, 4.6% of the population was 65 or older, a figure that rose to only 4.7% by 1900. Substantial aging of the population did not occur until the second decade of the twentieth century, distinctly separate in time from industrialization, urbanization, and most of the other factors associated with modernization.

Urbanization

The growth of cities was an important aspect of British development, for the rate of growth of urban areas can be broadly correlated with economic change. In 1800 England was still substantially a rural society, with more than half the population dwelling in small towns and villages. By 1891, 72.1% of the English population lived in towns of over 2000 inhabitants, and nearly 32% lived in cities of over 100,000 (Weber, 1967:144). By the turn of the century the rural sector had dwindled to only 23% of the whole (Census of England and Wales, 1911, vol. 55:35).

Cities were not monolithic entities of a single kind; rather, a variety of urban types existed with different occupational structures. London was a commercial and financial center where almost no large-scale manufacturing took place, as was York. In contrast, the textile manufacturing cities of Stockport and Preston were born with industrialization, and in these grimy factory towns most of the labor force, which included men, women, and children, was employed in textile manufacture. In the latter half of the century, cities like Sheffield grew with the expansion of heavy industry in iron and steel.

Both "push" and "pull" factors existed to stimulate urban growth. The major source of recruits to the expanding textile and steel industries was the labor surplus of the agricultural regions. The labor force in agriculture had continued to expand well into the nineteenth century in terms of numbers even though the relative contribution of agriculture to the economy had gradually declined, as shown in Table 2.2. However, in the latter half of the century the demand for agricultural labor slowed down, and a considerable increase in migration from rural areas to towns occurred. One "pull" factor was wages. As Table 2.3 shows, agricultural wages throughout the second half of the nineteenth century were approximately 50% of industrial wages. This gap in earnings, together with the demands of industry for more labor, drew agricultural workers away from the land and propelled them toward the factories and steel mills. There was a substantial rural out-migration in the 1850s, followed by a check in the 1860s and an even higher outflow in the 1870s and 1880s (Chambers and Mingay, 1966:186).

In the 1850s and in subsequent decades, labor shortages occurred periodically as workers migrated to towns (Jones, 1964:322). The situation was further exacerbated by an agricultural depression in the 1870s.[4] In response to the depression and the general shortages in

[4] A complex combination of events set off the depression in agriculture (Mingay, 1979:47). A few years of extraordinarily bad harvests coincided with an increasing flood of American grain into the United Kingdom and Europe, as the expansion of the railroads through the American grain lands and the development of the coal-burning steamship rapidly reduced freight rates on land and sea (Mingay, 1979:47). By 1902 a quarter of wheat could be brought by rail a thousand miles from Chicago to New York and then shipped across the Atlantic another 3000 miles to Liverpool for less than three shillings; 30 years earlier it had cost four times as much (Mingay, 1979:48). Although most European countries put up tariff barriers, England retained its free trade policies. This absence of tariffs gave foreign producers free access to a comparatively affluent and expanding British market (Perry, 1977:118). The contraction of British trade due to increased competition from abroad checked consum-

TABLE 2.2. *The Industrial Distribution of the National Income of Great Britain, 1801-1901 (percentage)*

Year	Agriculture, forestry, fishing	Manufacture, mining, building	Trade and transport	Domestic and personal	Housing	Income from abroad	Government, professional, and all other	Total national income
1801	32.5	23.4	17.4	5.5	5.3	-	15.8	100.0
1811	35.7	20.8	16.6	5.2	5.7	-	16.0	100.0
1821	26.1	31.9	15.9	5.7	6.2	1.0	13.1	100.0
1831	23.4	34.4	17.3	5.7	6.5	1.1	11.6	100.0
1841	22.1	34.4	18.4	6.0	8.2	1.4	9.6	100.0
1851	20.3	34.3	18.7	5.2	8.1	2.1	11.3	100.0
1861	17.8	36.5	19.6	5.2	7.5	3.0	10.4	100.0
1871	14.2	38.1	22.0	5.0	7.6	4.3	8.9	100.0
1881	10.4	37.6	23.0	4.9	8.5	5.8	9.9	100.0
1891	8.6	38.4	22.5	5.5	8.1	7.3	9.6	100.0
1901	6.4	40.2	23.3	4.8	8.2	6.5	10.7	100.0

Source: Deane and Cole, 1964:166.

TABLE 2.3. *Agricultural and Industrial Wage Rates, 1850-1914*

Year	Weekly wage rates		Ratio, agriculture: industry (percentage)	
	Agricultural	Industrial	Unadjusted	Adjusted
1850-1857	10s. 0d.	22s. 10d.	44	49
1858-1866	11s. 0d.	23s. 7d.	47	52
1867-1873	12s. 2d.	25s. 11d.	47	52
1874-1878	13s. 9d.	27s. 11d.	49	55
1879-1883	13s. 7d.	27s. 0d.	50	56
1884-1896	13s. 8d.	27s. 9d.	49	55
1897-1910	15s. 0d.	31s. 4d.	48	53
1911-1914	16s. 2d.	32s. 11d.	49	54

Source: Newby, 1979:35.

labor, farmers employed various strategies to limit their demand for workers. Some took up farming on a larger scale or altered methods of cultivation, and there was a general tendency to employ more relatives. Early in the century, the abundance of cheap labor had mitigated against mechanization. However, throughout the latter half of the century farmers turned increasingly to a growing range of machines that were now reasonably efficient and well advertised. If regular workers failed, the farmer could fall back on general laborers, the Irish, the half-employed "catch-worker," and the unemployed from the towns. Between 1861 and 1901, the decrease in total male agricultural laborers was just over 40%, and this flight from

---

ing power at home and returned demand to normal levels. The abnormal supply continued because of high agricultural productivity. Overproduction was the result, particularly in the most vulnerable and least competitive products: the basic bread grains (Saul, 1969:24). Tenant farmers were unable to pay the high rents to the landowners. The capital value of farms fell, and many were given up (Perry, 1977:76). Great stretches of land went out of cultivation, and the demand for labor decreased.

agricultural occupations contributed materially to the depopulation of the countryside (Saville, 1957:15).

One of the consequences of urbanization was the "aging" of the countryside. As with immigrants to other areas, those who left the countryside for the towns belonged to the younger age groups, and by the end of the century the age structures of rural and urban areas were markedly different. There were fewer males and females between the ages of 20 and 50 in the rural areas, and "in the highest age-groups there was a marked excess of old people compared with the proportions for the country in general, or the urban areas taken separately [Saville, 1957:31]."

Although a brief portrait of the major demographic events that occurred in the nineteenth century has been drawn, the entire process can be understood only within the broader context of the economic changes wrought by industrialization. It is to these changes we now turn.

Changes in the Mode of Production

What is notable in terms of the pace of industrialization is that mid-eighteenth-century Britain was already a monetary and market economy on a national scale. There was no peasantry in the Continental sense, and local and regional self-sufficiency had already been seriously undermined by a web of cash sales and purchases (Hobsbawm, 1968:15). The growing use of imported commodities expanded overseas trade and commercialized rural life.

Still, most of the industries and manufacturers were rural, and the labor force was of an unspecialized nature. Domestic industry was subordinate to agriculture, and occupational boundaries were fluid. Many laborers even in industries such as mining, building, or ironworking moved from industrial to agricultural occupations at times of harvest or planting (Deane, 1965:15).

The country craftsman or mechanic was a man with two or three strings to his bow. The thatcher might turn hay trusser for the summer seasons, the hurdle maker to repairing carts and wagons, the stonemason, when out of work, to jobbing carpentry. A Wiltshire thatcher . . . turned his hand to making sheep-cages when there was not thatching to be done; he also built cottages of wattle and daub, or chalk stone, letting them out to poor laborers at 1s. a week or selling them off [Samuel, 1975:5].

Early industrialization—that is, the phase known as protoindustrialization—occurred in rural villages and small towns, and there was a massive proletarianization of the labor force long before power-driven factories played a significant role in manufacturing. Proletarianization occurred as the village artisan or smallholder increasingly came to specialize in the manufacture of some product, such as cloth, hosiery, or metal goods. An undertaker usually gave out materials to the craftsman to be worked up to his order. The worker was paid by the piece for the work that was done. In some cases the undertaker also owned the worker's tools, and in a few cases even the domestic workshop. Thus, the industrial undertaker came to control, plan, and organize the whole process of production. The only difference between this form of production and the more advanced form of industrialization was that the actual work was scattered instead of being concentrated in factories (Dobb, 1926:291).

In the eighteenth and throughout the nineteenth century, the small farmer or independent artisan was increasingly likely to be a wage laborer, as the separate middle class of semiindependent, small masters began to disappear (Dobb, 1926:308). As of 1760, there was a total of 1.5 million families in England and Wales, and 100,000 of them were rural producers of wool, silk, and other fabrics; 100,000 were families of husbandmen; and another 200,000 were families of rural laborers (Tilly, 1981b:3). Approximately 40% of the population depended mainly on wages, and at least 13% received wages in manufacturing.

The nineteenth century brought about a great concentration of capital combined with an effort by capitalists to take control of the whole productive process (Tilly, 1981b:8). The market centers where merchants congregated to buy the village products, distribute (put out) the raw material, and rent out the looms or frames to cottage workers became towns of workshops where primitive manufacturers collected the finished goods from the scattered outworkers. In order to increase the return from labor, workers were grouped into common locales on coordinated work schedules and standard discipline. Villages where men and women alternated between farm labor and domestic manufacture became industrial villages of full-time weavers, knitters, or miners, and some of these industrial villages developed into industrial towns.

Gradually, in many industries the domestic system was replaced by factory production, as technological change and the needs of manufacturers for greater control over the productive process made large-scale production more profitable. The transformation occurred first in cotton.

The Decline of Domestic Production in Cotton

The cotton industry, like wool and other textiles, was a small, cottage industry of the protoindustrial type in the late eighteenth century. Production took place in the household, and all family members played a part. Children did preliminary operation such as cleaning and carding the raw cotton and assisted the weaver. Women spun the yarn, and men wove the cloth (Deane, 1965:84). In many households, it was subsidiary to agriculture, providing casual employment when seasonal demand for agricultural labor was low.

The technical problem that affected the mechanization of the cotton industry was the imbalance between the efficiency of spinning and weaving, for the spinning wheel could not supply the weavers with enough yarn quickly enough (Hobsbawm, 1968:42). Hargreaves's spinning jenny, patented in 1770, had the immediate effect of multiplying the amount of yarn that could be spun by a single operator, saving labor where it had been scarce (Deane, 1965:86).

The invention with even greater significance for the revolution in cotton was the water frame, patented by Arkwright in 1769. The water frame produced cotton yarn strong enough to serve as warp and weft, creating a sturdy cloth not mixed with linen. Initially powered by water and later by steam, it was a factory machine from the beginning and was central in spelling the demise of domestic industry. The third influential invention was Crompton's mule, also implying factory production, which combined the principles of the jenny and water frame to produce smoother and finer yarn. As steam power was applied, factories could be located where no water power was available, and this contributed to the increase in spinning as well.

Weaving initially kept pace with these inventions by a multiplication of hand looms and manual weavers (Hobsbawm, 1968:42). The attractiveness of weaving wages compared with those of other occupations, like agriculture or wool weaving, drew many families, and the number of weavers steadily grew from 40,000 in 1780 to 100,000 in 1790 and almost 200,000 by 1810 (Lyons, 1979:7).

Although a power loom had been invented in the 1780s, it was not introduced on a considerable scale until the 1830s and 1840s, and hand-loom weavers began to be displaced by the power looms. The power loom was not used earlier on a large scale because the relatively primitive state of machine making made it impossible to produce an efficient machine at an advantageous cost to manufacturers. Further, there was an ample supply of hand loom weavers, so that there was little incentive to introduce a costly, complex, and initially unreliable machine (Bythell, 1969:82). As power looms became more feasible, the main burden of adjustment fell upon the domestic producers, as their looms were rendered obsolete. By 1851, the number of hand-loom weavers had declined to 40,000 (Lyons, 1979:10).

When work was done in the household, regular hours were unnecessary. The craft worker owned the means of production and had considerable freedom in the manner and timing of work. Even under the putting-out system, where weavers received raw materials and returned the finished product to one entrepreneur on a weekly basis, there was little direct pressure that could be placed on a worker in regard to the finishing of work allotted.

As it became more profitable for the capitalist manufacturer to have greater control over the labor force, home industries declined. By 1841, about 70% of the cotton operatives were employed in factories. Of those employed in cotton factories, 48% were women and girls and another 13% children under 14. With a large, unorganized, and low-priced labor supply at his disposal, the manufacturer could easily expand or contract the working hours of his employees to meet market demands. The organization of weaving into factories changed the relationship between capitalist employer and worker, giving the employer the power of supervision over the entire labor process. Thus, although profits increased, workers' wages in the form of piece rates fell steadily from 1790 to the 1840s, with some cyclical variations (Lyons, 1979:11).

By 1850, the mechanization of the cotton industry was virtually complete (Deane, 1965:94). It continued to grow steadily until the cotton famine created by the American Civil War. The cotton industry also continued to employ women in factories, although child labor declined after the Education Act of 1876 made school attendance compulsory to age 14. In the last quarter of the nineteenth century, the total increase in growth was less, but imports continued to increase until the beginning of World War I (Deane and Cole, 1964:188).

Domestic Production in the Nineteenth Century

Although cotton presents something of an ideal-typical situation in terms of the pace of industrialization, development was considerably more irregular and incomplete in other industries, and extensive remnants of domestic production still existed well into the nineteenth century both in rural villages and in urban areas. The Inspector of Factories report in 1876 listed a variety of handicrafts found in villages, including pillow lace making, lace clipping, chair making, brickmaking, straw plait making, boot and shoe making, winding for hosiery, seaming for hosiery, knitting, and gloving (Kitteringham, 1975:117).

In some of these villages, the domestic worker retained a measure of independence. For example, plaiting was a major home industry, and plaiters typically obtained their materials in a variety of ways, buying direct from the farmer, from dealers who came around to buy the made-up plait, or from the local store (Kitteringham, 1975:123). They also sold their own finished goods at the plaiting market. The process has been recaptured in one descriptive account of a village market:

The markets were alive with the carts of straw being brought in and the bags and carts of plait being taken to the plait warehouses for transporting to factories to be made up into hats, bonnets, etc.—locally and in London. Haggling would commence the moment the bell rang, different twists and qualities fetched different prices, and there were also shifts from week to week in prices. The women had to stand out for the best bargain. Then there was the straw to be bought for the next week's plaiting and a round of the dealers to be made, and perhaps—if she had made a good sale—household goods to be bought at the stalls. Finally, there was the long journey home on foot. [Kitteringham, 1975:125].

Some women worked independently; in other instances a village middlewoman was involved, fetching the straw to the cottagers and bringing their finished product to market.

Domestic industry was also extensive in London late into the nineteenth century, but here as in many rural industries domestic workers had no control over the allocation of the factors of production, including their own labor power. Rather, the inability of London to compete with those industries engaged in large-scale factory production contributed to the expansion of the "sweated trades" (Stedman Jones, 1971:106).

The development of London as the commercial and financial center of the world market, as well as the center of imperial government, intensified the competition for scarce urban land and raised rents enormously. Large-scale factory production was made prohibitively expensive, and London simply could not compete with other areas in the production of raw materials, semifinished goods, or heavy capital goods (Stedman Jones, 1971:20). The solution in London was to subdivide production and dispense with the services of a skilled labor force in all but a few production processes. Manufacturers took advantage of a cheap, large, unskilled labor pool of women and immigrants who were willing to work at below subsistence wages, thus reducing London overheads to a minimum.

Sweating, then, was one solution to the problem of provincial factory competition. Instead of industrialization engendering a factory system, in London it involved the "vertical disintegration of production [Hall, 1962:55]." Although traditional London industries such as shipbuilding, silk manufacture, tanning, and rubber processing departed for the outskirts of London or the provinces, those trades that produced commodities of high value and low bulk, involved specialization in preparation, and required large inputs of labor and small inputs of power prospered (Stedman Jones, 1971:26). Ironically, the impact of the Industrial Revolution on London accentuated its preindustrial characteristics.

In any discussion of industrialization, the unevenness of development and change between one industry and another needs to be emphasized, for in many sectors technology and industrial structures remained traditional and unrevolutionized until the twentieth century (Saville, 1973:1). Two related heavy industries, iron and coal, both were affected by industrialization in quite different ways. The increase in coal production occurred without any labor-saving devices, but simply with an increase in the number of coal miners. Because of the rural location and traditional background of the labor force in mining, miners remained villagers. In contrast, iron production was immensely transformed by technological change, and the nature of the labor force changed as well.

Industrialization in Coal and Iron

At the beginning of the nineteenth century, the principal market for coal was the domestic market and the small domestic producer, which were often indistinguishable. The growth of both British and Euopean industry increased the demand for British coal (Taylor, 1968:38). By 1869 the iron industry consumed 30% of the coal produced, and general manufacturing, another 26% (Deane and Cole, 1964:219). Unlike cotton, the increase in the output of coal was accomplished without the use of any significant labor-saving devices. Rather, the expansion of coal produced a rapid increase in the number of coal miners, from 200,000 in 1850 to well over 1 million by 1914. Through the entire second half of the nineteenth century, more than 1 person in 20 was engaged in some form of mining (Benson, 1980:26).

The growth of the coal mining industry was inextricably tied to iron, since it was coal that fired the blast furnaces. In the first half of the nineteenth century, the iron industry was scattered, migratory, and intermittent in operation (Deane, 1965:103). As the steam-driven blast furnace allowed the concentration of large-scale units of production in regions where coal and iron were in ample supply and water-borne transport was available, the iron industry began to lose its migratory character. Stability increased capacity production, which grew from a maximum of 120 tons a week prior to 1850 to as much as 550 tons a day by 1870 (Clapham, 1932:50).

The stimulus to growth that made increased iron production profitable was provided by the railroads. Between 1830 and 1850, 6000 miles of rail were opened. Initially, the growth was in puddled iron rather than steel, as steel production was slow and expensive. The early railways were built of iron plates and run on iron rails. It was only gradually that technological advances made the puddler "sweating at his furnace" obsolete. The Bessemer converter, invented in 1850, and the open-hearth furnace, invented in the 1860s, reduced the cost of the production of steel, increasing its potential for large-scale mass production (Clapham, 1932:52). In 1872, the North-Eastern Railroad experimented with steel rails, points, and crossings, and by 1877 it had ceased to give orders for iron rails (Clapham, 1932:57). Despite its abandonment by the railways, puddled iron maintained some strength until about 1883 due to the demand for iron in shipbuilding. Eventually, steel, with its lower costs and higher durability, replaced puddled iron in the shipbuilding industry as well (Clapham, 1932:63).

Although the major demand for unskilled labor was in coal mining, steel also provided jobs for the unskilled. For example, in the steel and engineering works in Sheffield, there was a tremendous growth between 1851 and 1891 in numbers employed in the heavy trades. Employment increased over 300% compared to an increase of only 50% in the light trades (Pollard, 1959:159).

The growth of heavy industry meant a change in the scale of operations. In Sheffield, "John Brown employed 200 men in 1856, 2,500 in 1863 and 5,000 in 1872; Thomas Firth's staff rose from 20 or 30 in 1842 to 500 in 1857 and 2,000 in 1890; Cambell's from a handful in 1844 to 3,000 in 1865 and 4,000 in 1872 [Pollard, 1960:162]." As firms were faced with the problems of managing increasingly large numbers of workers, the details of administration changed. Increased numbers of workers meant increased discipline and regular hours, and throughout the century there was a steady growth of a managerial class of workers. Size created a further distance between employer and worker, as one writer explains:

> The "shareholder" as such had no knowledge of the lives, thoughts, or needs of the workmen employed by the Company in which he held shares, and his influence on the relations of capital and labor was not good. The paid manager acting for the company was in more direct relation with the men and their demands, but even he had seldom that familiar personal knowledge of the workmen which the employer had often had under the patriarchal system of the old family business now passing away [Trevelyan, 1956:573].

Furnaces, converters, and rolling and cogging mills represented considerable investments with a high rate of obsolescence (Pollard, 1959:162). The exceptional profits in the heavy trades enabled some firms to accumulate sufficient capital out of their own earnings, but virtually all the large works eventually had to turn to the open market and adopt limited liability before the turn of the century.

Still, it is important to recognize that production on a small scale had not disappeared. In London, for example, no more than a sixth of the adult labor force was engaged in factory production as late as the 1890s (Stedman Jones, 1971:29). Even in printing and bookbinding, where the average firm size tended to be large, nearly 60% of all London firms employed less than five men each in 1851, a situation that was not substantially modified in the next 40 years. Sawmills were usually aggregates of individual work benches hired to sawyers and turners, and similar types of subcontracting took place among boilermakers in the shipyards and in piano, carriage building, and light leather goods factories. Even those employed by major companies on the docks were hired on a subcontract basis (Stedman Jones, 1971:30).

By the dawn of the twentieth century, the rate of industrial growth in England had slowed down. To a large extent the slackening of growth was hidden by an increase in the proportion of products exported and the "invisible" exports of shipping, banking, insurance, and overseas investments (Perkin, 1969:411). As the first country to industrialize, Great Britain had a decided advantage in the world market, but this lead rapidly dissipated as Belgium, Germany, France, and the United States began to achieve more rapid rates of growth.

The relative decline in growth was accompanied by a movement of labor, initially from agriculture to industry and then to services, as trade, transport, and commerce created new demands (Deane and Cole, 1964:142–143). There was a significant expansion of middle-class occupations in both white-collar jobs and the professions and a decline in self-employed workers.

Changes in the economy altered the relationship of employer to employee and created an increasingly visible and vocal working class. Throughout the century working-class representatives increasingly demanded a voice in government and programs that would redistribute the wealth. The next section will explore alterations in the distribution of political power and the social reforms that accompanied the expansion of state responsibility.

The Changing Role of the State

The Distribution of Political Power

Before 1815, the distribution of political power was hardly an issue. At the end of the eighteenth century, the House of Lords consisted almost entirely of great landowners, whereas three-quarters of the House of Commons were also landowners or their near relations (Perkin, 1969:39). Government was a function of property and reflected its distribution. As Arthur Young, author of "Reports of the Society for Bettering the Condition and Increasing the Comforts of the Poor," wrote in 1794:

> The principle of our constitution is the representation of property, imperfectly in theory, but efficiently in practice . . . the great mass of property, both landed, monied and commercial, finds itself represented; and that the evils of such representation are trivial, will appear from the ease, happiness, and security of all the lower classes, hence possible virtual representation takes place even where the real seems most remote [quoted in Perkin, 1969:39].

Local government also reflected the proportional influence of graduated property and its institutions. Quarter Sessions, borough corporations, and parish officers were the forms by which a hierarchy of property holders governed (Perkin, 1969:40). The large country manors dominated village life, and the local squire exerted tremendous influence and social control over his tenants and villagers, manifested in the inevitability with which they followed his politics and religion (Perkin, 1969:42). Although the landowners had a large stake in maintaining the traditional structure of society that protected their property interests, they also played a role in stimulating industrialization, since the exploitation of their land for agricultural development and mining increased their rents (Perkin, 1969:75).

Interest politics rather than class politics predominated, and representatives of various trades, industries, and professions vied for patronage of their particular policies. Government and private patronage controlled nearly all appointments from bishoprics and apprenticeships to domestic service, and appointments were solicited among friends as a matter of pride and principle (Perkin, 1969:45). Patronage filled jobs, fostered talent, and provided pensions as well as meshed the continuing loyalties to the old society.

Gradually these relationships of patronage and dependency broke down, and contemporaries attributed the birth of class consciousness to the abdication of responsibility by the aristocracy. As a contributor to *Blackwood's Edinburgh Magazine* lamented in 1820:

> Everywhere, in every walk of life, it is too evident that the upper orders of Society have been tending, more and more, to a separation of themselves from those whom nature, providence, and law have placed beneath them. . . . The rich and the high have been indolently and slothfully allowing the barriers that separate them from their inferiors to increase and accumulate [quoted in Perkin, 1969:183].

In truth, there had been a decline in the traditions of protection for workers. The mercantile regulation of wages and prices no longer existed except in a few protected industries like silk, yet through the Combination Acts of 1799 and 1800 Parliament refused to allow workers to negotiate for themselves (Perkin, 1969:188). Similarly, the poor law was rewritten to prevent the rural practice of supplementing wages out of the rates.

From around 1770 to the 1830s, parochial and patronized forms of collective action gave way to national and autonomous forms, and the creation of a national social movement became an established way of accomplishing a set of political ends (Tilly, 1981a:6). Participants began to act on their own initiative, making claims for change on behalf of an unrepresented constituency and using mass demonstrations to draw attention to their cause. Public meetings replaced food riots and election brawls, and it became increasingly common for organized groups to hire a hall, print handbills, and make public displays of grievances and affiliations (Tilly, 1981a:20).

The first organized indication of the dissatisfaction of the working class appeared in the Parliamentary Reform Movement of 1816–1819, whose platform was household and then universal suffrage. It was the first time that working-class protest organized on a national scale for a nonviolent purpose, that of reform (Perkin, 1969:212). Although the movement failed, the same issue—the reform of the franchise—was taken up by the middle classes, who were incensed by the landowners' use of political power to protect rents at the expense of wages and profits. Their problem was symbolized in the Corn Law, passed by Parliament in 1815.

The Corn Law prohibited the import of corn until the price on the home market reached 80 shillings a quarter. The intent was to protect the price of corn sold by English farmers. The effect of the Corn Law was to keep the price of food high and cause drastic and disastrous fluctuations in prices (Thomson, 1950:36). A new Corn Law in 1828, which fixed a sliding scale of import duties, worked no better and only served to incense further industrialists who wanted to keep wages and manufacturing costs low. With increasing insistence, manufacturers argued for the repeal of the Corn Law, free trade, and a lessening of the power of agricultural and landed interests in Parliament.

The antiquated electoral system on which Parliament was based became increasingly anachronistic with the growth and shift of population and the rise of large northern towns. Although most wealthy farmers and small landholders in the rural districts could vote, many of the urbanizing boroughs were distinctly unrepresented. In the early 1830s, a movement for the reform of Parliament arose among many of the politically unrepresented—farmers, laborers, and shopkeepers who combined with mercantile and industrial interests to agitate for reform. The Whig spokesmen for these new forms of wealth were content to allow property rather than people to be represented, for their main interest was to allow industrialists and merchants into Parliament.

In 1832, a Reform Bill was passed that removed some of the disparities between the propertied middle class and the landowners by establishing the first middle-class franchise. The bill incorporated a principle of popular election and extended the franchise to ten-pound householders in certain districts and to tenant farmers. However, a system of open voting prevailed, so that considerable pressure could still be exerted by rural landlords on their constituencies. The extension of the franchise was narrow and complicated and benefited most of the wealthier merchants, who now had access to local government. The bill still left half the middle class and all of the working class without political representation, for the total net addition of new voters was only 286,000 to the old electorate of 366,000 (Thomson, 1950:74). Limited as it was, it symbolized a weakening of the power of the old order, entrenched in the House of Lords.

Ultimately, the more significant aspect of the reform bill was the redistribution of seats among the constituencies, as many of the old boroughs lost their separate representation or one of their two members in the House of Commons. Representation was given to 43 boroughs that had been without it, and in most cases they were the new, large industrial and commercial towns of the north. The over-representation of the countryside and small agricultural towns was diminished, and urban industry and business expanded its share of power. This reform measure, however, was soon made out-of-date by continued rapid urban growth.

In order to extend local representation further and at the same time institute tighter central control over the old paternalistic system, Parliament passed the Municipal Corporations Act of 1835, in which borough councils elected by the ratepayers became the regular form of town authority. Each of the new municipalities was empowered to levy a local rate or tax and gradually to assume the various functions, sanitary and other, that had previously been exercised by *ad hoc* local bodies (Treveylan, 1956:245). Thus, in every municipal area a powerful and at least partially popularly elected authority was set up and that in time absorbed nearly every local public activity. In contrast, the rural districts remained under the government of the squires for another half-century, and the spirit of the old regime continued to reign until 1888, when the establishment of County Councils followed the enfranchisement of the rural laborer in 1884.

The years between 1832, when the working class was denied the vote, and 1867, when urban household suffrage was conceded, were times of struggle for political representation. The major working-class movement in the first half of the century was Chartism. Organized initially in 1836 and given momentum by the new, harshly punitive Poor Law of 1834, Chartism sought universal (male) suffrage, annual parliaments, a secret ballot, equal electoral districts, abolition of the property qualification for parliamentary candidates, and payment of members (Beer, 1953:27). Although Chartism itself failed and eventually dissolved as a political movement in the 1840s, all its goals were implemented by the end of the century.

From the mid-nineteenth century until around 1875, the socialist fervor that had characterized earlier working-class movements remained silent. This was the heyday of liberalism, and when the voice of labor was heard, it came largely from Friendly Societies and the skilled trade unionists—small bodies of workers centering around three industries: the traditional crafts, textiles, and mining. Membership in these unions was generally confined to the more prosperous stratum of the working class, the labor "aristocracy," for two reasons. First, only the better-paid worker could afford the weekly subscription rate, so that many workers were automatically excluded. Second, only the well-organized trades were able to restrict entry to the occupation, creating a scarcity of labor that maintained high wages. These generally conservative unions worked with and through the traditional political parties and in the 1870s managed to gain several major concessions, including the complete legal recognition of trade unions (1871) and the legalization of trade disputes and all peaceful methods of pursuing them (1875). As representatives of the more successful of the working class, they aligned themselves with Liberal philosophy, emphasizing the widely held Victorian values of virtue, thrift, temperance, and self-reliance.

By the 1850s, it was apparent that the Reform Bill of 1832 was inadequate in terms of its structure of representation, but it took another 15 years before the franchise was extended further. In 1867, urban household suffrage was granted to all occupiers of houses in the boroughs rated at £12 or more and all leaseholders of property with a £4 annual value. At the same time, 45 seats were redistributed, which strengthened the representation of the counties and larger towns at the expense of the smaller towns. The effect was to increase the middle-class vote and extend the vote to skilled artisans and workers in the towns, the more trustworthy elements of the working class. Still, the electorate was less than 10% of the total population (Thomson, 1950:129). Further reforms occurred in succeeding years as the secret ballot in 1872 allowed workers to vote without fears of reprisals from employers. Public opinion became more of a reality in politics. Finally, in 1884 the vote was extended to agricultural laborers.

In the last quarter of the century, because of the tremendous expansion in the numbers of semiskilled and unskilled laborers in the heavy industries, a new type of unionism became disturbingly (to the middle class) visible. The economic problems of the new trade unionists were very different from those of the skilled workers who had long established unions, and their methods and tactics were also different. The old unions of labor "aristocrats" had rarely resorted to picketing in their strike actions, for they were able to rely on the scarce skills of their members as a crucial bargaining weapon. In contrast, the new unionists were subject to the pressures of an overstocked labor market, and the picket was a necessary tactic (Saville, 1960:318).

In 1886, the Social Democratic Federation (S.D.F.), a recently organized socialist group, seized upon the dissatisfaction of the unemployed to organize marches and demonstrations in Manchester, Birmingham, London, and elsewhere. Some of the demonstrations ended in violent confrontations that appalled the middle class and provoked retaliatory measures by the police but gave the S.D.F. visibility among the working class (Beer, 1953:262). Due to the tactics used by the new unionism and its association with socialism, public opinion became increasingly hostile, particularly during and immediately following a major dockers' strike in 1889. All through the 1890s a hostility toward trade unionism was expressed that at times bordered on the hysterical. The period after 1889 can be characterized as one of a developing counterattack by the propertied classes, triggered by the special characteristics of the new unionism that made it the particular target of middle-class fury (Saville, 1960:317).

Traditionally, labor had been aligned with the Liberal party, whose strategy of containment had been to run Labour candidates on the Liberal ticket, as Lib–Labs. The unions had generally been cooperative about working for reforms through traditional politics, but their newly gained political freedom inspired them to attempt more independent action. The S.D.F. was always ambivalent about the value of social reform as a tool for reaching socialist goals. This ambivalence concerning the relation between reform and revolution as well as its opposition to trade unions, which it saw as merely palliative, prevented it from becoming an effective political force (Beer, 1953:269). The S.D.F. made a temporary peace with unionism in 1897 by urging its members to join unions and work through them for reforms. Socialists and local unions began to put up independent labor candidates, while the Liberals put up a competing Liberal–Labour candidate. The result was often a split vote and a victory for the Conservatives. In 1899, the Trades Union Congress (T.U.C.) voted to make a concerted attempt to increase the number of Labour candidates in Parliament, and in 1900 they organized a Labour Representation Committee (L.R.C.). Initially, the S.D.F. was represented on the Labour Representation Committee. However, in 1901 the Labour party rejected the S.D.F. agenda and made it clear that their goal was a socialistic reorganization of society, not a revolution. The S.D.F. withdrew their support from the L.R.C., not regrouping until 1911, when they became the British Socialist Party (Beer, 1953:385). The withdrawal of the socialists weakened the conference, and membership waned (Rothstein, 1929:285).

In 1901, the Taff Vale and Denaby Main cases stripped the trade unions of many of the legal rights they had gained in the 1870s that had made combinations of workmen equivalent to combinations of employers (Saville, 1960:318). These judicial decisions were accompanied by a virulent campaign by the press against the unions as the cause of the failure of British industry to compete successfully with German and American competition. These attacks brought new life to the fledgling Labour party, and the total number of members affiliated with the L.R.C. rose dramatically. Labour began to score electoral victories, and in 1906, when 29 L.R.C. candidates were elected to Parliament, compared with only 14 of the Liberal–Labour group, they formally became the Labour party (Rothstein, 1929:286). Eventually they succeeded in reversing the decisions of the House of Lords and resecured their old rights.

Although landowners did not lose control of the House of Commons until the 1880s, the pressure of middle-class votes and the increasing coalition of interests between the two classes forced concession much earlier. In terms of overall effects, it was not so much that the landed gentry lost power, but that there was a fusion in politics and society of aristocratic and middle-class interests. Not until the closing decades of the century did workers gain a voice in government and begin to assert their interests through an organized labor movement. The changing political power structure was reflected in and supported by competing value systems, roughly summarized as mercantilism, laissez faire liberalism, and state socialism.

Political Economy and the Expansion of Government Responsibility

Mercantilism, the inheritor of feudalism, was a collection of policies based on the assumption that government could regulate internal industry and consumption and external trade. From the Restoration until the end of the eighteenth century, the right to regulate internal industry was maintained, as for example, the infamous law of 1666 requiring burial in woolen (Perkin, 1969:66). However, by the eighteenth century its power had weakened considerably. Internal controls were sporadic in nature and ineffectively administered, and English manufacturers had increasingly come to recognize the value of a less restrictive commercial policy.

The increasingly predominant view as the eighteenth century came to a close was that society was composed of isolated individuals who were capable of judging their own best interests. The individual, sovereign and freely competing in a free market, was the center of the universe. The welfare of the whole was seen as a function of the activities of its members, and any interference with individual behavior was deleterious to both the individual and the social good, which were synonymous.

The philosophic apology for individual initiative that unified moral philosophy and economic behavior into a new synthesis was provided by Adam Smith's *Wealth of Nations*. Smith expressed the view that human motives could be reduced to two: a desire to better our condition, which prompts people to save, and the passion for present enjoyment, which prompts people to spend. Both selfish, he argued for the construction of an economic commonwealth in which individuals seeking to further their own self-interest would unwittingly further the public good.

Smith was one of the primary exponents of the view that the greatest good would operate under conditions of competition within the free market, a view that conflicted directly with the mercantilist assumption that the regulation of industry was a part of the government's function (Checkland, 1964:384). Smith and other political economists rejected state regulation of industry, because mercantilists had used regulation to distribute monopolies and other privileges (Sorley, 1965:192). Smith made a comprehensive survey of state regulation in agriculture, home industry, and foreign trade and maintained that, in each case, every system of protection retarded the progress of society toward real wealth and greatness and diminished the value of land and labor. Natural liberty could establish itself, asserted Smith, only when all regulation was swept away.

Although Adam Smith was aware of the limitations of laissez faire in regard to the distribution of wealth, he believed that productivity, which was of prime importance to the welfare of society, depended on the free flow of the market. Any tampering with the distribution of wealth was likely to impede production and decrease the welfare of society. Competition, with its impartial judge of market forces, had replaced patronage as the guiding principle. These principles were used to reform British commercial and fiscal policy and found their expression in the free trade movement.

Jeremy Bentham expanded the political economy of Adam Smith and applied it directly to the role of the state. Bentham and his Utilitarian followers have often been associated with individualism, and the period between 1825 and 1875 has been described as the age of laissez faire, partly due to Bentham's influence upon government policy. It is true that, like other economists of his day, Bentham made a general obeisance to laissez faire, stating in his general rule that "nothing ought to be done or attempted by government for the purpose of causing an augmentation in the national mass of wealth . . . without some special reason. Be quiet ought on those occasions to be the motto or watchword of government [quoted in Taylor, 1972:34]." Yet his *Constitutional Code* published first in 1830 dealt in massive detail with every facet of government, asking among other things for the aristocracy to forgo power, recommending the reconstruction of the legal system, and asking for a large central government administration staffed by paid and trained experts chosen by examination (Roberts, 1959:194). Thus, there was always a role for central government in Benthamite thought, not necessarily for more government but for better government (Taylor, 1972:36).

Where there are clear indications of a successful policy of laissez faire, they occur in terms of freedom from economic regulation. In 1824 and 1825, some measures reducing import duties were successful in Parliament, and in 1826 there were further cuts (Deane, 1965:187). Yet the average rate of duty on net imports remained high. These measures were supplemented by others in the 1830s and 1840s. However, the first crucial step toward complete free trade was the repeal of the Corn Laws.

In 1838, the Anti–Corn Law League was organized for the specific purpose of advocating free trade; it undertook a program of education and lobbying into towns and villages, appealing to both humanitarian interests and self-interests of capital and labor. Ostensibly, the Anti–Corn Law League based its appeal on the economic advantages of free trade: cheaper food, more employment, higher exports, and greater prosperity. Coming at a time of high food prices and industrial distress, it had a great deal of popular appeal. However, the more important concern of the leaguers was with the political consequences of repeal, as they hoped that it would lead to a weakening of the landed interest and the overthrow of the Tory party (Chambers and Mingay, 1966:152). In the 1840s, the concerted political effort of the Anti–Corn Law League combined with a massive and damaging Irish potato blight and a poor British harvest to force concessions on the part of the protectionists, and in 1846 the Corn Laws, which had protected British agriculture for decades, were abandoned (Prothero, 1912:371).

Other restrictions on economic activity were also swept away, including a whole network of restrictions on the mobility of labor and capital. Among them were the Statute of Apprentices, which required a person to serve 7 years before he could follow a trade; the Usury Laws, which set a limit of 5% on the rate that could be charged for loans; and the Bubble Act, which prohibited the formation of joint stock companies except under special dispensation granted only by an act of Parliament (Deane, 1965:204).

Although the economy was, to some extent, deregulated, the more pervasive trend was toward expansion of the centralized state government. This expansion began in the 1830s with, among other issues, the Factory Act of 1833, which restricted the working hours of women and children. Administratively, the Factory Act created a system, however ineffectual, for the supervision of work in factories (Lubenow, 1971:139). In establishing controls over labor, the Factory Act signified a major departure from laissez faire economics, for it marked the beginning of economic regulation. Interestingly, in this, as in other political struggles, the opponents and proponents did not divide along expected lines. Although doctrinaire political economists argued that only long hours could enable England to compete with foreign manufacture, manufacturers favored restrictions to prevent smaller, more isolated mills from working longer hours (Roberts, 1959:199). As Marvel (1977) has shown, the large textile manufacturers, who had recently gained political power with the passage of the Reform Bill, supported the Factory Act of 1833 because they were less dependent on child labor than were the smaller manufacturers in the rural districts. Since the burden of the enforcement of the act was likely to fall more heavily on the small manufacturers, the large urban manufacturers stood to benefit, as restricted output raised prices and increased quasi-rents. Thus, even where laissez faire should have been a central issue since economic regulation was involved, other factors determined where the lines were drawn.

Further expansion of centralized government occurred with the

Poor Law of 1834, which established a central board of three commissioners to formulate policy; the Prison Act of 1835, which provided for the central inspection of prisons; the expansion of public education, and the regulation of railways. Yet the ambivalence of the Victorians toward an expanded central government was reflected in the reversal of the trend toward centralization for a period of approximately 20 years. With an act of 1844, the factory inspectors lost their power to make regulations and act as magistrates. The abandonment of the Railway Regulation Bill in 1847 marked a turning point away from public regulation of railways that was not resumed for two decades (Parris, 1960:26).

The Victorian ambivalence toward state growth was nowhere more evident than in the field of public health, where the issue was not so much laissez faire versus collectivism as it was a struggle between local and central government. Prior to 1846 improvements in public health had their origin in literally thousands of local acts of Parliament that had created some 300 local bodies of commissioners or trustees for paving, cleansing, lighting, and police. Poor law guardians, local boards of health, water and sewer commissioners, highway surveyors, select vestries, and others produced a maze of administrative duplication and inefficiency.

The expansion of England's industry, population growth, and rapid urbanization increased the necessity for national standards of health, as the sewage discharge from one factory or town polluted the health and water supply of localities situated downstream (Gutchen, 1961:86). Gradually, local act legislation was superseded by public general acts of Parliament, such as the Health of Towns Act of 1846 and the Town Improvement Clauses Act of 1847, which demanded uniformity in action.

Two years later, the Public Health Act, under the shadow of a cholera epidemic, established a new central body, the General Board of Health, to supervise the application of the act to the localities. The act also created local boards of health that were empowered to establish and maintain sewers, cleanse streets, remove nuisances, and provide the district's water supply. Since there were no provisions to enforce any of these duties, the local boards actually had a great deal of freedom to act as they chose (Gutchen, 1961:88). Thus, the appearance was one of increased centralization due to the creation of the General Board of Health, but the system was not really centralized.

Although the interventionist tendencies of central government in the field of public health provoked resistance, the arguments against intervention were not centered around laissez faire issues specifically. Rather, opposition to the expansion of central government came largely from the authorities that had come into existence as a result of the Municipal Corporations Act of 1835 and saw the centralizing force as trespassing on the rights of elected local authorities. Thus, resistance to the public health movement was only in the broadest sense a manifestation of laissez faire and basically outside the economic realm most crucial to the arguments of the political economists.

In 1871, the Local Government Board consolidated the functions of several agencies and created a ministry to supervise diverse local government activities. Power was further consolidated under the Public Health Act of 1875, which laid down in comprehensive terms the public health functions and duties of local authorities and was essentially the basis of all public health activity until well into the twentieth century (Fraser, 1973:70). Thus, in public as in nearly every phase of social and economic life, there was throughout the century, with occasional reversals, increased state intervention.

Social thought increasingly reflected the reality of Victorian life in a trend away from laissez faire. From John Stuart Mill on, classical economists began to think in terms of a society in which social cooperation would replace individual competitiveness. Not willing to abandon the principle of competition to which liberal economists attributed the progress of a century, their goal became the improvement of society through the improvement of the capabilities of its individual members.

T. H. Green, the most influential liberal philosopher of the later nineteenth century, provided a bridge between the atomism of earlier laissez faire thinking and the later liberal support of state intervention. Emphasizing the inseparability of the individual and society, Green defined freedom not as the ability to do as one pleases but as the capacity to choose the good identified with the common good.

2. England in Transition

Stressing that every injury to the individual was a public injury, Green gave support to the idea of social reform. He argued for a broad range of measures that would strengthen the ability of the masses to engage in the competitive system and help thwart socialism.

The main difference between the earlier and later orthodox economists, as exemplified by Alfred Marshall, was the latter's willingness to tolerate state intervention. Marshall believed that state intervention could be used for the purpose of increasing the total wealth and making more "just" the distribution of wealth. This intervention was not a substitute for the free economy but rather provided the means to make more effective the workings of the competitive system.

Marshall was also concerned, like Green, with using state socialism to woo the respectable working class, for he feared that laissez faire left the residuum of the working class, the more dangerous element, unregulated (Stedman Jones, 1971:303). State regulation, through forced migration or the establishment of labor colonies—an idea later supported by reformer Charles Booth—was the only solution to the control of a class that was both costly to society and industrially useless (Stedman Jones, 1971:307). As Booth explained, limited concessions to socialism were necessary for the health of individualism:

> Our Individualism fails because our Socialism is incomplete. In taking charge of the lives of the incapable, State Socialism finds its proper work, and by doing it completely, would relieve us of a serious danger. The Individualist system breaks down as things are, and is invaded on every side by Socialistic innovations, but its hardy doctrines would have a far better chance in a society purged of those who cannot stand alone. Thorough interference on the part of the state with the lives of a small fraction of the population would tend to make it possible ultimately to dispense with any Socialistic interference in the lives of all the rest [quoted in Stedman Jones, 1971:308].

Booth advocated a socialism "which shall leave untouched the forces of individualism and the sources of wealth [quoted in Stedman Jones, 1971:308]." This shift from concerns about production to concerns about distribution accompanied the growing recognition that interference with market distribution could have beneficial effects for the whole economy and ultimately defeat the need for socialist intervention. The neoclassical economists believed that by improving the capacity of the poor they would be able to increase their share of the wealth, as well as the total social wealth.

One of the major advocates of limited socialism was the Fabian Society. The theoretician of the Fabian Society was Sidney Webb, whose socialism was based on an extension of the theory of rent. For Webb and the Fabians, the struggle was not between capitalists and the working class, as other socialists believed. Rather, it was waged between the majority of the nation and the appropriators of differential rent. According to Webb, differential rent was the result of social labor that should be used for the good of the whole society. Since wealth was social in its origin, it must be social in its distribution. A government inclined toward social reform must therefore turn its attention to the industrial and agricultural rent and use it in the interests of the whole community, partly by means of taxation, partly by municipalization and nationalization.

The Fabian position was not to restore to the underprivileged their right or due but rather to command the general wealth for the common good. The Fabians concentrated on laying the foundation for a general system of social services that would benefit all members of the community, whether or not they were independent. Their major impact was in broadening the principles of government responsibility and clearly establishing the state's role.

The amount of influence actually wielded by the Fabians is debatable. However, their general policies were implemented between 1906 and 1914, when a series of major reforms were passed. This period has been described by some historians as the origin of the welfare state. Minimum wages were fixed in some industries, and legislation guaranteeing insurance against ill health and unemployment, school meals, medical services for children, and old age pensions was introduced (Hay, 1975:11).

A variety of explanations have been postulated as to why these reforms occurred when they did. Some writers have concentrated on explaining why attitudes toward social reform changed during this period. Others have focused on the political pressures that forced politicians to turn to social reform. Yet others have examined the underlying social and economic changes out of which these reforms emerged. Throughout the rest of this book all of these factors will be explored in terms of their influence on the passage of the old age pension.

To answer those questions raised in Chapter 1, to fill in those gaps in historical knowledge, it is necessary to try to return to early industrial England, if not in body then in spirit, for in the documents and records of the past lie some of the answers. Nascent industrial capitalism expanded and then discarded household production as the most suitable mode for maximizing profits. Although there are few extant records that allow systematic analysis of cottage industry, there were remnants of protoindustrialization that survived in both urban areas and in isolated villages well into the late nineteenth century. One of these was the tiny hand-loom ribbon weaving village of Chilvers Coton.

In the next chapter, both the empirical issue of how household production functioned and the theoretical issue of the impact of the decline of household production on the work and kinship relations of the aged will be examined through a case study of this one village. Chilvers Coton was unique in regard to the trade in which its inhabitants engaged, yet representative of many similar villages in which domestic industry had become a means of enhancing capitalist production

3

Household and Kin

A core feature of early industrialization was the creation and subsequent destruction of cottage industry. Although cottage industry existed to a significant degree for only a brief moment in history, many of the stereotypes of the golden age of aging are based on a romanticized view of cottage industry and the wrenching effects of industrialization and urbanization upon it. As Burgess (1926) states in regard to the aged:

> Their economic security and their social status were assured by their role and place in the extended family. The extended family was often an economic unit of production, frequently a household unit, and always a cohesive unit of social relations and of reciprocal services between the generations. But the balance of prerogatives of property, power and decision making belonged to the aging. The Golden Age of living for older persons was disturbed and undermined by the Industrial Revolution [p. 350].

Although little is known about family life in this protoindustrial period, historians have begun to piece together some descriptive material on how household production functioned. Most productive activity was centered in the household, and the labor needs of the household defined the work roles of family members. "The interdependence of work and residence, of household labor needs, subsistence requirements, and family relationships constituted the 'family economy' [Tilly and Scott, 1978:12]." Family members were maintained within the household according to household labor needs, and those whose labor was not needed left the household to find work elsewhere.[1] What was distinctive about household production was that people worked in their own homes, controlling the pace and organization of production. The family was the unit of production and consumption, and the household was the locus of work and residence (Tilly and Scott, 1978:14).

As the scale of production increased and the factory replaced the household as the center of production, domestic production declined. The family wage economy, which had characterized the family organization of those without property in the past, became a more common form of family organization among the working classes (Tilly and Scott, 1978:63). In these families, family membership meant shared consumption but not shared production, as each individual worked outside the home to bring in cash to meet the family's subsistence needs. While under the domestic mode of production, household labor needs were finite. There was no limit to the number of wage earners that a wage-earning family could use and no limit to the number of children who could live at home. The unit's need for wages, rather than for laborers, defined the work of the family members and the composition of the household.

The goal of working families throughout most of the nineteenth century was to earn enough to maintain a minimum level of subsistence. By the end of the century, the higher wages of men and the increased availability of cheap consumer goods raised the standard of living of working-class families. The family became a wage-earning unit that increasingly emphasized family consumption needs.

---

[1] For example, if there were more children in the family than the size of the landholding warranted in terms of labor needs, they were sent to other households to work as servants (Tilly and Scott, 1978:14).

Husbands and unmarried children, who were expected to contribute to the family income once they finished school, were most likely to work, whereas wives devoted more time to child care and household management (Tilly and Scott, 1978:176).

The position of the aged in the household varied under different modes of production. Anderson (1972:225) compared rural and urban regions of Lancashire in 1851 and found that more older people were living with married children in urban Preston than in the rural portions of the county. His findings contradict the hypothesis that industrialization destroyed the economic basis of the extended family. Rather, urban, industrial life initially increased the rates of co-residence between the aged and their married children.

Little is known about patterns of work over the life cycle under the domestic mode of production. The existence of retirement contracts among peasant farmers throughout northern and central Europe indicates that when property was involved, it was often exchanged for care and provisions in old age (Berkner, 1972; Gaunt, 1979). However, nothing is known about work patterns of the aged under other forms of domestic production. Since one premise of household production is that all family members contribute their labor, it seems likely that the aged would have continued working as long as possible. More research is needed to confirm this hypothesis.

Somewhat more is known about patterns of work of family members over the life cycle under the family wage economy. Men tended to work more continuously than women and children, but this pattern was disturbed in working-class families by sporadic and often extended periods of unemployment. Women tended to work when their children were young, leaving the labor force when their children were old enough to contribute to the support of the family. In old age, these women returned to work if there was employment available, although the labor market in general was more rigid for older people (Lyons, 1979:55). Older women were often substitute workers for ailing or unemployed husbands, and their "low levels of skill and sporadic employment experience restricted them to unskilled, irregular, and low-paying factory jobs [Tilly and Scott, 1978:128]." By the end of the nineteenth century, few married women of any age were employed.

Within the household, older people contributed by baby-sitting for their own married children or others. This was shown with evidence indicating that kin or lodgers were more likely to be present in the households of factory workers when there were young children present (Litchfield, 1978:192). This was particularly true when the wife worked in the factory or other employment outside the home, and often this relative was an aged parent (Anderson, 1971:143). Parents were also taken in if they had some source of support and could contribute to the family income (Anderson, 1971:231). Among workers in nonindustrial occupations, the incidence of coresidence was less, but when it occurred, it was often predicated on the debility of an aged parent (Levine, 1977:53). Generally, aged parents who had no source of support were found only in the more affluent households.

Older widowed people in the nineteenth century not living with married children usually had at least one unmarried child still at home. The average age of these children was likely to be higher than the typical age at which children usually left home, suggesting that children remained in the household to help support their widowed parents (Chudacoff and Hareven, 1979:81). Overall, few old people lived apart from a relative, and urban industrial life increased the proportion of families in which parents and married children coresided (Anderson, 1972:231).

The evidence thus seems to contradict the modernization view that associates industrialization with the demise of the extended family household. Rather, the nineteenth century was a turning point, if only for a transitional period, toward greater complexity. Income generation became more important than family production, and living with kin was one strategy for increasing the number of coresident wage earners (Levine, 1977:57). In this transition the aged were usually not neglected. Rather, by one means or another, they became a part of the family wage-earning unit.

Despite the extensive recent research on the effects of economic and social change on family structure, many of the essential questions posed by modernization theorists remain unanswered. The turning point in the transition from the extended to the nuclear family type is supposedly the demise of the household as an economic unit of production, yet few studies have addressed in detail the role played by family members under the household mode of production. We understand much about the family wage economy through detailed analysis of household census listings but less about the household mode of production. Most of the research on household production and family structure has analyzed farm families where there was property and control of land by the aged (Anderson, 1971:79–98). But what of the multitude of working-class aged, laboring in cottage industries where the only property might be a hand loom? Did they share in the household labor? Did they share in the special benefits of extended family membership? Was there reciprocity between genera- tions? How did the demise of cottage industry affect the response of other family members to the needs of the aged? Did the curtailment of household production reduce their work opportunities? In order to answer these questions, we must turn to a time and place when household production still existed.

The Ribbon Weavers of Chilvers Coton

In the early years of the nineteenth century, the characteristic in- dustrial workers were not employed in factories or mills but instead labored as outworkers in their own homes, receiving raw materials from undertakers or middlemen and returning finished goods for a set price per piece (Thompson, 1965:234). By 1850 throughout much of England, these casual outworkers had been replaced, transformed by technical innovations into factory laborers. However, here and there scattered in little villages and minor industries throughout the countryside, there were still remnants of the old system, of workers laboring in the old way. Among these was the little ribbon weaving village of Chilvers Coton.

George Eliot, who was born at Arbury Farm in Chilvers Coton, knew it well, and in her novel *Scenes of Clerical Life* (n.d.), she wrote of the weavers and the village:

> The roads are black with coal dust, the brick houses dingy with smoke; and at that time—the time of handloom weavers—every other cottage had a loom at its window, where you might see a pale, sickly-looking man or woman pressing a narrow chest against a board and doing a sort of treadmill work with legs and arms [p. 33].

3. Household and Kin

The village itself, shown in the map in Figure 3.1, lies to the south of Nuneaton, into which it was absorbed in 1920 (Salzman, 1947:173). The dust and smoke arose from the two major employers of the men of Chilvers Coton, the centuries-old coal mines and the Griff Brick and Tile Works. The wives, children, and aged parents of these coal miners and brickmakers wove silk ribbons.

In 1850, Chilvers Coton represented one of the last remaining examples of household production. Over the next 15 years, the British silk industry was virtually destroyed, as tariffs on French silks were removed. The decline of silk spelled the demise of the hand-loom ribbon weaving industry and permanently altered life for the residents of Chilvers Coton. Let us first examine in more detail the history of the silk industry before returning to Chilvers Coton at mid-century.

The Ribbon Weaving Industry

In the late seventeenth or early eighteenth century, silk ribbon weaving was introduced to the city of Coventry (Leggett, 1949:285). As part of the silk industry as a whole, ribbon weaving was dependent on imported raw materials and subject to the same market fluctuations, which varied widely according to political and economic conditions. In addition, it was highly dependent on fashion and thus particularly vulnerable to the whims of personal taste. In successive periods of prosperity, ribbon weaving spread among the wives of colliers in the villages to the north and northeast of Coventry (Prest, 1960:44). Chilvers Coton was one of those villages.

The chief European silk center was well established in Lyonnais by the seventeenth century. England was a relative latecomer to the trade, and, perpetually, the prime competitor of English silk was France. To a large extent, the fluctuations in the stability of English silks can be traced to alterations in policies concerning protection. Duties on foreign imports ranging from 10% to 20% were imposed or repealed as the advice of various interested persons or the exigencies of government required (Warner, 1921:489).

In 1773, at the persistent demands of silk weavers and manufacturers, Parliament passed an act strictly prohibiting the importing and wearing of all foreign silks, securing a home-market monopoly

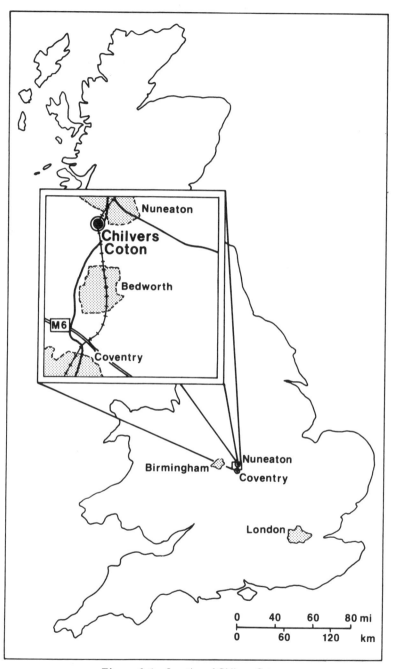

Figure 3.1. *Location of Chilvers Coton.*

for British manufacturers. This act remained effective until 1826, when the tariffs on imported silks were gradually reduced, although a wall of protection around the industry remained. From mid-century, pressure for free trade mounted, and on January 25, 1860, the Royal Speech at the opening of Parliament contained a paragraph announcing the conclusion of a commercial treaty with France. The terms of the treaty regarding the textile trade stated that cotton, woolen, and silk goods manufactured in France were to be admitted into England duty free, whereas English goods of the same nature were to be subject in France to a duty not exceeding 30% of their value. Prior to this treaty, English textiles had been strictly prohibited in France. Since the treaty opened a new market for exports, it was of great advantage to most British manufacturers. Although most of the silk manufacturers protested, Richard Cobden, the author of the treaty, scornfully replied to an advocate for the exemption of silk goods from the treaty list: "Let the silk trade perish and go to the countries to which it properly belongs [Warner, 1921:80]."

The immediate result of the treaty in the silk industry as a whole was one of despair. Business in the trade came to a standstill. Many firms gave notice to their employees that if the treaty became law, they would cease to give out work, as they would be able to purchase foreign silks at a cheaper rate than they could manufacture them (Warner, 1921:84). The net result was a steady decline in the trade throughout the rest of the century and a steady movement of weavers out of the industry. As Table 3.1 shows, the number of persons employed in the silk industry declined from 130,723 in 1851 to only 37,480 by 1901, as weavers took up other occupations or emigrated.

The Country Weavers of Chilvers Coton

One source of division in the silk industry was the distinction between factory and domestic weavers. In the larger city of Coventry, which supplied the weavers of Chilvers Coton, the influence of the master weavers, the self-employed artisans who hired journeymen and set prices, kept the factory system limited. Cottage "factories" predominated instead, as domestic weavers worked at home, placing

The Ribbon Weavers of Chilvers Coton

TABLE 3.1. *The Number of Persons Employed in the Silk Industry in the United Kingdom, 1851-1901*

Year	Males	Females	Total
1851	53,936	76,787	130,723
1861	43,732	72,588	116,320
1871	29,225	53,738	82,963
1881	22,205	42,630	64,835
1891	19,090	32,937	52,027
1901	11,058	26,422	37,480

Source: Warner, 1921:658.

steam engines at the ends of their rows of weavers' houses, with power being conducted down the row from one house to the next. Factory weavers were paid weekly wages. In contrast, the domestic weavers were paid by an agreed price list imposed by tradition, which they were able to maintain until the decline of the 1860s.

In addition to the division between factory hands and domestic weavers, there was a further division between town and country weavers. These country weavers were not the stereotypical master weavers, "men of character and high ideals who loved nature, poetry, philosophy and science [Warner, 1921:467]." Rather, they were women, children, and old people, serving as a large reserve pool of casual, semiemployed labor, working at debased rates (Thompson, 1965:260). Of the silk weavers in Chilvers Coton, only 28% were males, and of those males employed in weaving or subsidiary occupations like ribbon winding, 40% were under 20 or over 60. The young boys may have helped a parent or worked in the household of a weaver for a few years, but as soon as they could, they took the better-paying jobs in the coal mine or the brickworks in the nearby hamlet of Griff. In contrast, the female hand-loom weavers lived in almost complete subjection to Coventry, which exploited them and kept them permanently on the margin of unemployment (Prest, 1960:45). Employed when times were busy and laid off again when they were slack, these women were a necessary feature of the trade.

Several historical factors contributed to their subjection. The original ribbon weaving loom was a single hand loom that could weave one breadth at a time. Around 1770, the Dutch engine loom was invented, making it possible to weave several breadths of ribbon at once. Despite the large number of women employed, women were not allowed to work the new looms (Pinchbeck, 1930:170). Although a great demand for labor in the prosperous period of 1812–1815 allowed employers to ignore these regulations and put women on the engine looms, this advantage was never extended to the country weavers, who continued to work on the single hand looms. At the same time that women began using the engine looms in the more productive regions, manufacturers took advantage of the prosperity of the industry to break through the traditional apprenticeships (Pinchbeck, 1930:170). Because of the demand for labor, young people, usually girls, were employed for a varying period of years at half wages. These "half-pay" female apprentices were particularly prevalent among the country weavers. When the half-pay apprenticeship system died along with the regular apprenticeships, the rural weavers continued to earn very low wages, in some cases as low as two shillings a week (Pinchbeck, 1930:177). Never paid by the list of prices so treasured by master weavers, they struggled on at the hand looms, competing always against the more advanced power looms of the city.

Household Production and Patterns of Work

Four large masters in Nuneaton supported the weavers in Chilvers Coton and other small villages at mid-century, and the standard of living of the village weavers was miserably low, particularly if their total subsistence depended on the single hand loom. They were given work only when Coventry had more orders than it could manage, and it was said that they subsisted on bread, potatoes, a little tea, and sometimes a few scraps of bacon (Prest, 1960:70).

Since weaving alone could not support most families, the typical village family in Chilvers Coton combined wage-earning activities and household production as a survival strategy. As noted earlier, men typically worked in the mines, while their wives and children wove ribbons at home. In 1851, 23% of all employed males over the age of 10 were working as coal miners, and another 21% of employed males, the oldest and the youngest, worked as ribbon weavers.

For women, ribbon weaving was a lifetime occupation, performed as a cottage industry in the home, and because they could work at home, employment for females of all ages was universally high at mid-century.[2] As Figure 3.2 shows, more than 85% of women between the ages of 20 and 40 were employed. Even among those older than 70, over 50% were still occupied, as they helped with the less strenuous tasks like bobbin winding. In fact, labor-force-participation rates for women, even in old age, were nearly as high as they were for men.

In contrast to the typical British mid-century pattern, married women were nearly as likely as single women to be employed. As Table 3.2 shows, more than 79% of all married women were working in 1851. Almost the sole source of employment for women was in the weaving industry, for 70% of all females working were employed·in some phase of ribbon weaving.

Although the silk industry survived in the larger centers, ribbon weaving in the marginal villages like Chilvers Coton was essentially destroyed after the treaty with France, and the village itself changed in many ways. With the decline in silk, many Coventry manufacturers went bankrupt, and weavers began to leave the area (Prest, 1960:129). As shown in Table 3.3, there was a distinct drop in population due to the out-migration of weavers.

Gradually, other industries arose to take the place of ribbon weaving, and the village diversified occupationally, sharing in the general increase in the standard of living.[3] In 1851, there were only 118 oc-

[2] The census household listings for Chilvers Coton for 1851 and 1901 are the source of the quantitative data. The entire population is included in the analysis.

[3] Indexing wages to wholesale prices in coal mining and building from 1880, Bowley (1937:8) showed an increase in coal mining from 100 to 163 by 1900 and an increase in building from 100 to 115 by 1900. Bowley (1937:33) has also estimated that real wages overall rose about 45% between 1880 and 1896.

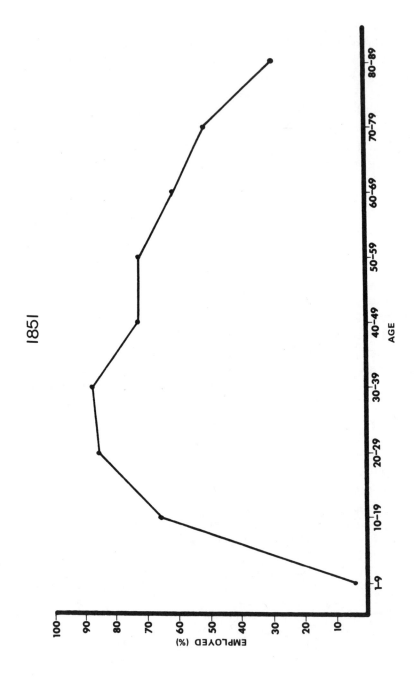

1851

1901

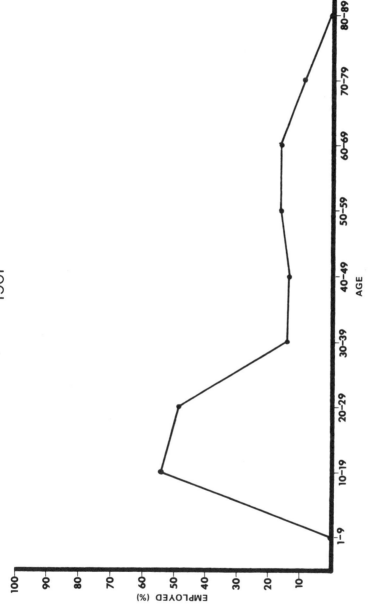

Figure 3.2. *Graphs show the life cycle employment pattern of females in Chilvers Coton in 1851 and 1901.*

TABLE 3.2. *Employment Status of Married and Single Women over Age Sixteen, 1851 and 1901 (percentage)*

Status	Year	Employed	Unemployed
Unmarried	1851	84.3	15.7
	1901	83.1	16.9
Married	1851	79.1	20.9
	1901	6.1	93.9
Widowed	1851	69.8	30.2
	1901	23.4	76.6

Source: Enumerator's Schedules for Chilvers Coton, 1851 and 1901.

TABLE 3.3. *Population of Chilvers Coton, 1831–1901[a]*

Year	Population
1831	2494
1841	2508
1851	2613
1861	2764
1871	2658
1881	3005
1891	3720
1901	5797

Source: Page, 1908:185

[a] Acreage = 3730.

cupations listed for men in the census; by 1901 this figure had nearly tripled to 320. Further, as Table 3.4 shows, there were significant changes in the occupational structure. In 1851, four occupations—ribbon weaving, coal mining, brickmaking, and agriculture—accounted for 63% of all jobs for men. By 1901 no single occupation

TABLE 3.4. *Employed Males over Age Ten in Selected Occupations, Chilvers Coton, 1851 and 1901[a]*

	1851		1901	
Occupation	N	Percentage	N	Percentage
Professional	9	1	29	3
Commercial	21	3	122	12
Conveyance of men, goods, and messages	23	3	53	5
Agriculture	101	12	17	2
Food, tobacco, drink, and lodging	32	4	104	10
Metals, machines, implements, and conveyances	11	1	55	5
Brick, cement, pottery, and glass	59	7	136	13
Building and works of construction	34	4	119	11
Textiles	169	21	41	4
Dress	25	3	53	5
Mining	186	23	74	7
Gas, water, electricity, and sanitary service	1	0	19	2

Source: Enumerator's Schedules for Chilvers Coton, 1851 and 1901.

[a] The percentages do not total 100 because only those occupational categories in which there was significant change are included here.

3. Household and Kin

dominated. Coal mining, ribbon weaving, and agriculture had declined in importance, but there was an expansion of white-collar jobs in commerce, as well as significant growth in those occupations concerning consumer goods and services, that is, food, dress, travel, and gas and electricity. The building industry had also expanded, which increased jobs in the brickworks. Chilvers Coton was no longer an isolated village, for improved communication and transportation and an expanding middle class had altered its preindustrial character.

Population began to rise in the 1870s and then grew at a more rapid pace through the rest of the century as Chilvers Coton became incorporated into the larger borough of Nuneaton. Partly because of the out-migration of ribbon weavers in the 1860s as well as other factors relating to the growth of the region, the age distribution of Chilvers Coton was altered. As Table 3.5 shows, the proportion of people over 60 declined from around 10% in 1851 to less than 6% in 1901.

By 1901, there were only 17 silk ribbon weavers left in Chilvers

TABLE 3.5. *Population of Chilvers Coton by Sex and Age, 1851 and 1901*

	1851				1901			
	Males		Females		Males		Females	
Age	N	Percentage	N	Percentage	N	Percentage	N	Percentage
0–9	355	28	303	23	392	24	405	25
10–19	260	20	305	27	307	19	306	19
20–29	175	14	201	15	363	23	326	20
30–39	142	11	172	13	226	14	211	13
40–49	115	9	121	9	145	9	164	10
50–59	113	9	123	9	100	6	113	7
60–69	76	6	70	5	44	3	59	4
70 and older	51	5	46	4	28	2	26	2

Source: Enumerator's Schedules for Chilvers Coton, 1851 and 1901.

Coton. The result was a drastic reduction in employment for women, particularly married women. Now only 6.1% of married women were in the labor force, employed as charwomen and servants, dressmakers and seamstresses. In contrast, the labor-force participation of unmarried females remained high. Most of the young working women had moved into domestic service, which accounted for only 8.7% of the female labor force in 1851 but 20% in 1901. The widowed, who were most likely to be old, struggled on, working when they could but most often (76.6%) not being employed. The demise of household production had drastically reduced work for married women and for older women.

Male employment was not affected nearly so drastically as women's employment, but it was affected, again among the more marginal workers, the young, and the old. As shown in Figure 3.3, employment for males between the ages of 10 and 19 declined from 73% in 1851 to 61% in 1901.[4] For old men, the effect was more striking. In 1851, 87% of men between the ages of 60 and 69 were still working, 74% between ages 70 and 79, and 60% of those in their 80s. By 1901 no very old men were employed. For those over 70, the figure had dropped to 37% and was now 77% for those in their 60s.

When ribbon weaving thrived as a cottage industry, married women could work at home, and there were many subsidiary tasks that older people could perform. The decline in employment for married females, youth, and the aged can be explained by the fact that the work they had traditionally done disappeared and no other form of employment had taken its place. The next question, then, is whether the position of the aged in the household was also affected by the decline of domestic production.

Ribbon Weavers in the Household

The changes in employment opportunities reverberated through all aspects of village life, affecting the types of households families maintained and the position of the aged in these households. In Table

[4] Much of the decline in employment among young people can be attributed to increased school attendance. The Education Act of 1876 made school attendance compulsory for children from ages five to fourteen, but ten year olds were permitted to attend school half-time and hold jobs. In 1899 the minimum age for employment was raised to 12.

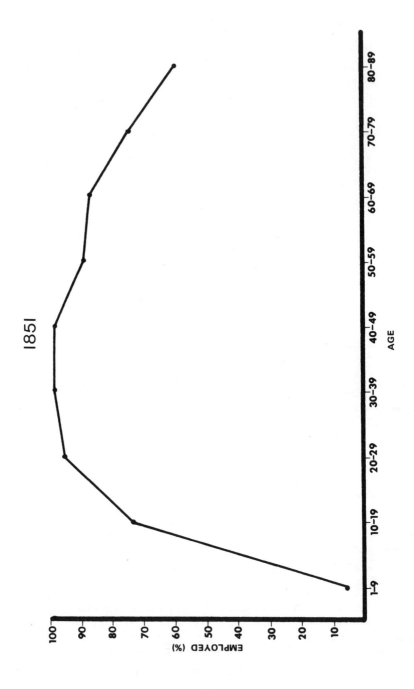

1851

AGE

EMPLOYED (%)

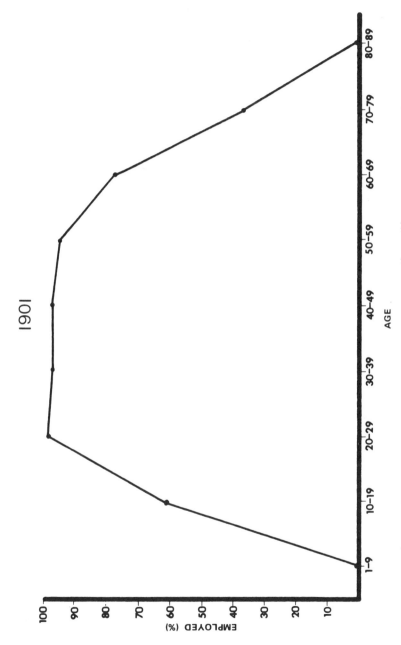

Figure 3.3. *Graphs show the life cycle employment pattern of males in Chilvers Coton in 1851 and 1901.*

3. Household and Kin

3.6, the household structure of the elderly is presented for 1851 and 1901. Certain significant shifts in the pattern that are related to a variety of factors can be discerned.

The most immediately obvious change is the increase by 1901 in the percentage of both married and widowed older people living in their own houses with their own unmarried children (Types 5 and 6). In 1851, 18% of the older married men and 13% of older married

TABLE 3.6. *Structure of Households Containing Older People, Chilvers Coton, 1851 and 1901 (percentage)*

	Males		Females	
	1851	1901	1851	1901
Household type	(N=130)	(N=77)	(N=117)	(N=76)
1. Solitaries	5	8	6	7
No family household				
2. Coresident with kin	2	0	3	3
3. Coresident with nonkin	22	9	16	9
Simple family households				
4. Married couple without children	23	16	20	13
5. Married couple with children	18	38	13	28
6. Widowed with children	6	10	4	14
Extended family households[a]				
7. Extension upward	1	1	2	2
8. Extension downward (grandchildren only)	4	3	8	4
9. Extension sideways (siblings)	1	0	1	0
Multiple family households[b]				
10. Households with secondary units disposed upward from head	1	6	4	12
11. Households with secondary units disposed downward from head	18	8	18	8
Total	100	100	100	100

Source: Enumerator's Schedules for Chilvers Coton, 1851 and 1901.

[a] This refers to conjugal family units having kin-linked individuals.

[b] This refers to two or more kin-linked conjugal family units.

women were living with unmarried children, that is, in a conjugal family setting.[5] By 1901, this figure had increased to 38% for males and 28% for females. When the widowed are included, the average for men and women rises from approximately 20% in 1851 to nearly 45% in 1901. At the same time, the aged were less likely to be living with a spouse alone (Type 4)—the classic "empty nest." The percentage of married couples living alone declined from 23% (males) and 20% (females) in 1851 to only 16% and 13%, respectively. This pattern contradicts traditional wisdom that describes the "empty nest" phenomenon as a creation of modern, industrial society. How can it be explained? Were children staying home longer? Were they marrying later? Was there a difference in life expectancy between 1851 and 1901? In reality, several factors combined to create this pattern.

One explanation for this shift relates to work opportunities for young people. Anderson (1971:124) found that when children had independent opportunities for earning, they tended to leave their parents' houses earlier. We have already seen that work opportunities for young people decreased with the decline of the silk weaving industry. This made them less able to live on their own as apprentices or lodgers.

This same phenomenon, the independence of youth, also affects age at marriage and, again, the likelihood that children would be living at home. In 1851, young people could set up an independent household if the husband was working, usually as a coal miner, and his wife engaged in silk weaving, since miners attained their maximum earnings while still young (Benson, 1980:120). In fact, this was

---

[5] Conjugal family units are formed by married couples with or without children and lone parents with at least one child. If there are more than two generations in the household, the conjugal family unit is formed from the youngest generation upward. For example, in the case of a widowed household head living with her widowed daughter and that daughter's child, the widowed household head remains outside the conjugal family unit. Extended family units contain conjugal family units having kin-linked individuals, such as a married couple and the husband's widowed mother or a married couple and a grandchild. Multiple family households contain two or more kin-linked conjugal family units, such as a widowed mother living with a married child and grandchildren (definition used by the Cambridge Group for the History of Population and Social Structure).

3. Household and Kin

a typical household pattern. It has been said that "the girls all kept company and were pregnant before they married at 16 or 17. Bastardy was common, and no stigma was attached to it [Prest, 1960:71]." Age 16 is an exaggerated estimate, for only a few ever married in their teens (Benson, 1980:120). However, age at first marriage was lower in 1851 than in 1901, as is shown in Table 3.7. In 1851, nearly half of the men and women were married by age 23; in 1901, 74% of the males and 65% of the females had yet to marry by that age.

There are several possible explanations for this change. First, marriage in areas where cottage industries predominated tended, in general, to be early (Tilly and Scott, 1978:95). Thus, the demise of cottage industry and subsequent loss of work opportunities for women may have made it more difficult for young couples to establish an independent household. Second, early marriage was highly characteristic of mining areas (Hewitt, 1958:45; Haines, 1977:270; Tilly and Scott, 1978:96). According to Haines (1977), early marriage among miners can be explained by their expectation of a

TABLE 3.7. *Those "Never Married" by Age in Chilvers Coton, 1851–1901 (percentage)*

	1851		1901	
Age	Male	Female	Male	Female
15 and under	97	100	100	100
16–17	96	100	100	100
18–19	92	88	100	97
20–21	80	57	97	81
22–23	53	53	74	65
24–25	31	44	57	41
26–27	31	36	40	29
28–29	23	36	24	13

Source: Enumerator's Schedules for Chilvers Coton, 1851 and 1901.

"relatively short working [life] at peak efficiency" so that "it should not be surprising that miners 'discounted' their futures by marrying earlier and providing more children to care for them in old age [p. 267]." In all likelihood, the combination of a high proportion of males employed in mining and the availability of domestic industry for females created the early marriage pattern of 1851.[6] By 1901, there were substantially fewer men in Chilvers Coton employed in mining, and cottage industry had disappeared. Third, toward the end of the nineteenth century, there was a general tendency in wage-earning households where the income of children was needed for parents to keep older children home longer, perhaps delaying marriages (Tilly and Scott, 1978:141). Thus, the increase in the number of children living at home with their aged parents and associated decline of older spouses living together alone can be partially explained by comparatively delayed marriage among those under 26.

A second explanation for the decrease in the proportion of older people in the "empty nest" phase of the life cycle has to do with demographic change. If life expectancy for the aged had increased, then this could explain why more were living alone. As Table 3.8 shows, there were no distinguishable improvements in life expectancy for the aged in the latter half of the nineteenth century in England, so it seems unlikely that this factor explains the change in household composition. However, improvements in mortality for those between the ages of 5 and 20 did occur after 1860 (Greenwood, 1936:678). This may have affected the children of the 1901 cohort of older people, whose children would have been born between 1865 and 1880. Further, after 1880 mortality declined for those between the ages of 20 and 35 (Greenwood, 1936:678). Aged men and women may have had more unmarried children still at home because more survived through adulthood. Thus, a combination of reduced mortality for the young people and delayed marriage kept unmarried children at home longer and reduced the proportion of aged in the "empty nest."

[6] In his analysis of marriage and fertility patterns in coal mining areas for 1851, 1861, and 1871, Haines (1977:267) used 10% of the male population in coal mining employment as his criteria for identifying mining districts. In 1851, 23% of all males in Chilvers Coton were employed in mining.

TABLE 3.8. *Life Expectancy for Males Aged Sixty-Five and Above in England, 1861–1911*

Age	1861	1911
65–69	10.65	10.95
70–74	8.37	8.47
75–79	6.16	6.50
80–84	4.38	4.93
85 and older	3.16	3.66

Source: Keyfitz and Flieger, 1968:520–526.

Generally, evidence from mining communities indicates that adult sons and daughters did their best to look after their aging parents. As one old miner recalls of norms in mining communities: "It was a code of honor strictly adhered to to show respect for old people . . . and everybody would help old people to get from A to B, or run messages or fill pails of water or coals. We thought nothing of it, but that it was the done thing [quoted in Benson, 1980:141]." According to Benson (1980), "The nineteenth century mining family was strong and resilient and altogether more responsible than it is given credit for [p. 141].

This view of family resiliency and reciprocity is supported by the data from Chilvers Coton. In 1851, 18% of the aged were living in three-generation households that they headed (Type 11). Nearly all of these households were working units. The norm was reciprocity, and the family operated as an economic unit, as parents and children shared work and housing. In three-generation households composed of one or both parents, married children, and grandchildren, 71% of the older generation worked. Often their work was part of the family production unit. For example, in one typical household, a 63-year-old coal miner lived with his 68-year-old wife, who worked as a silk winder. Their married daughter, who had an infant child, was a ribbon weaver, and her husband worked as a laborer. The combined family income allowed them all to survive. In contrast, the child-care role, which has been found to have been crucial in industrialized areas where mothers worked in factories, was of minimal significance in Chilvers Coton. Although 64% of those over age 60 living with married children were in households where there were children under 7 present, in every case the wife was either not working or, more usually, working in her home as a ribbon weaver.

More than half of these households consisted of a parent, a single child, either unmarried, separated, or widowed, and grandchild. These households were often fragile economies, subsisting on the marginal labor of mother and daughter, as in the case of the 70-year-old ribbon weaver Martha Copp, living with her 29-year-old unmarried daughter, also a ribbon weaver, and 7-year-old granddaughter. Widowed men, too, occasionally combined resources with children, most often daughters, and the household of the 74-year-old laborer James Natliff, living with his separated daughter and grandchild, provides a typical example. The fragility of these household economies meant they could not survive the loss of women's work, and in fact, by 1901 there were almost no households composed of older widowed women with single children and grandchildren.

As Table 3.9 shows, no solitary married couples were living in their parents' households in either year. The tendency was to establish a separate residence upon marriage. However, economic circumstances often forced married or separated children to move back into their parents' household after children were born. Taking married children back was a common reaction to crisis. In his autobiography, the Coventry ribbon weaver Joseph Gutteridge (1969) describes a period when he and his family were near starvation due to lack of work: "Notwithstanding the efforts made to conceal our poverty, it soon came to the knowledge of my wife's mother, who insisted upon our going to her house as soon as my wife could be safely removed, and we were to stay until our circumstances brightened [p. 120]."

By 1901, the situation had altered quite dramatically. There was a significant increase in the percentage of older men and women living in the households of their children and a decrease in the percentage of aged men and women taking children and other kin into their own households. Older widows had always been more likely to be taken in

TABLE 3.9. Households of Older People Living with Children as a Proportion of All Older People[a] 1851 and 1901

Status of Aged	1851				1901			
	Males		Females		Males		Females	
	Married	Unmarried	Married	Unmarried	Married	Unmarried	Married	Unmarried
In own household with:								
Single child/ren and grandchild/ren	.06	.04	.06	.08	.04	.04	.04	.00
Married child/ren and grandchild/ren	.03	.05	.02	.02	.00	.00	.04	.00
Married child/ren	.00	.00	.00	.00	.00	.00	.00	.00
In household of child:								
Single child and grandchild/ren	.00	.00	.00	.00	.00	.00	.00	.03
Married child and grandchild/ren	.00	.01	.00	.02	.00	.06	.00	.09
Married child	.00	.01	.00	.02	.01	.01	.00	.01

Source: Enumerator's Schedules for Chilvers Coton, 1851 and 1901.

[a] This table refers only to older people living with children, types 10 and 11 in Table 3.6.

by their children, but the proportion of widowers living with children also increased substantially. In a sense, this change may be more symbolic than real, for there were many instances in 1851 where an older person was a nominal head of the household but was most likely supported by his or her children. For example, in 1851, the 61-year-old widower Joseph Bresley, a basket maker by trade, lived in his own house with his married son, a coal miner, his daughter-in-law, a silk weaver, and their three young children. In other households, aged bobbin winders, weavers, and laborers all maintained the status of head of the household but most certainly combined resources with children to survive. One possible explanation for the increased number of aged living in the households of children and also other kin in 1901 is that the reduction in work opportunities reduced their ability to maintain the nominal position of head of the house.

It was not only parents and children who shared reciprocally in household arrangements in 1851. There are many instances recounted of relatives sharing households in hard times. Joseph Gutteridge (1969) tells a tale of family tensions and reciprocity:

> My youngest brother, George, who since leaving the old home had lived with his uncle—the man to whom I have already referred to as having tried to prevent my marriage—expressed a wish to come and live with us, not withstanding our limited accommodation. He came, and the uncle and other members of the family taxed me with having enticed him away from a comfortable home to a "poverty-stricken hole," as they pompously designated our humble abode. The breach between me and my relatives was widened, but the love I felt for this younger brother—the one whom my father on his death-bed had asked me to care for—was so intense that for his sake I could have suffered more calumny and vituperation than I actually endured . . . we enjoyed each other's confidence, and he only left us for a home of his own [p. 125].

Grandchildren and other kin were also taken in by older people, combining labor and other resources. As Table 3.6 shows, the number of older people taking in grandchildren (Type 8) and siblings (Type 9) declined in 1901. These kinds of households may have disappeared, as it became more difficult for the aged to maintain their own households. However, it also may be that the out-migration of the 1860s dispersed kin, so that in 1901 fewer older people had siblings living in Chilvers Coton

By 1901, there was no clear role for the aged to play within an extended-family household. Few married women were working, so there was little need for an aged parent to help with child care. There was a scarcity of employment for older people, so they could not contribute either labor or wages. Yet there was an increase in the proportion of older people taken into the households of children. Under what circumstances, then, did children take aged parents into their households?

The change in the local economy that had occurred after the demise of the ribbon weaving trade was one of the factors that affected the household position of the aged. In 1851, half of the children who took in aged parents did so because the parents contributed directly to household production or the family wage economy. As shown in Table 3.10, this was the case among weavers, farmers, and coal miners. The other half were more affluent tradesmen who could afford to help a widowed parent even if he or she made no direct contribution to the household. In 1901, when the aged were rarely

TABLE 3.10. *Occupation of Head in Households with Aged Dependent Parent (percentage)*

Occupation	1851 (N=15)	1901 (N=19)
Professional or manufacturer	0	19
White collar	0	31
Skilled trade	50	31
Farmer	14	0
Semiskilled or unskilled[a]	29	19
Weaver	7	0

Source: Enumerator's Schedule for Chilvers Coton, 1851 and 1901.

[a] Includes coal miners and brickmakers.

employed, it was nearly always the more affluent who took in an aged parent, with the head of the household employed as a skilled tradesman, white-collar worker, or professional. For example, among the occupations of heads of those households that included an aged parent were an engine driver, carpenters, a clothing manager, insurance agents, a minister, a colliery deputy, a butcher, and a barman. In general, these households were not so carefully balanced between poverty and absolute destitution. They reflected the more general affluence of an expanding village, and often the family was a consuming rather than a working unit.

Although the village of Chilvers Coton changed dramatically between 1851 and 1901, in neither period were the aged neglected by kin. In 1851, 81% of all older people were living with a spouse, a child, or some other relative. The aged were not solely dependent on the young, for there was reciprocity in these arrangements. Many older people took in grandchildren and even more frequently allowed a daughter with an illegitimate child or a widowed child and offspring to return home, to share together the financial and familial management of the household. For both young and old, the family was a major source of support and a place to turn in times of crisis. In a precarious economic environment, family members pooled their resources to survive.

In 1901, the community was different, and the economic strategies devised under the household mode of production no longer applied. Still, the aged were not neglected. Of all people over 60, 84% were living with some family member in 1901. New household arrangements accommodated family members with new needs. Unmarried children lived longer with their parents. Successful children or perhaps another relative took in the widowed. Although there were tensions in family relationships, there was also reciprocity between generations.

The analysis confirms some previous theories of family organization and amends or contradicts others. Industrialization, at least temporarily, increased the number of older parents living in their own homes with their unmarried children. It also increased the number of married children taking aged parents, particularly widows, into their households and, surprisingly, decreased the proportion of older people in the "empty nest." Although there was no overall change in the proportion of older people living with kin, the considerable shift in household composition indicates that families operated as a unit, responding to structural changes through flexible internal rearrangements.

This discussion also adds to our knowledge of work for the aged under domestic production. Nearly all older people worked at some job when ribbon weaving was a local industry. Retirement was almost nonexistent. When household production disappeared, work for the aged disappeared along with it. Certainly, the demise of cottage industry was not the sole aspect of industrialization that affected work opportunities for older people, but it did have a major impact. In Chapter 6, other factors relating to work and retirement will be explored.

In this chapter, we have seen that the family provided a buffer for the aged against the impact of a major change in the economy, the decline of a once-thriving cottage industry. Ribbon weaving in Chilvers Coton was partially destroyed because of economic changes that made the hand-loom weaving of all textiles inefficient and ultimately vulnerable. However, an equally important cause of the demise of hand-loom ribbon weaving was the changing political climate that increasingly emphasized free trade over protection. When French silk ribbons were admitted into England duty free, the British could not compete with the more finely woven French products.

In other spheres, too, alterations in the power structure due to clashes of interests between manufacturers and the landed gentry created political changes that both directly and indirectly affected the lives of the aged. One of the most significant of these battles was fought between local authorities and central government over the administration and control of the poor law. As we shall see in the next two chapters, it was often the aged, those most likely to be dependent on poor relief, who became the inadvertent victims of that battle.

4

Poor Law Policy and Old Age Pauperism

December, 1889, Boreham, man, 73, lived twenty years as hermit, called each morning by neighbor; on Christmas Eve not satisfied with reply, and later forced door. Man quite naked, on bundle of rags, very weak, cottage most filthy; no furniture. Attended by neighbors, died next morning.

February, 1910, Chignal, widow, 71, eccentric, feeble, alcoholic; lived nineteen years with son, sister visited weekly; would not have doctor. Had fallen on fender, so son tied her in chair; Constable found chest and neck bare, quite black, also hands, hair matted; room full of rags and rubbish; told son to get help, which he did; died five days later.

October, 1906, Vange, man, 70, cut throat; four shillings Relief; according to widow, for days together no food. Two lodgers at cottage, to one of whom two sons objected; sons would help parents if lived in small cottage. Not fully elucidated.

May, 1908, High Ongar, woman, 85, in caravan many years, partly paralysed, re-fused enter infirmary; found dead.

September, 1898, Margaret Roothing, widow, 83, on Relief, refused enter Infirmary; fell downstairs. Three days later son visited her, next day found her dead by bedside; jury thought Guardians should have provided nurse.

March, 1899, Hadfield Peverel, woman, 81, house most filthy, death from fire, small lamp in bed.

(Cuttle, 1934:363–365; records from several Essex poor law unions)

4. Poor Law Policy and Old Age Pauperism

Poverty in old age was a centuries-old problem, but not until the late nineteenth century did the British become aware of the conditions of absolute destitution in which the working classes were forced to live their final years. In a pattern that was typical of nineteenth-century social reform, a social evil was discovered (MacDonagh, 1958:58). Particularly influential in revealing just how much poverty was due to old age was Charles Booth (1891, 1892, 1898, 1899), who drew attention to the plight of the aged poor in a series of books and articles published in the 1890s. Booth determined that the average rate of pauperism among those over 65 was more than 29% with 21% of the aged receiving outdoor relief and another 8% incarcerated in workhouses (see Table 4.1).[1] Further, pauperism in old age was not evenly distributed across the whole population, for "amongst the working population and small traders, who survive to sixty-five years of age, the proportion who come to the poor law for assistance is not less than 40 percent [Booth, 1894:14]."

TABLE 4.1. *Twelve-Month Count of Paupers by Age, 1891*

Age	Indoor paupers		Outdoor paupers		Total paupers	
	N	Percentage	N	Percentage	N	Percentage
Under 16	111,781	1.0	441,805	4.1	553,587	5.1
16–65	232,284	1.4	385,299	2.3	617,583	3.7
Over 65	114,144	8.3	287,760	21.0	401,904	29.3

Source: P.P. XIV, Report, 1895:xiii.

[1] There was some controversy regarding the accuracy of Booth's figures, which reflected the total receiving relief over a period of a year. Some believed that this method overestimated the number of truly destitute, since many older people might seek temporary relief to tide them over a period of illness or other emergency. However, the Royal Commission on the Aged Poor (P.P. XIV, Report, 1895) concluded, "We think it is right, however, to point out that an aged person above 65, who comes only at long intervals for relief, may often be a person who is generally averse to such assistance and only accepts it under pressure of illness or severe distress. The ordinary condition of such persons must be only just removed from pauperism and calls for sympathy and consideration [p. xiii]."

Booth also estimated that rates of pauperism were directly correlated with age, so that increased age meant increased risk of pauperization. Although Booth did not have the statistical information to support his belief, his estimates were confirmed in a more systematic analysis presented by Lord George Hamilton as the presidential address to the Royal Statistical Society in 1910 (see Table 4.2). Basing his figures on the pauper census of March 31, 1906, in which ages were precisely tabulated, Hamilton demonstrated that pauperism did indeed rise with advancing age.

Pauperism was a distinct feature of old age in nineteenth-century England, and poor law authorities had the greatest power to intrude directly into the lives of older people and their families by restricting the amount of outrelief provided, by refusing outrelief entirely, "offering the house," or by enforcing the law of settlement and removing a pauper from his or her parish of residence. Thus, no analysis of ag-

TABLE 4.2. *Estimates of the Effects of Advancing Age on Pauperism*

	Booth		Hamilton
Age	Paupers (percentage)	Age	Paupers (percentage)
20–60	1–8	Under 5	1.4
60–65	10	5–15	2.6
65–70	20	15–25	.3
70–75	30	25–35	.7
Over 75	40	35–45	1.3
		45–55	1.7
		55–65	4.3
		65–75	16.3
		75–85	27.6
		Over 85	35.3

Source: Booth, 1894:13; Hamilton, 1910:7.

ing can be complete without a comprehensive discussion of poor law policy and its effects on the aged poor.

The History of the Poor Law

For centuries, the idiom of the poor law represented rural class relationships (Newby, 1977:41). As early as the fourteenth century, the Poor Law Act of 1388 tried not only to fix wages but also to prevent the mobility of labor that would allow wages to rise (Fraser, 1973:28). In 1536, with a decline in indiscriminate almsgiving through the church (Martin, 1972:28), the state acknowledged minimal responsibility for those who were unable to work by authorizing parishes to collect money to support the impotent poor so they would no longer need to beg. In 1601, the Elizabethan Poor Law was passed, establishing a system of local government in which each parish administered its own relief through overseers appointed by magistrates who were empowered to levy poor rates on property. The parish was required to find a convenient stock of flax, hemp, wool, thread, and iron to set the ablebodied poor to work. The poor rates were to be used to relieve the lame, impotent, old, and blind as well as others among the poor who were unable to work (Martin, 1972:28). Thus, from its inception, the poor law distinguished two categories of poor: the impotent and the ablebodied, "sturdy rogues and vagabonds [Prothero, 1912:433]."

The earliest evidence of distinctive poor law institutions is from the 1630s, when several parishes, chiefly in textile towns, reported to the Privy Council that they had established workhouses where their unemployed could be given supervised employment (Oxley, 1974:80). In 1696, Bristol authorities passed an act for erecting hospitals and workhouses (Martin, 1972:31). The Bristol example was followed by numerous other towns. Although the poor law was characterized by extreme local variation in policy and administration, in philosophy the distinction between impotent and ablebodied was maintained. For those impotent paupers who required institutionalization, poorhouses were to be established. In contrast, the ablebodied poor were to be sent to work on hemp or some other appropriate material in workhouses or, as they were initially termed, houses of correction (Fraser, 1973:30). In practice, separate institutions were rarely established, and poorhouses began to disappear early in the nineteenth century (Martin, 1972:32).

Various changes in poor law policy in terms of the collection and expenditure of funds were made in the seventeenth and eighteenth centuries. The change that probably had the most far-reaching impact on the aged was the Act of Settlement in 1662. The theory behind the law of pauper settlement held that each parish was financially responsible for its own poor. The Act of Settlement grew out of the general disorganization of administration of the poor law, which was amplified during periods of political disorder when vagrancy increased. Increased vagrancy caused confusion in administration through the system of dispute and litigation that had evolved as each parish, required to look after its own poor, attempted to absolve itself from responsibility for paupers whose place of residence was in doubt. Overseers, conscious of the desire of ratepayers to keep rates down, did all they could to prevent paupers from becoming chargeable to their parish. The problem centered around how a person was to be considered as "belonging" to a certain parish (Brundage, 1978:2). In the mid-seventeenth century, the vagrant population had increased, to the consternation of political authorities. The ex-highwayman, Stanley, wrote that there were "not so few as 80,000 vagrants that prey upon the commonwealth [quoted in Prothero, 1912:434]." It was against these vagabonds and squatters who might become chargeable to a parish that the Act of Settlement was directed, specifying that every man was required to have a settled domicile within 40 days and be enrolled in some fixed community.

Settlement was gained by birth, marriage, apprenticeship, payment of parish rates, or purchase of an estate.[2] In each case, the most recently acquired settlement cancelled earlier acquired or derivative settlements. This complicated the determination of a person's settlement, since it meant searching through a number of acquired set-

[2]There were many other qualifications for establishing settlement, and implementation varied tremendously from parish to parish. Changes in regulations throughout the nineteenth century further complicated the legal issues (Rose, 1976:27).

tlements to locate the most recent one. If no settlement had been acquired, then the paternal or, failing that, maternal settlement had to be found (Rose, 1976:26). Thus, administrators and poor-relief recipients found themselves enmeshed in a complex legal tangle.

In 1795, an act was passed specifying that no act of removal could be taken out against an individual unless he or she actually applied for relief. This act linked the law of settlement more closely to the system of poor relief, since only actual rather than potential paupers were now removable.

The poor law had been geared to a preindustrial economy and as such was incapable of coping with problems related to population growth, increased social mobility, industrialization, and economic fluctuations that occurred in the latter years of the eighteenth century. Parliament's inability to cope with problems induced by wages at below-subsistence levels led to the development of the Speenhamland system. In 1782, Gilbert's Act sanctioned the principle of relieving the "ablebodied" without requiring them to enter the workhouse (Blaug, 1963:151). In 1795 at the Pelican Inn at Speenhamland in Berkshire, local magistrates and overseers, responding to an expected rise in the price of wheat, endeavored to fix a "fair wage" by using the rates to supplement earnings in proportion to the price of bread and size of families. In the following year, Parliament confirmed this principle and in effect sanctioned outdoor relief, or the dole, abandoning the workhouse test of destitution. Overseers and justices were empowered to grant relief at their discretion to the industrious poor (36 Geo. III, c. 23). The new law allowed employers, who were often poor law authorities, to raise or lower wages according to the price of food, compensating workers when wages were low by granting them poor relief.

Various interpretations have been suggested regarding the impact of the Speenhamland plan. Some historians have perceived it as a laudable attempt to deal with problems of structural and seasonal unemployment in a lagging sector of the economy that probably contributed to economic expansion (Blaug, 1963). Others, while admitting that it was a form of labor control, also interpret the plan as basically humanitarian in intent (Fraser, 1973:34). In fact, research has demonstrated rather convincingly that the Speenhamland plan acting in combination with the law of settlement furthered the interests of the landed gentry by subsidizing the running of their estates (Brundage, 1978:5).

As with other aspects of poor law administration, Speenhamland was a way of manipulating the rural labor supply, and the way it worked can be understood only in the context of the distinction between open and closed parishes. Closed parishes were those owned entirely (or nearly so) by one landowner who controlled the amount of housing available by restricting the number of cottages built and thus the opportunity for laborers to acquire settlements. By recruiting labor from adjacent open parishes where there were many small landowners with no control over housing, the gentry could pay low wages and force farmers in the open parishes to subsidize this labor from their rates (Brundage, 1972:29). If the ratepayers of an open parish, either in their vestry or through their overseers, tried to withhold relief from destitute laborers, the nearby squire, in his capacity as magistrate, could order the parish to grant relief (Brundage, 1978:4).

The accepted belief about the overall effect of Speenhamland has been that it depressed wages, promoted population growth by giving larger sums to those with more children, reduced rents, compounded the burden on ratepayers, and pauperized almost the entire working class (Blaug, 1963:151). The extent to which this portrayal is accurate is still the subject of intensive debate. Regardless of the facts, this was the view taken by the commission appointed in 1832 to amend the existing poor law.[3] Although various solutions were proposed to combat the evils of the existing system, the common thread that ran through them all was the notion of self-help. The tendency of the poor law was to create dependency; the aim of all individuals should be independence. The report of the commission led by Nassau Senior, one of the leading laissez faire economists, and Edwin Chadwick, former secretary to Jeremy Bentham, concluded that the allowance system not only demoralized labor and depressed wages but also encouraged idleness by inducing workers to quit the less eligible class of laborers and enter the more eligible class of paupers (Fraser, 1973:41). The philosophy of the "less eligibility" principle, as it came to be known, was based on the inference that pauperism was willful and that the

---

[3] Blaug (1964:231) has found that the Speenhamland system had generally disappeared by 1832.

condition of the pauper who was relieved should be worse than the condition of the poorest, independent, self-supporting laborer.

In order to put the "less eligibility" principle into practice, the workhouse test was reinstated. Distinguishing between the indigent or destitute (proper recipients of relief) and the poor (everyone who in order to obtain subsistence is forced to have recourse to labor), the report clarified that it was inappropriate and contrary to the original Elizabethan Poor Law to give relief to laborers in work. Thus, the parish no longer had the duty of finding work for paupers while paying an allowance to make up for inadequate wages. All outdoor relief was to be abolished, and only offers of institutional relief in the workhouse were to be made. The intent of the New Poor Law was to deter pauperism, not to reduce poverty.

A significant aspect of this act of 1834 was the creation of a central authority, consisting of three poor law commissioners who were empowered to issue orders regulating every detail of the administration of relief. In order to oversee better the administration of large, "well-regulated" workhouses, the commissioners grouped the old parish divisions into unions. Relief was to be administered by relieving officers under the direction of an elected board of guardians. Thus, two new principles were introduced into the poor law: elected local bodies and centralized control.

This new system generated antagonism among the landowner class that had administered the old system of relief, parish overseers, magistrates, and members of select vestries, who were outraged at the prospect of interference by the new central authority and who still bore the costs of the responsibility of relieving their own poor (Rose, 1972:10).[4] The result was that considerable freedom was given to local boards of guardians in the administration of relief, so that many elements of the old system remained. Thus, the demise of parish sovereignty was at least initially tempered by the fact that boards of guardians were usually composed of local landowners and farmers, enabling employers to maintain their control over labor (Newby, 1977:42).

[4] The struggle between local and central government over control of poor law policy is discussed in more detail in Chapter 5.

The report of 1834 generally confirmed that relief giving was indiscriminate and wasteful and that poverty was an indication of individual failure calling for rebuke and stern treatment. However, the evidence on the elderly indicated that "even in places distinguished in general by the most wanton parochial profusion the allowances to the aged and infirm are moderate [Parliamentary Papers XXXVII, 1834:24; hereafter cited as P.P.]." The authors of this report accepted the almost universal practice of relieving the aged and infirm in their own homes with small weekly allowances and suggested no alteration in this practice (Webb and Webb, 1909:311). It is uncertain, however, that this policy was consistently practiced. For instance, Alfred Power, the first assistant commissioner for Lancashire and the West Riding, argued that in his district the workhouse test was needed most for the aged and infirm because of the "dissimulation and fraud constantly practiced by the relatives of the paupers at the expense of the poor rates [Ashforth, 1976:131]." Since no clear policy in regard to the relief of the aged was formulated, it was left to the poor law commissioners to formulate their own policy, using the report of 1834 as a guide. Thus, in 1839, the central authority declared that "we do not require the aged and infirm paupers to be relieved only in the workhouse" and that "it is not our intention to issue any such rule [P.P. XX, 1839:53, 61]."

For those who were accomodated in the workhouses, the report recommended that they have a separate building to themselves in order that "the old might enjoy their indulgences [P.P. XXXVII, 1834:307]." However, the suggestion that separate institutions for the aged be constructed was never enacted, as later investigators feared the deleterious consequences to the working classes of so benevolent an arrangement:

With regard to the aged and infirm, there is a strong disposition on the part of a portion of the public to so modify the arrangements [of the workhouses] as to place them on the footing of almshouses. . . . If the condition of the inmates of a workhouse were to be so regulated as to invite the aged and infirm of the laboring classes to take refuge in it, it would immediately be useless as a test between indigence and indolence and fraud, it would no longer operate as an inducement to the young and healthy to provide support for their later years, or as a stimulus to them whilst they have the means to support their aged parents and relatives. The frugality and forethought of a young laborer would be useless if he foresaw the certainty of a better asylum for his old age than he could possibly provide by his own exertions, and the industrious efforts of a son to provide a maintenance for his parents in his own dwelling would be thrown away and would cease to be called forth, if the almshouse of the district offered a refuge for their declining years in which they might obtain comforts and indulgences which even the most successful of the laboring classes cannot always obtain by their own exertions [P.P. XX,1839:470].

The Poor Law Commission lasted until 1847, when it was replaced by the Poor Law Board, under a minister responsible to Parliament (Rose, 1971:135). In general, the policy of permitting outdoor relief to the aged did not change, and in the 25 years following the administrative change only two references to the aged were made. In 1852, in commenting on the provision requiring the weekly payment of relief, the Poor Law Board wrote to the Board of Guardians of Barnsley Union, "As to cases in which the pauper is too infirm to come every week for the relief, it is on many accounts advantageous that the relieving officer should, as far as possible, himself visit the pauper, and give the relief at least weekly [letter to the Board of Guardians, Barnsley Union, 26 October 1852]." The second statement occurred in the first edition of the *Out-relief Regulation Order* of 1852, in which the central authority ordered for persons helpless from age "one-third at least of such relief should be given in kind," that is, food and provisions rather than money [Rose, 1971:146]. Upon protests from boards of guardians throughout the country, the provision was withdrawn in reference to the aged. Although the protest was phrased in humanitarian terms as imposing undue hardships,[5] the

[5] The protest that arose from boards of guardians was phrased in humanitarian terms:

That the carrying into effect of various provisions of this Order would, in many cases, involve the infliction of extreme hardship upon poor and deserving persons who are, or may be compelled to apply to the local poor law authorities for relief. That although it is important and advantageous to make a distinction in the nature of relief to be given to indigent and deserving poor persons above a certain age (the age of 60 years, for instance), as compared with that given to younger and able-bodied persons; yet the recent Order draws no such distinction, and the same rule is applied in all cases to the relief of the indigent and helpless out-door poor. . . . That it would be extremely difficult for Guardians to determine (especially for aged and sick poor), what kind of food or articles should be given [Rose, 1971:149].

real issue was the usurpation of the authority of the boards of guardians, who again felt their discretionary power was being undermined. As they protested, "That, considering the respectability of Boards of Guardians, and the attention and economy with which they devote themselves to the fulfillment of their gratuitous duties, a full *discretionary power* might be entrusted to them [Rose, 1971:150]."

Between 1848 and 1874, the public health movement grew, culminating in the creation of a central board of health similar in organization to the Poor Law Board. This board was abolished in 1858 but was then recreated in the 1860s because of concern over outbreaks of cholera. Local authorities were compelled to appoint sanitary inspectors and to undertake the provision of sewers, water supply, and refuse disposal, and a Local Government Board was set up to supervise this work (Thomson, 1950:134). The Poor Law Board was absorbed into the new Local Government Board, whose jurisdiction encompassed the poor law under a broader spectrum of social support, usurping local authority further and placing poor law administration more clearly under the jurisdiction of the central government. The president of the Local Government Board was a member of the Cabinet, and there was a new concern with implementing deliberate policy rather than allowing decisions about relief to be dependent on temporary statutes and the whims of local authorities. This tightening of control was accompanied by a steady pressure on boards of guardians to reduce outdoor relief, beginning with the publication of the *Circular on Outdoor Relief* in 1871 (Rose, 1971:228). Even the sick and the aged, who made up at least half and perhaps as much as three-quarters of the adult population receiving outdoor relief, were to have their applications for relief scrutinized (Webb and Webb, 1910:149).[6] In a period of increased concern with record keeping, tables showing the amount of relief given by each union were published and circulated. Unions that gave disproportionate amounts were held accountable, regardless of the proportion

[6] Although poor law returns were not tabulated by age until 1890, there was a separate category termed "aged and infirm." According to the Poor Law Commission's annual reports, over half of the adult paupers on outdoor relief were aged and infirm from at least as early as 1840 (Rose, 1972:19). The Webbs (1909) had estimated an even higher figure.

of aged in the population. This was particularly hard on rural unions, where the aged made up a disproportionate share of the population.

The reduction of outdoor relief implied an increased reliance on the workhouse as a test of destitution. For the aged, this was to be mitigated by the extraction of support from relatives. According to Inspector Longley, the author of the "Report on the Administration of Outdoor Relief in the Metropolis," a rigid adherence to the policy of "offering the house" would induce the relatives of the aged poor to provide for them. As Longley argued:

> One of the chief defects in the present administration of the law in respect to the disabled class, and especially of that section of it which consists of the aged and infirm . . . is its failure to relieve the rates from the burden of the maintenance of paupers whose relatives, whether legally liable or not, are able to contribute to their support. It is, I believe, within the experience of many boards of guardians, that while there are persons who, even when in prosperous circumstances, readily permit their aged relatives to receive out-relief, an offer of indoor relief is frequently found to put pressure upon them to rescue themselves, if not their relatives, from the discredit incident to the residence of the latter in a workhouse [quoted in Rose, 1971:188].

Beginning in the 1880s, there was growing criticism of the failure of the poor law to alleviate poverty, let alone find any solution to it, and the present administration of the poor law came increasingly under attack. There was a growing liberal sympathy with the plight of the poor, stirred by such publications as *The Bitter Cry of Outcast London* (1883) and General William Booth's *In Darkest England and the Way Out* (1890) (Rose, 1971:235). Socialist bodies criticized the dichotomous distinction between deserving and nondeserving poor, thus attacking the very heart of poor law philosophy. As Robert Blatchford, publisher of the socialist paper *The Clarion*, wrote in 1892:

> We now come to the second class—the industrious poor who are indigent from age or from misfortune and through no fault of their own. Of these I have to say that they are indigent in their old age after a life of toil because they have been robbed of the fruits of their labor by the class from who our guardians and magistrates are mostly drawn. To these men the State is not only a debtor, it is a fraudulent trustee. It is not for the State, then, to speak of "charity" to these men, but of reparation, of reverence, and of honour [*The Clarion*, September 17, 1892].

In addition, there were pressures from an increasingly well-organized and articulate labor movement. The inclusion of unskilled workers into trade unions occurred in 1889 and 1890, and the electoral reform acts of 1867 and 1884 extended the franchise to the working class.[7] In 1894, the Local Government Act removed both the property qualification for prospective poor law guardians and plural voting, which had allowed landowners as many as six votes for electing guardians (Brundage, 1972:27). Elections for boards of guardians became more open, and many of the critics of the poor law were elected to the boards, as political organizations such as the Social Democratic Federation or the Independent Labour Party ran candidates (Rose, 1971:238).

In 1895, a Royal Commission on the Aged Poor was formed to investigate the plight of the aged. The testimony of witnesses combined with the figures of Charles Booth created public sympathy for the elderly for whom life under the poor law seemed unduly harsh.

Life under the Poor Law

Theoretically, the aged could receive either outdoor relief in their own home or indoor relief in the workhouse. Practice varied tremendously from union to union, however, so that in some unions nearly all older people received outrelief and in others it was uniformly denied (Webb and Webb, 1909:310). Even where outrelief was the common practice, the amount given was universally meager, the expectation of boards of guardians generally being that this amount would be supplemented from other sources. Booth showed that this was in fact the case in most instances, as only a small proportion of all older people managed to survive on the sole support of the parish. As Table 4.3 shows, only 5% of the aged had outdoor relief as their only source of support.

For those who did rely solely on outdoor relief, life was a desperate struggle, as indicated by the testimony of a witness before the Royal Commission on the Aged Poor:

[7] Working-class politics are discussed in detail in Chapter 1.

TABLE 4.3. *Sources of Maintenance of the Aged*

Source of maintenance	N̲	Percentage
Parish only	458	5.0
and charity	469	5.1
and relations	462	5.1
charity and relations	293	3.2
earnings	326	3.6
Charity only		
and relations	368	4.0
earnings		
relations and earnings	534	5.8
Relations only	486	5.3
and earnings	369	4.1
and means		
earnings and means	310	3.4
Earnings only	2224	24.4
and means	692	7.6
Means only	2134	23.4
Total	9125	100.0

Source: Booth, 1894:339.

A. One other case is Benjamin Atkins and wife in the village in which I live; he receives 2s/6d per week, and a stone of flour.

Q. Have they any other source of relief?

A. None whatever, and they have rent to pay out of this.

Q. They are alive of course?

A. Yes, it is going on now.

Q. How can they manage to live having rent to pay out of 2s 6d a week, supplemented by a stone of flour?

Life under the Poor Law

A. They are in the greatest destitution, my Lord.

Q. You have mentioned that they were in great destitution, but would it not be a case of absolute starvation?

A. Well, it would be [P.P. XIV, Mins. of Ev., 1895:347].

The idiosyncratic method of poor law administration also meant that the amount of outrelief could be reduced when an aged person had a supplementary income source, so that it was often no particular advantage to work, belong to a club, or have savings. For example, in one union one elderly couple received 2s. 6d. from a local club that they had paid in through their work lives. When they applied for relief, their relief was reduced by that amount. As a witness explained:

> And there are other cases in the same way, in all of which the provision that they have been able to make for themselves by thrift is handicapped, as it were. It is not sufficient for them to live on, and when they come to the board for relief it is taken into consideration against them, so that they receive less, whereas those who have attempted to make no provision at all for old age, or who have no present provision, receive the full amount of out-door relief [P.P. XIV, Mins. of Ev., 1895:308].

Some writers have suggested that there was no loss of self-respect associated with outdoor relief and that "allowances were regarded as the certain outcome of a life of low wages [Digby, 1978:162]." However, many older people held quite different attitudes. In those unions where the guardians were reputed to be harsh and stringent in their denial of outrelief, there were reports of people starving rather than having to face refusal and perhaps the workhouse. The following tale was told by a laborer:

A. The man got no chance of getting a living. He had got with him at that time a daughter, with two little children, and he had got his wife, and all they had to depend on in the house was what one daughter earned at the stay work. It so preyed upon this man's mind that he had to be taken away; but before he was taken away I fetched Dr. Harper down to see him, and I went back again to his house, where I said to him, "Sir, what is the cause of this man being like this?" and he says, "It is all through weakness, through his body being in a low state; what the man wants" [he said] "is something to nourish him." They had not got anything in the house, only a drop of toast and water, and they had not got much bread at all, and I took a jug and went up the the Rev. John Alford, the vicar of Brixworth, and asked him if they could give me something. . . . It so happened that nobody had got anything made at the time; and I went to the butcher, and the lady at the shop gave me some meat to make some beef tea for him. I shall never forget it; how that man ravished it in; how he sucked it. I thought he would take the tin out of my hand.

Q.   And he never applied for relief?

A.   Your Lordship, there have been scores applied, but it is continually refused.

Q.   What happened to this man afterwards?

A.   Well, he lived for some, I should think, six or nine months afterwards; but he worked and did his best. It was cruel to see the man go backwards and forwards to work after he had come back. . . . He came home from work and was dead in about a week. [P.P. XIV, Mins. of Ev., 1895:841–842].

The fear of being denied outrelief was not the only problem for the aged. Those who did receive relief often found the experience degrading and unpleasant. Another witness testified:

The fourth part would be that the relieving officer is, as a rule, uncivil to those in receipt of poor-law relief, and many poor people have informed me that they would as readily meet the police officer as they would the relieving officer. Cases have come under my notice where the relieving officers have been complete bullies. One place in particular, the poor people have to go and wait in places appointed a long time for their money, and if they were not there when the relieving officer was there he would take the money back [P.P. XIV, Mins. of Ev., 1895:348].

As negative as the experiences of many older people were with outdoor relief, it was infinitely preferable to the other option, the workhouse. Both older people and their children perceived the workhouse as the ultimate disgrace. As one witness testified: "It is perfectly true that people will allow their relations to be kept at the cost of the poor rates without making any effort for them as long as they get out-door relief, but the moment they get in-door relief they will make every effort to help them [P.P. XIV, Mins. of Ev., 1895:117]." Booth (1894) verified the extensiveness of these attitudes: "When they, themselves, as well as their parents, are poor, children have, as a rule, no scruple about letting their parents apply for out-relief. To allow them to go into the workhouse would be differently regarded [p. 7]."

Stigmatization was only one aspect of attitudes toward the workhouse; the more pervasive feeling among older people was one of fear, fear of incarceration and of death. This can be seen in the case of an elderly brother and sister:

> They struggled along for a long time, but they had got nothing to do. People gave to them for a time, but for people who have to pay rates and that it is very hard for them to keep people as well; they say: "We pay rates for the purpose, and you ought to make application." Very well, they did make application. They walked right over to Brixworth, and when they got there they had the offer of the house, and they pleaded very hard to have a little out. They said they thought they should not want it for long, and they were refused and I believe they went back home, but I cannot speak definitely about it, but they ultimately went into the house, and after they had been in for a time the women went to the guardians again, and she pleaded that they allow her a little outside as she could not live in the house; she felt that it would be the cause of her death soon if she stopped there; she felt that she could not make her home there, and the guardians refused the application, and on the following Saturday the woman insisted upon going out, and she walked back to her native village, and she was in the village at ten o'clock at night. A farmer, Mr. Mather, took her into his house, and she said: "I will rather die in the street than I will go back to the union." The farmer kept her all night, and coaxed her to go back, drove her over in his trap on the Sunday morning, and I think it was hardly so long as a fortnight before they took her back as a corpse to her own village [P.P. XIV, Mins. of Ev., 1895:845].

The dread was so great that people often sought desperate measures to avoid the workhouse:

Q. You said the poor old man, though lame, ran creeping up a hill to escape from a visit of the relieving officer?
A. No, I did not say that.
Q. What was it?
A. What I said was this, that he went up the hill to seek for shelter; that is, to leave the house in which he was residing. The one reason or one argument used by the relieving officer for removing the old man to the workhouse was that he had no one to attend to him.
Q. And the old man, rather than be taken to the workhouse, crawled up a hill to seek protection from a neighbour or friend?

4. Poor Law Policy and Old Age Pauperism

A. Just so. I brought that case principally to show their reluctance to go to the workhouse.

Q. And, in your opinion, many of the old people in your union would rather die than go into the workhouse?

A. Very many of them; they would rather, sir [P.P. XIV, Mins. of Ev., 1895:314].

There were many reasons why the aged felt such dread of the workhouse. Descriptions of typical workhouses depicted them as drab and monotonous:

> The inmates, over 900 in number, were congregated in large rooms, without any attempt to employ their time or cheer their lives. There was a marked absence of any human interest. . . . It could not be better described than as a "human warehouse." The dormitories, which in some cases accommodated as many as sixty inmates, were so full of beds as to make it impossible to provide chairs, or to walk, except sideways, between them [P.P. XXXVIII, 1909:169]

Dietary in workhouses were universally meager and limited in variety, typically consisting of gruel and bread, with occasional allowances of tea, butter, and sugar for the aged. A typical workhouse dietary is depicted in Table 4.4. However, it was not the monotony that caused the feelings of absolute terror felt by many older people when confronted with an "offer of the house." Their terror was associated with the loss of personal freedom that accompanied workhouse entry—the freedom to come and go at will, to make decisions about daily existence—due to the imposition of authority reflected in institutional life. A remarkable piece of testimony from an aged inmate of a workhouse verifies the problems of authority and loss of freedom inherent in workhouse life:

Q. We have now to ask about the aged poor; those above 60?

A. They have to go and pick oakum for eight hours a day, in twisting little pieces of corded string for eight hours a day, until the people nearly become imbecile; they do not know what to do.

Q. Up to what age are they kept at this work?

A. They are kept at it from 65 until—well, there were some there 70. There was one man there 79, at least he said he was.

Q. Were they all alike, worked for eight hours a day?

TABLE 4.4. *Dietary for Ablebodied Men and Women*[a]

Day	Group	Breakfast		Dinner				Supper		
		Bread (oz.)	Gruel (pt.)	Cooked meat (oz.)	Potatoes (lb.)	Soup (pt.)	Suet or rice pudding (oz.)	Bread (oz.)	Cheese (oz.)	Broth (pt.)
Sunday	Men	6	1.5	5	.5	–	–	6	–	1.5
	Women	5	1.5	5	.5	–	–	5	–	1.5
Monday	Men	6	1.5	–	–	1.5	–	6	–	1.5
	Women	5	1.5	–	–	1.5	5	2	–	1.5
Tuesday	Men	6	1.5	5	.5	–	–	6	–	1.5
	Women	5	1.5	5	.5	–	–	5	–	1.5
Wednesday	Men	6	1.5	–	–	1.5	–	6	2	–
	Women	5	1.5	–	–	1.5	–	5	2	–
Thursday	Men	6	1.5	5	.5	–	–	6	–	1.5
	Women	5	1.5	5	.5	–	–	5	–	1.5
Friday	Men	6	1.5	–	–	–	14	6	2	–
	Women	5	1.5	–	–	–	12	5	2	–
Saturday	Men	6	1.5	–	–	1.5	–	6	2	–
	Women	5	1.5	–	–	1.5	–	5	2	–

Source: Rose, 1971:165.

[a] Exceptions were: "Old people of 60 years and upwards may be allowed one ounce of tea, five ounces of butter and seven ounces of sugar per week, in lieu of gruel for breakfast, if deemed expedient to make this change. Children under nine years of age to be dieted at discretion; above nine, to be allowed the same quantities as women. Sick to be dieted by the medical officer."

4. Poor Law Policy and Old Age Pauperism

A. Eight hours a day; they have a quarter of an hour to go out and smoke a pipe.

Q. Did you find that work severe? . . .

A. No, not severe; monotonous. You did not know what to do. You could not go out to write a letter, or to read, or to do anything: you had no time of your own; in fact, it was a place of punishment, and not relief. . .

Q. Would you state any other objections you have to the treatment of the aged poor?

A. I think that the taskmaster is very much more severe than he should be.

Q. In what way?

A. Well, when you go to dine, or to breakfast, or anything like that, he says, "Come quicker," and pushes you partly into the seat; that is a very trifling thing. I had a sore throat, and he objected to my wearing a scarf round my throat, and he said, "I will pull those rags off you when you come back again here." That was, if I went back again. "You must not wear such things as this." I said, "I have a sore throat," and he says, "I don't care whether you and your father and your grandfather had sore throats." My father died of starvation through his throat growing together, and he suffered with sore throat. I suffered with sore throat, but not much; still, sufficient.

Q. Did you complain to the master of the workhouse of the language and treatment by the man you called the taskmaster?

A. No, my Lord.

Q. You did not?

A. No, my Lord; not the slightest good in doing that.

Q. Why?

A. Whatever the taskmaster wished the master to say, the master would say. They were all under one control, even the doctor and everybody was the same. [P.P. XIV, Mins. of Ev., 1895:836].

As tales such as these became public knowledge, popular support for the pension grew, and what had been a political issue for more than 30 years finally became a reality.

From Pauper to Old Age Pensioner

As early as 1878 Canon William Blackley proposed a scheme of compulsory contributions early in life into an annuity fund that would finance sick pay and a pension later in life. This proposal was effectively crushed by the Friendly Societies, who voiced strong op-

Officer investigating Old Age Pension claims. "WELL, MRS. BRADY, AND HOW OLD MIGHT YOU BE?"
Mrs. Brady. "SORRA WAN OF ME KNOWS, INDEED, SOR."
Officer. "THINK NOW. DON'T YOU KNOW THE DATE OF YOUR BIRTH?"
Mrs. B. "THE DATE OF MY BIRTH, IS IT? SURE, THERE WAS NO SUCH THINGS AS DATES WHEN I WAS BORN!"

From *Punch, or the London Charivari,* October 28, 1908.

position to either a compulsory contributory scheme that would compete for working-class earnings or a state-backed scheme of insurance
such as that supported by Booth, which they viewed as dangerous interference (Collins, 1965:254).[8]

Although not yet ready to accept any form of a pension that was
viewed as prohibitively costly, the Royal Commission on the Aged
Poor did suggest reversals in poor law administration in regard to the
relief of the aged. The Royal Commission condemned both the giving
of inadequate outdoor relief to old people and the confinement of
some of them in unsuitable workhouses, as also did a Parliamentary
Select Committee on the Aged Deserving Poor in 1899. In 1896, the
Local Government Board issued a circular that extended liberal outdoor relief to the *deserving* aged poor, those who had been "of good
character, thrifty according to their opportunities, and generally in-

[8] The opposition of the Friendly Societies to the pension was a complex political
issue. For an extensive discussion, see Gilbert (1966) and Chapter 7.

dependent in early life [Circular of July 11, 1896]." This policy shift coincided with a general trend in the poor law system toward greater specialization of care and differentiation of paupers into categories.

Four years later, the Local Government Board took an even more decisive step, declaring as the definite policy systematic and *adequate* outdoor relief to all aged persons who were destitute and deserving.[9] With the emphasis on "deserving" retained, the board declared that the aged "should not be urged to enter the workhouse at all unless there is some cause which renders such a course necessary, such as infirmity of mind or body, the absence of house accommodation or of a suitable person to care for them, or some similar cause, but that they should be relieved by having adequate outdoor relief granted to them" [Circular of August 4, 1900]." In addition, it recommended a considerable upgrading of the situation of the elderly in the workhouse, including extra dayrooms for the aged, freedom regarding hours of going to bed and waking up, greater facilities for visits by friends, and provisions of tobacco, tea, and sugar.

Around the turn of the century, Seebohm Rowntree published his scientific analysis of poverty, not only tabulating rates but also attempting to identify causes. His work represented an ideological shift from the philosophy of self-help embodied in the "less eligibility" principle, for Rowntree located causes of poverty in environmental factors external to the individual rather than in internal personal failure. In a very basic sense, this was nothing new. Men such as Richard Oastler, leader of the factory movement, had proclaimed in the 1840s that fluctuations in the industrial economy made paupers of factory operatives, caught without means of subsistence in periods of unemployment. However, Rowntree's approach and his message were more suitable to twentieth-century collective thought.

Among Rowntree's more significant findings was the discovery that poverty was not a permanent condition but was instead related to phases in the life cycle of the laborer. According to Rowntree (1901):

> The life of a laborer is marked by five alternating periods of want and comparative plenty. During early childhood, unless his father is a skilled worker, he probably will be in poverty; this will last until he, or some of his brothers or

[9] The definition of *adequacy* was still left to local authorities.

sisters, begin to earn money and thus augment their father's wage sufficiently to raise the family above the poverty line. Then follows the period during which he is earning money and living under his parents' roof; for some portion of this period he will be earning more money than is required for lodging, food, and clothes. This is his chance to save money. If he has saved enough to pay for furnishing a cottage, the period of comparative prosperity may continue after marriage until he has two or three children, when poverty will again overtake him. This period of poverty will last perhaps for ten years, i.e., until the first child is fourteen years old and begins to earn wages; but if there are more than three children it may last longer. While the children are earning, and before they leave the home to marry, the man enjoys another period of prosperity—possibly, however, only to sink back again into poverty when his children have married and left him, and he himself is too old to work, for his income has never permitted his saving enough for him and his wife to live upon for more than a very short time [p. 171].

Rowntree (1901:155) also showed that more than 20% of those living in primary poverty did so due to either the death of the chief wage earner in the family or the illness or old age of the chief wage earner. Figure 4.1 portrays his life cycle of poverty.

Inexorably, political and social factors drew public opinion toward a pension plan, the central dilemma being a choice between a contributory and a noncontributory scheme. In 1899, Charles Booth, with the support of the Fabians, the T.U.C., the co-operative movement, and the Labour party, launched a national movement to promote a noncontributory pension financed out of taxation. The Friendly Societies, heavily in debt because of imbalances in the funds created by large sums paid out to older members, began to see the value of supporting a noncontributory scheme (Gilbert, 1966:196). The threat to Liberal preeminence by the growing power of the Labour party further spurred interest in reform measures.[10]

The pension thus gained widespread support, and in 1908 the Old Age Pensions Act was passed. It provided that every person of British nationality who had resided at least 20 years in the United Kingdom

[10] At the turn of the century, the fledgling Labour party was just beginning to gain strength and support, and several observers judged the emergence of a strong Labour element in the House of Commons as the most significant element of the 1906 election (Fraser, 1973:137). For a more detailed discussion of the rise of Labour, see Chapter 2. Chapter 7 describes the political factors associated with the pension issue.

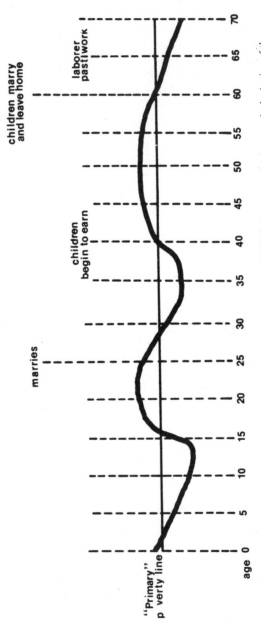

Figure 4.1. *Seebohm Rowntree's graph (1901:171) portrays the life cycle of poverty of the British laborer at the beginning of the twentieth century.*

was entitled to a pension at age 70. Excluded were those whose incomes exceeded £26 a year, those who "habitually failed to work . . . according to ability, opportunity and need for the maintenance of themselves and those legally dependent on them," lunatics, prisoners, and those receiving poor relief (Webb and Webb, 1909: 332). National pensioners were removed from the jurisdiction of the poor law authority and transferred to County Councils that administered pensions through the Post Office. In 1911, the pauper disqualification was removed, extending state income maintenance to even the poorest aged.[11] The amount granted was meager (five shillings), and although it was externally a radical measure, in reality it was largely cosmetic since it did not provide the minimal amount necessary to sustain life. As late as the 1930s, older people were still found in destitute conditions (Cuttle, 1934:363-365). Still, it was significant in lifting the insecurity from the lives of the aged. According to Gilbert (1964-1965):

> To the aged poor it seemed unbelievable that one could collect 5s. simply by coming to the post office on Friday. Particularly in the country villages, unsuspecting postmistresses found themselves showered with apples and flowers from pensioners' gardens in gratitude for the simple act of distributing money [p. 226].

Many more applied than had been anticipated. Clearly, the poor law had acted as a deterrent because of the moral stigma attached to receiving funds from it. The extent of old age poverty was even greater than Booth had estimated. When enacted, the pension depauperized the aged population, removing the stigma attached to receiving funds from the state. It was revolutionary in the sense that it was noncontributory, financed from national taxation, truly a departure from the self-help philosophy that had permeated the poor law.

The centralization of poor law administration was one aspect of state growth tied to the expansion of industrial capitalism. The New Poor Law of 1834 was not as radical a change as many believed, since

[11] In the Pension Act of 1908, any person who had received poor relief since January 1, 1908, was disqualified. A few years later, after much heated debate, the pauper disqualification was removed (Collins, 1965:259).

it continued to favor the landed interests and formalized procedures that had become policy earlier in many districts. However, other shifts in policy later in the century did usurp the power of local authorities and transfer it to the central government, now dominated by new interest groups. The late nineteenth-century conflict over poor law policy was between local authority and the distant state bureaucracy. The next chapter will explore the impact of this conflict on the indirect participants in that battle, the older men and women who became inadvertently involved in a struggle for the control of government because of their dependency on the poor law.

5

The Impact of Government Growth

"I am a woman and living in Merton Papage and have 63 years of age," wrote Esther Radford in 1874 to the Cambridgeshire Board of Guardians in a plea to establish settlement and eligibility for relief.

> I was married on Sept. 7, 1812 to James Radford at Oakington who left me 14 years ago whilst we were living in a house site at the corner of Gloucester St., Cambridge, after about 6 months residence there. I have been living in Cambridge ever since Michelmas 1860 and have never lived in any other place. My husband previous to coming to Cambridge resided at Oakington where he was owner of a freehold estate consisting of a dwelling house and presented with an acre of land which my husband bought of Dr. Stanley and gave him £300 for it. We lived there those 14 years when he sold it to Ian Allard of Histon. About 7 years ago last April my son Hy Radford who is now resident at Oakington and a builder by trade informed me that he had been to America and seen his father who was alive. I have not heard from my husband since. [Cambridgeshire Settlement Papers, G/C/A.S.10].

Despite that Esther Radford had lived in Cambridge for 14 years after she was abandoned by her husband, the Cambridge Board of Guardians determined that her legal settlement was Oakington, in

Chesterton Union, the previous residence of her long-departed spouse. They thereby ordered the Guardians of the Poor of Chesterton Union "to remove and convey by yourselves, or by some person employed by you, the said Esther Radford [Cambridgeshire Settlement Papers, G/C/A.S.10]" to Chesterton Union, where she should be provided for according to law.

Esther Radford was one of the many unfortunate victims of compulsory removal under the law of settlement, as parishes clung to removal as a protection against increased poor rates (Rose, 1976:41). The practice of settlement and removal reflected the intensely local nature of the English system of poor relief. Much of the opposition to the abolition of settlement and removal sprang from the fear that it would lead to the financing of poor relief from national rather than from local funds. When ideas for a system of national poor law financing to accompany the repeal of the law of settlement were proposed, they were rejected on the grounds that a national system would remove the check of local experience and knowledge (Rose, 1976:42). Those who provided the funds would no longer be directly involved in their expenditure, and fraud as well as the destruction of local self-government would be the result. Thus, settlement and removal were maintained, despite numerous arguments against them, because they guaranteed local responsibility for poor relief against those who wished to increase the powers of central government (Rose, 1976:43).

The settlement issue was just one aspect of poor law policy. Although those favoring the expansion of central government were comparatively unsuccessful in regard to the law of settlement, other less controversial aspects of poor law policy were more amenable to alteration. Ultimately, the erosion of local control was accomplished by the mundane pursuits of bureaucrats rather than by the flamboyant issues raised by politicians.

Centralization and the Poor Law

The Old Poor Law, which had evolved gradually since the Elizabethan Poor Law of 1601, was well suited to the political and social structure of the country. Overseers, drawn from the ranks of farmers and shopkeepers, dealt with applicants for relief, and the gentry, in their capacity as magistrates, provided a place of appeal for the poor. The gentry's involvement in parliamentary politics gave them the further power to devise and implement legislation. According to Brundage (1978), "The system thus not only controlled the poor but also enhanced the notion of hierarchy, bolstered the ethos of paternalism which was its corollary, and provided an efficient feedback mechanism into the national lawmaking mechanism [p. 2]."

Although there were common principles of administration under the Old Poor Law, its hallmark was local autonomy. In 1832 the poor law was administered through 15,000 independent parishes (Lubenow, 1971:32). The complexities of the law of settlement, the abuses of the Speenhamland system, as well as inequities in the assessment of rates caused increasing criticism of the Old Poor Law on the grounds that the parish was too small a unit of administration.[1]

In 1834, a bill for the amendment of the poor law was brought before Parliament. After extensive debate, it was passed with overwhelming support. The key policy issue was to return paupers to a condition of economic and moral independence by implementing the twin principles of the "workhouse test" and "less eligibility." This policy was to be applied on a uniform basis throughout the country, with a permanent central authority, the Poor Law Commission, to direct the system. Parishes were to be consolidated into unions, and relief was to be administered by relieving officers under the direction of an elected board of guardians.

The New Poor Law has been described as an administrative revolution, and the issue of centralization that theoretically removed power from the landed gentry and local authorities was one that was raised by opponents of the new law. A typical criticism referred to:

> the tyrannical and arbitrary power of the Central Board of the irresponsible commissioners which completely nullifies and destroys the representative system so congenial to the feelings of the people of this country—so essential to their liberties and so indisputably the cause of all the prosperity of

[1] Since the increase of England's wealth after 1760 was chiefly in manufacturing, new wealth was located in the manufacturing centers. Thus, those communities with the highest poor rate (in rural areas) were not always most able to pay (Lubenow, 1971:32).

5. The Impact of Government Growth

England—and places the individuals whom the people may elect to regulate their affairs entirely and helplessly subject to the baneful coercion of government hirelings [quoted in Fraser, 1976:19].

Persistently, critics focused their attack on the issue of the central board, which they viewed as an arrogation of power from legitimate local authorities (Lubenow, 1971:45).

Although the creation of a central board was a visible departure, the New Poor Law was not as radical as it appeared. In practice, it incorporated many features that had already been present in many parishes under the Old Poor Law (Brundage, 1978). Further, there is ample evidence to suggest that the landed gentry did not lose power to the new central board and may, in fact, have gained power by becoming ex officio members of boards of guardians, by exercising influence through plural voting, by using their decision-making power in the consolidation of parishes into unions, and by their selecting persons to run for boards of guardians in elections that were often uncontested (Brundage, 1972).[2] In effect, then, the "revolution" created a network of powerful local boards that administered policy. The role of the Poor Law Commission was supervisory, with the main change being the introduction of central inspection to the system of social administration. Centralization as a principle had little meaning in terms of actual application. Local government was never administered by agents of the central government, and the real struggle was that of the government to impose national, uniform standards within the framework of local autonomy (Gutchen, 1961:86). Perhaps the most novel feature was the extension of bureaucratic values into a society still dominated by the social controls indigenous to a landed society where landed estate and social status still constituted the most legitimate justification for political authority (Lubenow, 1971:40).

Although landed magnates continued to dominate poor law administration until nearly the end of the nineteenth century in some areas, they were ultimately dislodged by the accelerating impact of

[2] Dunkley (1973) has argued that the New Poor Law consolidated but did not extend the power of the landed gentry and that even this occurred only in a few unrepresentative rural districts.

social change (Brundage, 1975:349). Gradually, local act legislation was superseded by general acts of Parliament. Various statutes provided more uniform standards of rating, and at the same time different kinds of rating were increasingly based on a standard poor-rate assessment. Particularly significant was the Union Chargeability Act of 1865, which made the union the proper fiscal unit and enabled the Poor Law Board to establish viable audit districts and, thus, close supervision (Midwinter, 1972:201).

The Poor Law Board was absorbed into the new Local Government Board in 1871. According to one interpretation, 1894 was the critical year for the breakup of the magistrate-dominated machinery when the Parish Councils Act removed justices of the peace from the boards of guardians and abolished plural voting and property qualification for guardians (Brundage, 1975:349). However, this act was basically a reflection of a shifting alignment of power that had already been accomplished. In all probability, many of the acts and policy circulars eroded the power of local authorities. In the subsequent pages, the 1871 "Circular on Outdoor Relief" will be used as an example of how this was accomplished.[3] The circular provided a means of control by allowing the Local Government Board to exert considerable pressure on local boards of guardians to conform to policy. Before examining how the circular was implemented, let us turn to the wider issues contained within it, that of kin responsibility for the aged and the impact of state intervention on family relationships.

Familial Responsibility and Old Age Dependency

Responsibility for income maintenance of the aged originally resided within the kin group. The belief that children are responsible for the care of their aged parents can be traced back to at least the fifteenth century. According to Macfarlane (1978):

[3] A similar fiat took place in the field of public health in regard to the little noticed Sanitary Act of 1866, which transformed the permissive powers of local authorities into compulsory ones and placed the localities under the tutelage of central government (Gutchen, 1961:91).

5. The Impact of Government Growth

There is a good deal in the pamphlets and sermons of the time to say that it was a father's duty to leave his property to his children, or that children ought to support their parents financially if they were poor. For example, Thomas Bacon wrote in the sixteenth century that "if their parents be aged and fallen into poverty . . . then ought the children, if they will truly honor their parents, to labor for them unto their necessities, to provide necessaries for them [p. 205].

Whether children actually fulfilled this duty is open to question, but then, like now, the normative proscription existed. This moral duty was turned into a legal stipulation in the Elizabethan Poor Law (Eliz. I, c. 2, 5.6), charging kin with responsibility for the aged while simultaneously formally transferring ultimate economic responsibility for the impotent aged to the parish. Lists of paupers from parishes indicate that throughout the next 2 centuries the aged were among those receiving the greatest amount of support (Richard Smith, personal communication). The extent of this support is difficult to calculate, but it is apparent that a disproportionate share of relief was given to the aged.

The issue of filial duty was brought before the hearings on the poor law in 1834. Some arguments against support of the aged by the parish were presented on the grounds that it would further erode familial ties: "Social ties [are] now in the course of rapid extinction by the Poor Laws. It is to be feared, indeed, that feelings and motives are gradually becoming lost to the laboring orders [P.P., XXXVII, 1834, 258A]."

The commission concluded that it was necessary to replace familial support with parish support, because the English working classes were totally deficient in natural filial affection. Echoing a Benthamite view, the commissioners stated:

The duty of supporting the parents in their old age is so strongly enforced by our natural feelings that it is often well performed, even among savages, and almost always so in a nation deserving the name of civilized. We believe that England is the only country in which it is neglected. To add the sanction of the law in countries where that of nature is found sufficient, to make that compulsory which would otherwise be voluntary, cannot be necessary; and if unnecessary, must be mischievous. But if the deficiencies of filial affection are to be supplied by the parish, and the natural motives to the exercise of those virtues are thus to be withdrawn, it may be proper to endeavor to replace them, however imperfectly, by artificial stimulants [P.P. XIV, Report, 1895: xliv].

Thus, it became general policy to allow small amounts of outrelief to the aged without specific concern about pressuring children to contribute.

In the early 1870s, the Local Government Board and its inspectorate launched a campaign against outdoor relief in an attempt to return the poor law to the principles of 1834. The 1871 "Circular on Outdoor Relief," which was one of the first policy recommendations of the Local Government Board in regard to the poor law, condemned the outrelief system and suggested that all applications for relief be more carefully scrutinized with an increased reliance on the workhouse as a test of destitution. New stress was placed on getting contributions from kin, for it was implied that if the aged were confronted with the workhouse, their relatives would come forward to maintain them (Webb and Webb, 1910:150).

What was ultimately more significant in terms of the erosion of local control was the emphasis on implementing deliberate policy rather than on allowing decisions about relief to be dependent on temporary statutes and whims of local authorities. There was increased concern with record keeping, and tables showing the amount of relief given by each union were published and circulated. Unions that gave disproportionate amounts were held accountable, regardless of the proportion of aged in the population.

Between 1871 and 1885, steady pressure was placed on boards of guardians to reduce outrelief despite that the sick and aged made up at least half and perhaps as much as three-quarters of the adult population receiving outrelief. This policy remained in effect (with great regional variation in administration) until the 1890s, when the first return of paupers by age was made (Collins, 1965:246). Reformers' arguments were supported by the data gathered by Booth on the condition of the aged poor, showing that the average rate of pauperism among those 65 and above was over 29% and in many districts over 50% (Booth, 1891, 1894). Two royal commissions were organized to investigate the state of the aged poor. Their findings combined with pressure from Parliament led to a reversal of poor law policy administration in regard to relief to the aged.

Despite the liberalization of relief policy, the issue of filial responsibility remained a concern. The 1895 Royal Commission on the Aged Poor read into the hearings the preceding quotation from the

1834 report regarding the neglect of kin by the working classes. The issue was also apparently a concern among unions. For example, in 1905 the Fulham Board of Guardians felt it necessary to specify formally that sons and unmarried daughters of sufficient means were responsible for the maintenance of aged and infirm parents:

> Legitimate children (sons, whether married or single, and daughters, if unmarried) are bound to maintain their parents when unable to work through sickness or other cause . . . it is only relatives of sufficient ability who are liable, and proof of ability is required by justices before an order can be made [Wall, 1977:60].

In 1909, the same year that the pension was implemented, the Royal Commission on the Poor Laws, referring to those aged still ineligible for a pension due to their pauper status, argued that a decline in filial duty was a major cause of the increased economic dependence of the aged: "We believe that if the position is clearly defined and a consistent policy laid down both as to pensions and Poor Relief, the natural feeling between parents and children will again assert itself [quoted in Collins, 1965:249]."

In 1909, most older people were effectively depauperized with the implementation of the Old Age Pensions Act, although substantial numbers remained in poverty. The specific provisions of the pension were discussed in Chapter 4. The pension was also significant in that it spelled the demise of local control of the support of the aged, shifting that responsibility to the state bureaucracy. This shift represented a major break with tradition in that funding was moved from local rates to national taxation.

The Effects of the Crusade against Outrelief

The 20 years between 1871 and 1891 were a period of specific policy change in which a "crusade against outrelief" was vigorously enforced. As noted earlier, there were two aspects to this crusade. First, the inspectors of the Local Government Board wished to decrease significantly the amount of funds deployed for outdoor relief. Second, a determined policy was instituted to bring pressure to bear upon family members to contribute to the support of aged kin.

Anderson (1977) has already shown that the total percentage of older people who were institutionalized in England and Wales increased in the latter portion of the nineteenth century. He attributes this increase to the harsh implementation of the 1871 circular. This chapter will expand on his findings by describing the decision-making factors at the local level of one union that led to increased institutionalization.

The union of Cambridgeshire was selected as a case study for two reasons. First, Cambridgeshire was a rural union. In 1871, the year the circular ordering the tightening of outdoor relief was released by the Local Government Board, 53% of all working males in Cambridgeshire were employed in agriculture (Census of England and Wales, 1871, vol. 17). Like other rural unions, Cambridgeshire bore the burden of outdoor relief to the aged quite heavily, so any order to reduce outrelief would affect both administrative policy and the well-being of the aged quite directly (Digby, 1976:164). Second, as a rural union that had been administered by local farmers and shopkeepers, Cambridgeshire aptly illustrates the struggle of local government officials to maintain control against the insistent intrusion of central government directives.

A detailed examination of the implementation of the 1871 "Circular on Outdoor Relief" in Cambridgeshire through the use of minute books and other records of the Board of Guardians will be used to illustrate how the expansion of bureaucratic requirements for standardization decreased local autonomy. Some suggestions will also be made as to whether the need for a state pension arose because of a decline in family relationships or whether other factors were more important. Throughout, the impact of policy change on the aged will be described.

The Response to the Circular

The first reaction of the Cambridgeshire Board of Guardians to the "Circular on Outdoor Relief" of 1871 appeared in the minutes on January 31, 1873, where it was moved that "greater care be taken in the administration of Out Relief [Minute Book, vol. 26:25]." The board also voted to print and publish a list of paupers receiving outrelief "by affixing on the usual places for exhibiting parochial notices in each parish." This was apparently too stringent a measure for the board, for at the next meeting it voted to rescind the order concerning the publication of the list.

For 2 years, no further action was taken, and the amount of outrelief given remained approximately the same. However, policy was made explicit in response to a letter from St. Ives Union soliciting the scale of out-relief granted in Cambridge. It was ordered that the clerk reply "by stating that there is no particular scale for the administration of out-relief in this Union but that each case depends upon its special circumstances and relief administered accordingly [Minute Book, vol. 27:79]." Clearly, the system of administration was particularistic, and policy decisions were subject to the whims of the board and the composition of board members.

During the next few years, there was increased external pressure on the Board of Guardians to both reduce outrelief and rationalize its procedures. Demands were made by the Local Government Board for lists of paupers in which relief recipients appeared in alphabetical order. This led to a brief rebellion from relieving officers who were unhappy with the extra work required in preparing lists in alphabetical order, but they did comply. What appeared to be a major policy change took place on November 21, 1877, when the Board of Guardians voted that "out-relief be forthwith discontinued [Minute Book, vol. 28:316]." Despite this vote, the amount of outrelief actually rose from £146 8s. in 1877 to £152 2s. in 1878. Obviously, this policy change was not implemented.

Even more concerted pressure was brought to bear on the union in 1879, when the Local Government Board inspector indicated that there was an unusually high rate of pauperism in Cambridgeshire Union. The following letter was read into the minutes:

Ordered that the Local Government Board Inspector having called the attention of the board at their meeting held on the 30th as to the high rate of pauperism in this Union it be referred to the following members of the board to enquire into the circumstances and report as to whether any and in what manner alterations should take place in the administration of relief and the classification of paupers receiving the same [Minute Book, vol. 30:276].

This direct pressure could not be ignored, and a committee of 15 guardians was appointed to investigate the matter. After holding seven meetings consuming at least 3 hours each, the committee, in a rather lengthy report, made a series of minor recommendations regarding the reporting and listing of paupers, including a new categorization of permanent and temporary poor and the inclusion of ages on the lists. It made no recommendations to reduce outrelief, and it took no measures to do so. Thus, the report addressed only the administrative aspects of the edict, those concerning classification, while ignoring the suggestion for a major policy change in regard to outrelief.

It is apparent that until the 1880s, a particularistic, non-bureaucratized system of relief administration predominated in Cambridgeshire but that there was continuing external pressure to standardize procedures and reduce the amount of particularistic decision making. External pressure centered around the issue of the reduction of outrelief, which was the overt goal of the Local Government Board. However, the latent function of the circular of 1871 and its follow-up was a centralization of control, gained by increased bureaucratization of the system. Minor—but increasingly demanding—organizational changes were easier to implement and less threatening to local autonomy than were major policy changes. In reality, by losing local control of information through a reorganization of the system by which information was transmitted, the Cambridgeshire Board of Guardians became increasingly ineffectual and less able to resist policy change as well.

By the early 1880s, Cambridgeshire, along with the rest of England, was beginning to realize that the agricultural depression of the 1870s was not a short-term fluctuation due to a series of poor harvests but rather a long-term economic decline in agriculture. Feeling the effects of the depression, local ratepayers began to place additional pressure on the Board of Guardians to reduce outrelief. This pressure is indicated by the board's note of November 30, 1881, to insert an advertisement in the Cambridge newspaper announcing that "any ratepayer may have a gratuitous copy of the List of Paupers receiving out-relief during the last half year on applying at the clerk's office [Minute Book, vol. 30:409]."

In 1883, the system of parish representation was reorganized, and an unprecedented 11 new members were elected to the Board of Guardians. One of the newly elected guardians had campaigned on a platform of reducing outrelief, as reported in the local newspaper: "It has been too easy a matter for persons to obtain relief. They knew that too often when people got into trouble the first thing they did was to go to the guardians instead of trying to meet their difficulties in other ways [*Cambridge Independent Press*, April 1883]."

This election was a critical turning point, for it meant that national and local interests now coincided on the issue of outrelief. On June 5, 1883, a new committee composed largely of new board members was appointed to investigate outrelief. The committee met throughout the summer of 1883, holding a total of 19 sessions. At each session it examined the relieving officer's lists and either reduced or eliminated outrelief, with an "offer of the house" being made in lieu of outrelief. In all, over 450 paupers had their relief either reduced or eliminated in the course of a single summer.

Prior to 1883, the policy of extracting support from children, one of the mandates included in the 1871 circular, was never mentioned. All policy discussion centered solely around the reduction of outrelief per se. As the summer wore on, the new board began to implement this aspect of the circular as well and placed pressure on relatives, particularly sons, to contribute to the support of aged parents.

Three factors based on board policy can be identified that distinguished those who received outrelief from those who were "offered the house." First, having a son with whom the board could negotiate for a maintenance contribution offered a source of protection for the aged, particularly widows.[4] The board allowed an older woman outrelief in a reduced amount if a son could be induced to contribute to her maintenance. In effect, this often became a bargaining procedure, with sons negotiating reductions in the amount of re-

[4] In only rare instances were sons asked to contribute to the maintenance of a father, largely because fewer men were receiving outrelief as a result of the harsher application of the "less eligibility" principle to males.

quired contributions, as indicated by the following letter from a relieving officer to the board:

Dear Sir:

I have enclosed you Mr. H. Coe's consent to pay 1s./6d. toward his mothers maintenance but Mr. David Coe of 12 Adam Row will not sign and he will attend the board on Wednesday and would like to be called in early. I have seen the amount of his wages for the year which is about £61. He has a wife and five children. The oldest is 12 years of age and his wife is near her confinement. I have sent you this in case I should not be able to see you in time.

Yours truly,

C. M. Hills [Union Letter Book, July 15, 1883].

Second, it was stated board policy that "where a person is residing with relatives and the circumstances of the family show that destitution does not exist in-maintenance only [the workhouse] should be given (Minute Book, vol. 32:417]." Whereas previous outrelief to the aged had often subsidized whole families, the removal of this subsidy through this policy change probably broke up extended-family households. Since families functioned as economic units, the elimination of a contribution by one member jeopardized the family economy, making it impossible for a child to keep an aged parent in the home.[5] Third, the board determined that "persons over 70 years of age should not be permitted to live alone, but should reside with those who can be held responsible for their cleanliness and safety [Minute Book, vol. 32:417]." When this policy became manifest, any aged person who had no one responsible for his or her care was placed in the workhouse. Statistics for Cambridgeshire, shown in Table 5.1, confirm that the policy was implemented, for the greatest increase in institutionalized aged during this period was among the very old. Very old women were particularly affected, as the number of women over age 75 in the workhouse doubled, from 51 to 102.

The reason that the policy change affected older women in such a

[5] Until the census records of 1881 and 1891 are available, it will be impossible to demonstrate a change in household composition as a result of changed outdoor relief policy. However, I predict that there would be fewer families living with an aged parent.

5. The Impact of Government Growth

TABLE 5.1. *Number of Paupers in Workhouse in Cambridgeshire by Age, 1871–1891*

	Males				Females			
Year	65+	75+	85+	Total all ages	65+	75+	85+	Total all ages
1871	190	130	17	923	42	37	14	645
1891	202	139	32	717	55	81	21	410

Source: Census of England and Wales, 1871, 1891.

disproportionate manner can be determined by examining the Cambridgeshire records on paupers in receipt of relief. Beginning in 1888, Cambridgeshire Union made periodic reports to the Local Government Board, summarizing data on paupers in receipt of outdoor relief. These reports were one more aspect of the trend toward increased bureaucratization of poor law administration that emphasized accurate and complete record keeping. The records for Cambridgeshire indicate two important aspects of outrelief policy, as

TABLE 5.2. *Proportion of All Outdoor Relief in Cambridge Union Received by Aged in Selected Years[a]*

	Paupers receiving outdoor relief			
Year	Males all ages (N)	Aged males (percentage)	Females all ages (N)	Aged females (percentage)
1888	123	.53	335	.64
1891	140	.54	329	.63
1895	133	.50	306	.60
1900	137	.46	300	.63

Source: Report to the Local Government Board. Paupers in Receipt of Relief. Cambridge Union, 1st and 2nd Districts.

[a] Figures prior to 1888 on outrelief by age are not available. Thus, any radical change that occurred in response to the 1871 circular would not be illustrated by this table.

shown in Table 5.2. First, a disproportionate share of all outdoor relief was received by the aged. Aged men received approximately half of all the outrelief given to males over more than a 10-year period, and aged women received approximately two-thirds of all outrelief given to females.[6] Clearly, any reduction in outrelief would affect the aged more severely than any other group, if reductions were applied unilaterally.

These figures also tentatively explain the increase in the number of aged women in the workhouse. Women in general and older women in particular received outrelief to a much greater extent than men, as in 1888, for example, when 215 older women were listed as recipients. Apparently, then, the crusade against outrelief negatively affected older women in Cambridgeshire simply because they were numerically more likely to be affected.

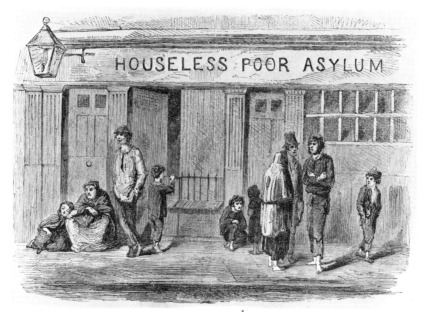

"Asylum for the Houseless Poor, Cripplegate"

From Henry Mayhew, *London Labor and the London Poor.* London: Dover, 1861.

[6] Data for England and Wales as a whole, quoted earlier, indicate that these figures are probably typical.

5. The Impact of Government Growth

The implementation by the newly composed Board of Guardians of the 1871 circular in terms of both the reduction of outrelief and the extraction of contributions from sons as well as the additional clarification of policy increased the number of institutionalized aged in Cambridgeshire. The effect was greatest on women, on the very old, and most likely on the childless, although those living with children who were unable to prove destitution were also likely to have been affected. The Cambridgeshire records definitely prove that women and the very old were institutionalized during this period, but data showing that family membership had an effect are more difficult to locate because of the unavailability of census household listings after 1870. However, one study of workhouse populations did show that the "belongingless poor," those with no living family members, made up a disproportionate share of workhouse populations (Sellars, 1908). Further, the 1891 Census of England and Wales showed that 59% of all males and 56% of all females in workhouses were unmarried. Thus, although direct proof is not available, indirect evidence supports the supposition that family membership did provide some protection for the aged.

Further Resistance to Centralization

Support for the argument that the real battle was not over outrelief and income maintenance of the aged but over challenges to local control and authority is provided by records concerning two other issues that emerged late in the century. One challenge came from the growing power of labor, as workingmen gained the right to be elected to boards of guardians. The issue of the time of board meetings was one obstacle that boards hostile to working-class members used. On two occasions in 1893 and again in 1895, a motion was introduced to alter the time of the board meetings on Wednesday from 10 A.M. to 6 P.M. in order to accommodate any prospective working-class members. On both occasions, the motion was defeated.

Opposition to growing state control also appeared in regard to the issue of old age pensions. On February 17, 1892, a committee formed to study the issue made its report, coming out clearly against state pensions:

That while ready to consider any proposals for the prevention or extinction of pauperism or to improve the condition and prospect of the aged and deserving poor, the Board is not prepared to support the recommendations in detail of the National Providence League with regard to old age pensions.

The board deprecates any legislation which would have a tendency to undermine the principle of voluntary associated thrift, self help and self dependence, discourage provident habits and forethought or in any way interfere with the excellent work done by the industrial classes through their own Friendly Societies [Minute Book, vol. 33:417].

Although the report is phrased in terms of a concern with maintaining the poor law philosophy of thrift and self-help, it is apparent that the extension of state intervention was of equal concern.

In the battle between the local and national interests, the aged paid a price. The state used the issue of the reduction of outrelief, coupling it with increased bureaucratization, as a means of wresting control from local authorities. The outrelief issue arose during a time when ratepayers were troubled by economic difficulties so that boards of guardians were pressured from two sources. The victims were the aged, the major recipients of outrelief. The boards of guardians again resisted state intervention in regard to the pension, and it is likely that pockets of local resistance were a factor in delaying the passage of the pension act.

The Effects of Intervention on Family Relationships

The external consequences of administrative policies can be determined by examining administrative records and census data, but there is no extant comparable data source for determining internal effects on familial relationships. Testimony of witnesses from a series of Royal Commission Hearings on the Aged Poor held in the 1890s does provide some clues, indicating at least three consequences of bureaucratic interference in family affairs. First, the arbitrariness with which the 1871 circular was administered caused financial hardships for both the aged and their families. Second, the aged lost independence, as their ability to contribute to household income was removed. Third, tensions between generations were increased.

5. The Impact of Government Growth

Financial Hardships

Individual financial hardship was caused by a lack of follow-up procedures in regard to collecting maintenance payments from children in some unions. Whereas some boards required a son to make payments directly to the relieving officer, who then paid the aged parent, others made no systematic attempt to determine that maintenance orders were carried out. The effect was simply a reduction of outrelief and subsequent lowering of the standard of living of the older person with no compensation. As one witness testified:

> What is frequently done in the case of an old man and an old woman is this: I have an instance here, the one aged 80 and the other aged 77; they live in the parish of St. Giles; they have 3s. a week allowed them by the guardians, and instead of doing what they used to do, allowing 4s/6d and calling upon the son to contribute 1s/6d of that money, they now allow simply the 3s and let the son or sons do what they can [P.P. XIV, Mins. of Ev., 1895:248].

Financial hardships were also caused when children of little means were forced to pay parental maintenance, particularly when the children were themselves aging. The following case was reported by one witness:

> Thomas Potter of Winfarthing; he has to pay sixpence a week in support of his father, who is 82 years of age. This man's age is 55 years, and he has a family of six children and is keeping a benefit society himself. This is a remarkable case. Three years back this old man received outdoor relief. It was cut off by the board of guardians, and he was ordered to go to work or go to the workhouse. The old man dreaded it so, he tried his hand to do a little work, but it did not last long. This might be an experiment to find out whether the old man had any more work in him, but strange to say the very man whom he worked for a number of years was the guardian of this parish where this poor old man lived, and it did look like giving him the last kick [P.P. XIV, Mins. of Ev., 1895:363].

This example also illustrates the hazards of a paternalistic system that uses particularistic criteria in decisions of eligibility for support. Another instance provides an even more extreme example:

The Effects of Intervention on Family Relationships

In the year 1887, two brothers, William and Robert Stokes, living at Wood Daling, in Norfolk, their ages were, respectively, 58 and 60 years, were summoned before the Reepham bench of magistrates by the Aylsham Board of Guardians for not contributing to their mother's maintenance. Robert answered the summons; William did not, through being sick, lame and unable to walk. William, 58 years of age, had been earning 8s. per week for some months. Robert was not in good bodily health and had been out of work for some time. Both had wives and families, and at the same time were heavily in dept. . . . These two brothers refused to pay to the support of their mother, because they were not able to do so. . . . Both were sentenced to a fortnight's imprisonment [P.P. XIV, Mins. of Ev., 1895:345].

The punishment was extreme in this case, but the financial hardship imposed by the maintenance order was a common problem.

Increased Dependence

There was considerable testimony that the aged preferred the comparatively impersonal relief provided by the union to direct assistance from children.

Q: Do I understand that you consider the case a hard one where a mother with a number of unmarried sons is supposed to be assisted by them, instead of being relieved by the poor rates? Does that seem to you hard?
A: My Lord, the only distinction I can draw is, that what little allowance would be allowed by that union would not be sufficient to keep the widow in any shape with a home, and the sons making provision for themselves and willing to find a home and to supplement what little allowance there would be, they feel it is a hardship, and these widows themselves feel it is a hardship. They do not like to feel dependent fully upon their sons [P.P. XIV, Mins. of Ev., 1895:362].

This desire for independence is illustrated dramatically by one instance in Cambridgeshire Union in which a widow applied for relief. It was judged that her sons were able to maintain her, and the board voted that relief be provided, contingent on the contributions of her sons (Minute Book, vol. 35:277). At the next meeting of the board a letter from John Payton, the son, was read stating that he was willing to contribute to the maintenance of his mother and had offered her a home with him. However, she refused to go, preferring to live independently. Upon hearing this, the board voted to discontinue outrelief based on her ingratitude and instead make an offer of the house (Minute Book, vol. 35:283). Clearly, some older people preferred the workhouse to dependence on children.

Increased Intergenerational Tension

There was considerable evidence presented at the hearings that increased family tension arose from the forced maintenance orders, as in the following instance:

> A: I know it causes a good deal of ill feelings among their wives and that, and causes things very unpleasant.
> Q: Family bickering?
> A: Yes, it does sir [P.P. XIV, Mins. of Ev., 1895:783].

Children who were barely able to maintain their own families also expressed resentment toward the aged in terms of the burden placed upon them. As one witness noted, "It is to my mind practically impossible that they can contribute anything towards the support of their parents out of their very limited incomes; and that being so, they, instead of desiring a lengthened existence to their parents, almost, in some instances, wish that that existence were terminated [P.P. XIV, Mins. of Ev., 1895:248]."

Government Growth and Family Relationships

The 1871 "Circular on Outdoor Relief" represented one of many battles fought over the issue of local government autonomy. The success of Local Government Board demands for compliance with the circular could not be estimated without accurate information on paupers in receipt of relief, and for approximately 10 years the Cambridgeshire Board of Guardians successfully resisted the implementation of the circular by making minor administrative changes in the listing and reporting of paupers. However, the more accurate records that evolved gave the Local Government Board the precise information it needed to identify Cambridgeshire as a noncompliant union, and as a result more concerted pressure was placed on the guardians to reduce outrelief.

The pressure from central government coincided with local ratepayers' dissatisfactions, and the issue came to a head in the 1883 elections, when a major campaign issue became the reduction of outrelief. The newly elected, expanded Board of Guardians immediately began the process of reducing outrelief, and the result was a period of brief but unremitting economic pressure on aged paupers and their families. That the numbers of paupers receiving outrelief remained remarkably stable from 1888 to 1900 indicates that the economic issue was short-lived and that other matters such as the struggle to keep working-class members off the board took precedence in later years over outrelief reduction.

Two arguments have been postulated about the impact of government growth on family relationships. One suggests that the decline of family ties created a need for increased state support of the aged. However, a realistic appraisal of the prepension period shows no evidence of family breakdown, although it is undeniable that tensions existed. The refusal of children to maintain aged parents was due to economic hardships imposed by the withdrawal of outdoor relief rather than to filial neglect. Working-class families simply could not survive as an economic unit when aged members did not contribute to the family economy.[7] A second argument asserts that government growth and increased bureaucratization *caused* the breakdown of family relationships. Bureaucratization of the poor law did have an impact, but not in the sense usually postulated. Bureaucratization was used as a tool by the state to remove control from local authorities. In fact, the establishment and legitimation of a centralized mechanism of administration paved the way for the passage of the pension by making large-scale economic aid conceptually possible. The growth of government is not the relevant factor in the argument. Rather, it is

[7] Not until 1948 was the responsibility for maintaining an aged parent removed from children with the passage of the National Assistance Act (Rheinstein, 1965:251).

the nature of the policy itself and the harshness of the manner in which it was implemented. The content of social policy needs to be recognized as significant in and of itself.

No national figures are available to help determine whether old age pauperism actually increased in the nineteenth century. We do know that it was extensive. By the time the Old Age Pensions Act was finally passed, it was perceived as a necessary measure to compensate for the lack of work for older people whose energies had been absorbed by machine technology and whose job opportunities had decreased. In the following chapter, the political and economic factors that reduced work for the aged and led to the battle for the pension will be described.

6

Work and Retirement

Work for Older Men

In 1898, the general manager of the Barrow Steel Company posted the following notice for the employees of his firm:

> From this date forward please note that no men are to be engaged who are known to have any defects, such as the loss of a limb, defective sight or hearing. Further, no men to be engaged in any department who are older than fifty years of age. Any man already in the employ of the company in the excess of this age may be retained, but in case of their leaving they are not to be reengaged! [quoted in Metcalfe, 1899:31-32].

Not reengaged! How harsh, even cruel, this notice must have appeared to some aged steelworker, perhaps recently recovered from a bout of influenza, who could not help but wonder how much longer he could go on. Yet, the apparent harshness of this directive becomes more comprehensible in the light of conditions of the time. This policy was not merely a reflection of a personal whim on the part of the general manager of Barrow Steel but rather a rational reaction by employers to the Workmen's Compensation Act, which was intended to compensate industrial workers for injuries on the job. Excellent as the intent of this act may have been, it had an unintended consequence for older workers, reducing their employment opportunities and forcing many out of the labor force (Hamilton, 1910–1911:10).

In the not too distant past, older workers could always struggle on, finding sporadic work at low wages under the benevolence of some manufacturer who believed he had an obligation for the welfare of his "hands." As firms grew larger and the workplace became the factory, it was increasingly less efficient to keep older workers around for the few odd chores they might perform. The cadre of new managers who replaced the old foremen felt responsible to the company, not to some elderly workman whose frequent ailments were costly and disruptive. The distinction between the old paternalistic business and the modern firm was readily recognized by workers, who patiently explained the difference to examiners at the hearing of the Royal Commission on the Aged Poor. "So far as private firms are concerned," responded one Friendly Society representative when asked if employers attempted to find work for their older hands,

> there is very great sympathy with the old workmen, and I believe that masters in the district I came from do their best to find such employment. But so far as firms are concerned, limited firms, I mean companies, well, the same sympathy is not experienced and the same help is not afforded. One can well understand that, because the managers feel the responsibility to the shareholders and also the directors feel such responsibility [P.P. XVI, 1895:816].

The practice of keeping older workers on at wages substantially lower than those of younger workers was resisted as well by unions, who feared a general lowering of wage rates (P.P. XLV, 1898:172).[1] This was a particularly strong issue among the Amalgamated Society of Engineers, one of the largest unions. One trade unionist testifying before the Royal Commission explained the union position:

[1] See Chapter 7 for a more extensive discussion of the concerns of trade unions.

But we have to remember this, that if we allowed that man, when he arrived at a certain age to work for less wages than what may be termed the strong and lusty, the employers would at once take the opportunity of causing a downward tendency to the wages of the general body of workmen [P.P. XIV, Mins. of Ev., 1895:797].

Since employers in some industries refused to pay the aged wages equal to those of younger workers, a consequence of union policy was to reduce work opportunities for older workers. However, practice varied from one manufacturer to another, depending not only on union policy but also on whether the employment of the elderly was efficient and functional for the employer. Sometimes a compromise was reached, as in the wireworking industry, where there were many minor tasks that an older worker could perform:

I will give you an illustration: one man was permitted to work. He was 74 years of age, and he was just able to do a little. The employer did not want to get rid of him, and he was permitted to work at 6d. per hour when he did what we call "hour" work, as against the 8d. and 9d. of an ordinary man, and no objection was raised because of his age [P.P. XIV, Mins. of Ev., 1895:742].

By distinguishing "hour" work from regular work, the manufacturer could allow an older man to do odd jobs, and the union pay scale was not threatened.

Even those who were able to hold on to jobs suffered lower incomes due to illness. The Manchester Unity of Oddfellows reported that whereas the average member received 17s. 11d. a year in sick allowance, equivalent to about 8 days of illness a year, those members over 65 received on the average £7 40s. 9d. each, a loss of approximately 60 days a year (Turner, 1897:3). These workers were ill for almost one-fifth of the working year, and yet they were fortunate, for countless other workers had no Friendly Society or club to fall back on in times of distress.

In the countryside, too, older laborers were having difficulty finding jobs in the last decades of the nineteenth century. At one time, it had been common practice for parish authorities to hire older men to work on the roads. For example, Raymond Williams (1973) recalls the story of his grandfather, who lived during the era when rural life had not yet been transformed: "My grandfather was a farm worker until middle age, when he lost his job and with it his cottage, and became a roadman: cutting and clearing along a length of the road that led away to the Midlands [p. 4]."

In 1888, the machinery of local government was completely overhauled in the rural areas, and power was transferred from local nonelected justices of the peace to elected county councils (Thomson, 1950:179). Again, without apparent malice, a reform measure had the unfortunate effect of adding to the obsolescence of the aged. As one witness testified before the hearings of the Royal Commission on the Aged Poor:

> Q: You have noticed, I understand, an increasing difficulty in aged workmen obtaining employment?
> A: I have sir.
> Q: That is, that the new county council gives better wages, but they demand youth and vigour?
> A: They only employ their own men, and not what I might call, roughly speaking, used up laborers on the farms.
> Q: And in the case of the old parish authorities, they were not so exacting?
> A: They employed the old people as long as they could be employed on the roads.
> Q: So that a considerable source of employment for those only partially able to do a good day's work is now removed in consequence of the new Local Government? [P.P. XIV, Mins. of Ev., 1895:323].

Those fortunate enough to be able to continue working into old age were plagued by other difficulties. For elderly agricultural laborers, who comprised the highest proportion of aged workers, employment was both sporadic and hazardous. Seasonality was a difficulty encountered by all agricultural laborers, but younger workers were freer to follow work opportunities from one season to another, one locale to another (Samuel, 1975:5). In contrast, evidence indicates that for the aged the only work was often during harvest times, which gave them their chief, and sometimes only, earnings of the year (Morgan, 1975:45). During harvest the elderly were often employed at loading the wagons or building the ricks, which was less strenuous than, say, pitching hay but not without risks. Between 1872 and 1898

Jackson's Oxford Journal reported a series of farm accidents involving older workers:

> At Great Twe near Deddington in July 1872 an aged agricultural laborer (seventy-seven) slipped off a wagon load of hay, head downwards, and expired about 6 o'clock. At Deddington four years later an old man of seventy-five who was working on a straw rick, "tumbled therefrom to the ground and thereby received such injuries that he died". At Bampton on 10 August of the same year John Martin, farm laborer aged sixty-one years, had just emptied a load at the rick and was standing on the raves of the cart when the horses suddenly moved forward and "he fell to the ground striking his head against a ladder . . . died the same evening". At Murcot in July 1899 a sixty-two-year-old laborer had a fatal fall when he was climbing down from a hay rick. Falling from a straw rick George Woodwar aged fifty-six, a laborer of Appleton, died from haemorrhage of the brain at the end of harvest in 1898. A shepherd aged fifty, employed by Mr. Salmon of Luffield Abbey near Silverstone, Buckinghamshire, engaged with others building a rick in 1873, "overbalanced himself and fell from the top of the rick to the ground, a distance of 27 feet", and died the next day from injuries to his spine. [quoted in Morgan, 1975:33–34].

Work was risky, certainly, but for the unskilled, there was no alternative.

Life Cycle Patterns of Work for Women

Women in nineteenth-century England tended to work while they were young and unmarried and then withdraw from the labor force until necessity brought about by their husbands' unemployment, widowhood, or old age drew them back. When married women did work, they tended to be found in the least industrialized segment of the labor force. That their lives were tied to their families meant they had little chance to develop a skill. Only a minority of employed women worked at skilled trades, and the percentage of married women workers in such jobs was even less. Those who worked outside the home often did charing or worked as laundresses, where jobs were readily available, and other married women worked at home (Meacham, 1977:99). For example, numerous women, rather than taking work in factories, took in boarders when their children were young as a means of supplementing the family income (Tilly and Scott, 1978:125). Those who did work in factories were most often the wives of men in casual or low-paying employment. In general, women formed a floating population of temporary or casual laborers who were part of a vast secondary labor force.

Because of women's sporadic labor-force participation, their work was considered as temporary or supplementary, a factor that contributed to a disparity between men's and women's wages. The problem of low wages, particularly in home work, plagued all women but was exacerbated for older women. As they grew older, women found themselves less capable of maintaining the required pace, and so their wages dropped. For instance, the case is recounted of one dressmaker who found her wages dropped by two shillings a week when she reached 45 (Meacham, 1977:101).

The compensation for sacrifice throughout life was ideally a secure place within the family in old age. Certainly, many examples can be found of grateful children supporting aged mothers in their declining years. One assistant relieving officer in London, interviewed by social workers in 1891, attributed his ascent on the social ladder to the work and encouragement of his mother, whom he continued to support in her declining years (Meacham, 1977:22).

Further, in many households an aged parent had a distinct role to play:

> (A women biscuit maker in Reading): Her job is to feed the ovens, but she says she cannot stand it much longer; indeed, her husband is just beginning to work again and if her mother-in-law can get a job of charing she hopes to be able to leave it off. Meanwhile her one and only child (a year old baby) is in the charge of her mother-in-law [quoted in Meacham, 1977:56].

In this household, the older woman's presence was important because mother and daughter-in-law shared child care and wage-earning activities. On the other hand, there is also evidence that aged relatives were a mixed blessing:

> However much help they give in the house before the days come when they can carry on no longer, they are very definitely another mouth to feed, another oc-

cupant of a much needed bed; it is pretty certain that the young woman of the working classes would not have a helper of any sort if there were no old relative present. Thus the old folks' food and houseroom would be saved [quoted in Meacham, 1977:57].

Since clear assessments of the impact of social change on older women's work opportunities are difficult to make because of the sparse evidence available and the sporadic nature of their employment patterns, let us turn to a case study of one major type of employment for women: domestic service.

The Case of Domestic Service

Outside of agriculture, domestic service was the single largest occupational category for women in the nineteenth century (Dawes, 1973:9; McBride, 1976:11). Domestic service constituted a transition from rural to urban life, as thousands of rural emigrants moved to cities between 1820 and 1856. Until 1880, young women between the ages of 18 and 24 from the homes of impoverished tenant farmers were continually drawn into service by the lure of comparatively high wages and the relative security of a job that included room and board. The experience of working as a servant was common for a high proportion of young women. In 1861 in London, one in every three women between the ages of 15 and 24 was a servant, and more than one in every six women between the ages of 10 and 95 was listed as a domestic. The total number in service increased until 1891 to a maximum of 1,549,502 and then gradually diminished, as the expansion of educational requirements and the growth of available white-collar jobs offered young women other work opportunities (McBride, 1976:14).

After 1880, there was a gradual aging of the servant population, and those who still found refuge in domestic service were older married or widowed women who sought domestic jobs after many years of child rearing or as a result of widowhood. This increase can be seen in Table 6.1. After 1890, the percentage of servants who were married or widowed and over the age of 45 rose gradually, and service at-

"The Crossing-Sweeper That Has Been a Maid-Servant"
From Henry Mayhew, *London Labor and the London Poor.* London: Dover, 1861.

tracted a higher percentage of women over 60 than any other occupation (McBride, 1976:101).

Most of the older women who were employed as domestics did not live in, as did younger women, but were part of a class of charwomen who worked on a daily or occasional basis (McBride, 1976:112). Charing fitted in with the cyclical pattern of occasional work for lower-class women when the husbands' wages were inadequate or nonexistent.

Life Cycle Patterns of Work for Women

TABLE 6.1.   *Ages of Female Servants in England and Wales, 1851–1911 (percentage)*

Age	1851	1861	1871	1881	1911
Under 15	8.7	8.9	11.6	8.0	3.1
15–19	31.7	38.1	30.2	35.0	28.3
20–24	26.0	23.6	23.6	24.5	25.4
25–44	26.0	26.3	19.7	24.0	32.3
45–64	8.8	8.8	5.3	7.2	9.5
65 and over	1.9	1.9	1.7	1.4	1.3

Source: Census of England and Wales, quoted in McBride, 1976:45.

Usually, domestic service was an apprenticeship for marriage, and only a small proportion attempted to stay on. Some fortunate women who remained in service were well cared for by employers and received adequate pensions or a room or cottage on the family estate where they might spend their last few years (Dawes, 1973:95). For example, the 11-year-old orphan Annie Jones was taken into service by the Cook family of Bristol in 1864. She remained with the family until she died at the age of 91 and was buried in the family grave, where the headstone recounts that she was ''the faithful servant and friend of the Cook family [quoted in Horn, 1975:122]. Similarly, Harriet Sizeland, who became nurse to the Chorley family in 1867, was still employed by them over 60 years later. She was then retired with an annuity to her native Leeds (Horn, 1975:23). On the Apethorpe estate of the Brassey family a financial statement prepared in 1911 indicates a regular expenditure of eight shillings per week for pensions to several retired, long-serving servants (Horn, 1975:164).

Yet for every servant who remained within the bosom of the family, there were many others who were cast aside in illness or old age. Contemporary sources indicate that there was considerable prejudice against hiring servants over the age of 45. The British Women's Industrial Council advised an unmarried servant to invest her savings in a lodging house with a partner, keep house for a relative, live on her savings until a government pension started, or seek occasional work in charing (Butler, 1916:68). The future for an older servant was bleak if her savings were limited and she could not do charing or keep house for a relative, and unemployment was even bleaker for someone who had always worked at a job where at least the security of room and board was guaranteed.

In general, for a former domestic old age meant loneliness and, at the end, the workhouse. As Joseph Chamberlain testified in 1893 before the Royal Commission on the Aged Poor, no one would employ a servant "past 50 years of age and accordingly, almost by necessity of the case, they would have to go to the workhouse [quoted in Horn, 1975:164]." Evidence from workhouses tends to confirm this impression. In 1871, 1 of every 3 female inmates at Fullham, Kensington, and St. George's workhouses had been a domestic, and these inmates included the more elite of the servant class as well as the general servant. Of the 63 female servants over 60 in Kensington workhouse in 1871, 3 were former cooks, 2 were housekeepers, and 1 was a governess. Similarly, at Kensington Hall Infirmary of 35 inmates over age 60, 9 were cooks, 7 were housekeepers, 1 was a former governess, and one was a lady's maid (Horn, 1975:165). In 1911, when former occupations of pensioners were recorded, more than one-fourth of the 88,000 women who applied had formerly been in domestic service (Horn, 1975:165).

Women shared the problem of unemployment in old age with men; but this problem was exacerbated by the tendency for women to leave the labor force when they married. When loss of a husband's income through widowhood or unemployment forced a woman to return to the labor force in her later years, one of the few work opportunities available was the low-paying, insecure, and degrading occupation of charing.

Aging and Unemployment

Around the turn of the century, when the concept of "unemployment" was recognized, statistics confirmed the growing impression that the aged were experiencing difficulty finding work. In 1905, the

Conservative government passed the Unemployed Workman Act, requiring the establishment of distress committees in every large urban area of the country. In addition to providing employment for those thought to be genuinely in need, the committees were also empowered to set up labor exchanges, keep unemployment registers, and assist the migration or emigration of unemployed workmen (Rose, 1972:43). This was the first time unemployment statistics were available on a nationwide basis. As the figures were tallied, it became apparent that unemployment was a major problem for the aged and one that was initially obscured by the tendency for older people to move from the category of unemployed to that of pauper. As Table 6.2 shows, men were likely to be classified as unemployed until they reached the age of 65, only to disappear from this category and reappear as paupers.[2] "There can be no doubt," concluded the report on unemployment, "as to the difficulty experienced on the part of men engaged in certain occupations to obtain employment as their

TABLE 6.2. *Unemployed Males in Selected Industries and Male Paupers by Age, 1906*

Age	Proportion of unemployed per 1000, in selected industries	Proportion of male paupers per 1000
15–19	5.1	1.7
20–24	17.8	1.6
25–34	23.6	2.9
35–44	29.2	5.8
45–54	24.7	11.4
55–64	26.7	28.7
65–74	11.4	70.3

Source: Morrison, 1911:865.

[2]Unemployment was most certainly underestimated in this first attempt at systematic calculation. This is partly because unemployment registers were used as a resource to recruit strikebreakers, generating hostility from labor unions (Rothstein, 1929:296).

age increases [quoted in Morrison, 1911:865].'' Clearly, older men became out of work and, finding no employment opportunities, eventually were forced to apply for relief. As another witness testified before the Royal Commission on the Aged Poor in regard to the case of a 75-year-old man:

> Well, he has got on as well as he could; perhaps got a day's work now and again. I was vexed to see him, this very case, yesterday; he was going to try to get employment, and the answer he got was he was getting old, and they had sufficient young men, and he does not feel inclined to go to the house [P.P. XIV, Mins. of Ev., 1895:363].

In the nineteenth century, retirement meant a choice between unemployment and pauperization.

As unemployment, poverty, and government reform became national rather than parochial issues, and as industries abandoned paternalistic practices, new burdens were placed on aged workers. Was it just perceptions of reformers sympathetic to the aged, urging a pension on a reluctant society still imbued with the philosophical tradition of laissez faire, that made the plight of older workers appear more urgent? Or, had changing political, social, and economic conditions actually led to decreased economic opportunities for the aged?.

The Concept of Retirement

Although patronage had provided pensions to a privileged few, retirement as a general concept did not appear until the closing years of the nineteenth century. Of course, in preindustrial times retirement occurred when a parent handed over the farm to a child in return for care in old age. Industrialization decreased the opportunity for this form of old age security to be implemented, but it created new sources of protection for the middle classes.

The wage-earning family went through a poverty cycle, whereas the successful middle-class family went through a series of consumption decisions involving savings and the allocation of resources to different forms of investment that coincided with different needs through the family life cycle—a pattern that has been identified as the property cycle (Morris, 1979:91). Until around age 40, the typical successful middle-class male invested in business capital. After age 40 he switched his investments to assets that produced a rentier income (Morris, 1979:108). This allowed him to accumulate assets that produced a rate of return lower than that expected in trade or business but allowed him to gain an income that fluctuated less and that required less effort and attention to maintain. This switch to asset acquisition fulfilled the social purpose of preparing an income for old age and allowed the middle-class male gradually to withdraw from business (Morris, 1979:110). Unlike the twentieth-century form of retirement, this break with business was partial and took place over several years.

Industrialization improved the ability to purchase assets by creating a wider range of commercial, industrial, and professional opportunities, and at the same time the investor's willingness to move capital provided financing for industry, finance, urban house construction, mortgages for public utilities, and the transport system. The retirement pattern of the middle class was created from a symbiosis of social and economic needs.

In the last decade of the nineteenth century, the concept of retirement was given official recognition. The year 1891 was the first census year in which the retired were classified as a separate category. Prior to then, they had been classified according to former occupation, regardless of present work status. Although age was recognized as a major factor associated with retirement, the definition was broader than it became later. As originally defined, the retired included both those who had discontinued their previous activity and those who were physically or mentally incapacitated. Thus, all inmates of lunatic asylums were tabulated with the retired (Census of England and Wales, 1911:146).

In examining labor-force trends for older males, we find definite indications that rates of retirement were gradually increasing. As shown in Table 6.3, in 1891 approximately 35% of men over age 65 were not employed; by 1911, this figure had risen to 44%. Such high rates of retirement signify that it was no longer the preserve of the middle class. The pension was partially responsible for reducing the

6. Work and Retirement

TABLE 6.3. *Labor-Force-Participation Rates of Men by Age, 1891–1911*

| | Percentage employed by year | | |
Age	1891	1901	1911
15–20	91.2	91.8	91.7
20–24	96.9	97.4	97.4
25–34	97.9	98.3	98.6
35–44	97.5	97.8	98.2
45–54	96.2	96.0	96.7
55–64	89.7	89.0	89.5
65 and over	64.8	60.6	56.0

Source: Census of England and Wales, 1911.

labor-force-participation rates of older males, but it is obvious by the fact that more than one-third were not working 20 years before the pension came into effect that other factors were also operating.[3]

It is impossible to assess even short-term changes in rates of retirement for women due to inconsistencies in the census records from year to year in classifying females engaged in domestic duties at home.[4] In 1901, an attempt was made to estimate the percentage of retired females by age, excluding housewives, who in that year were classified separately. Table 6.4 shows the percentage of women in 1901 who had declared that they were retired from an occupation (as opposed to those who were no longer working due to marriage, who were defined as "living on own means"). Overall, labor-force-participation rates for women were low, and, as it was for men, retire-

[3] The maximum pension allowed was five shillings, and 15 years earlier the Royal Commission heard testimony that seven shillings a week was the lowest on which a single aged man could live without starving (P.P. XIV, Mins. of Ev., 1895:130).
[4] See the 1901 and 1911 census reports, for discussions of how females engaged in domestic duties were classified.

TABLE 6.4. *Labor-Force-Participation Rates of Women and Percentage Retired by Age, 1901*

Age	Percentage of all females in labor force	Percentage of females retired[a]
15-20	41.5	-----
20-24	35.0	-----
25-34	20.4	.65
35-44	17.1	1.86
45-54	17.2	2.68
55-64	16.9	8.40
65-74	13.3	28.14
Over 75	6.5	91.78

Source: Census of England and Wales, 1901.

[a] This does not include women engaged in domestic duties at home, who were classified as "living on own means."

ment was most clearly associated with advanced age. What is notable, however, is that most older women who did have an occupation continued to work past age 65. Their rates of retirement were lower than those for older men. Only those past age 75 had high rates of retirement. For older women, work was necessary for survival.

The preceding data indicate that retirement was not unusual for older people and that for men at least it was becoming increasingly prevalent. Some of the reasons why retirement was increasing have already been discussed. In Chapter 3, we saw that the decline of household production reduced work opportunities for the aged. It also appears that policy changes such as workmen's compensation and the creation of county councils may have played a role.

Other arguments have attributed increased retirement to the technological and social changes that accompanied industrialization. Let us examine these arguments and see what other factors may have been responsible for the decline in work among the elderly.

6. Work and Retirement

The Rise of Technology

Some writers have speculated that industrialization and the technological change that accompanies it move production from the home to the factory or office, creating a labor force of "employees" who have little control over the timing or mode of withdrawal from work (Burgess, 1960:20; Friedmann and Orbach, 1974:610). The new technologies and assembly-line production lead to obsolescence of traditional skills and patterns of work relationships. Whereas younger workers are more mobile and adjust more readily to technological change, any shift, even within the same occupation, can put the older worker at a disadvantage (Brennan, Taft, and Schupack, 1967:18). Thus, older workers carry on obsolete work roles, which are less valued and less highly remunerated (Cowgill, 1974a:12). The result of these combined factors is the increasing withdrawal of older workers from the labor force (Friedmann and Orbach, 1974:611).

As noted in Chapter 2, the latter half of the nineteenth century was a period of rapid and sustained technological change in the heavy industries, textiles, and agriculture. Did technological change, with its increased demand for wage labor combined with competition from younger workers, push the aged into obsolete work roles and lead to their increased withdrawal from the labor force? Certainly contemporaries believed this to be the case. According to one Fabian pamphlet:

> Wages of men from forty-five years of age upwards, show a gradual and persistent decline. The roughest forms of labor are the first to suffer; but in skilled trades where deftness of handiwork is the first condition of efficiency and of continued employment, the attainment of fifty-five years of age is usually accompanied by a reduction of earnings. The Bradford weaver has to abandon one of his two looms as he advances in years; the Lancashire cotton-spinner and the head-piecer who has never become a spinner, have to seek for work in mills where the machinery is older and does not run so rapidly; the bricklayer is unable to lay as many bricks, and the compositor to set as many ems; the seamstress's sight fails; the dock-laborer, rheumatic through exposure to the weather, finds his place occupied by more vigorous competitors from the country villages [Turner, 1897:3].

A cursory glance at the age distribution of the new occupations created by industrial advance compared with the distribution in the more traditional occupations shows that older workers were disproportionately represented in traditional work. Workers 65 and older comprised 4% of the labor force in 1901 (Census of England and Wales, 1901, vol. 44:187). In the occupations of commercial clerk, railway engine driver, and electrical apparatus maker, which were all growing rapidly, the relative proportion of aged workers was quite low, less than 1%. In contrast, older occupations that were declining in importance had a high proportion of older workers. For example, 7.4% of bootmakers, 8.6% of agricultural laborers, and 5.6% of fishermen were over 65. General laborers also tended to be disproportionately old, but in this case it is more likely that men shifted from other occupations to the ranks of casual labor in later life.

The issue of expansion of the casual labor force and the movement of older men into it is one of the more significant trends in the late nineteenth century and one of the less readily identifiable consequences of technological change. Casual labor was particularly predominant in London, and in nearly every trade there was a nucleus of permanently employed men and a casual fringe, whose size varied enormously from one occupation to another (Stedman Jones, 1971:56). The major source of casual labor, aside from juveniles, was a steady trickle of skilled or permanent workers ousted from their regular occupations (Stedman Jones, 1971:73). For example, when sails were replaced by steam, shipwrights fared badly, and older skilled shipwrights were forced into the casual labor force (Stedman Jones, 1971:105). As Mayhew (1861) observed in his description of the London docks:

> Those who are unable to live by the occupation to which they have been educated, can obtain a living there, without any previous training. Here we find men of every calling laboring at the docks. There are decayed and bankrupt master butchers, master bakers, publicans, grocers, old soldiers, old sailors, Polish refugees, broken down gentlemen, discharged lawyers, clerks, almsmen, servants, thieves—indeed everyone who wants a loaf and is willing to work for it [p. 301].

Thus, men past their prime who were dislodged from skilled trades drifted into the ranks of the casual labor pool.

The question is how this expected distribution of older workers in traditional occupations contributes to an explanation of the increased proportion of retiring older workers. This can be answered only by examining the internal dynamics of the flow of the labor market in terms of the supply and demand of workers. Even though agricultural work, fishing, and bootmaking were all traditional occupations in the

"The Bearded Crossing-Sweeper at the Exchange"

From Henry Mayhew, *London Labor and the London Poor*. London: Dover, 1861.

sense of being old and relatively unchanged, they were different in the important sense that the bootmaker was a skilled, self-employed artisan, whereas the agricultural worker was a wage laborer. Bootmaking remained relatively unmechanized until relatively late in the nineteenth century, so that the aged bootmaker was not subject to competition from machine products (Clapham, 1932:131). Further, bootmakers had control over entry to the occupation with their strong union and could continue working in old age (Hobsbawm, 1964:287). In this occupation, then, and others like it, the "aging" of a traditional occupation was an advantage rather than a disadvantage, delaying the transition from self-employed to employee.

Even if the older worker was not self-employed but producing piecework for an employer, he maintained an advantage as long as the trade remained unmechanized. "In cases of piecework trades," testified another witness, "men are able to go on very much longer than they are in daywork trades . . . . In piecework trades so long as men can maintain the standards of quality of the article they produce, the employers are prepared to allow them to go on, knowing that any loss of speed falls upon the men and not the employers [P.P. XIV, Mins. of Ev., 1895:910]."

Not all pieceworkers could go on indefinitely, for their ability to keep pace with the machine was limited. The fate of many skilled craftsmen was sealed as mechanization increased the rate of production:

The hand-loom weavers whom we employed could weave about one piece per week, for this work they received twenty or twenty-one shillings, or a little less or more, according to the quality of the weft used or the quantity put into the piece. When the power-loom took up the weaving of these goods the first drop in weaving wage was to nine shillings per piece, and soon after it was down to six shillings. For a time, but not very long, the old hand-looms went on alongside the power-looms, the weavers getting as much more for their hand woven pieces as a generous manufacturer would give, but as the power-loom pieces were as good as the hand woven ones there was nothing for it but for the young weavers to learn to mind the power-loom and for the old men or women nothing but to sell their old looms and try to get some little odd jobs about the factory where the power-looms were used, live on their friends, or go to the workhouse [Metcalfe, 1899:17].

The impact was even more direct in those occupations where hand-work was completely outmoded, and here technology extracted its toll. The older the man, the greater was his difficulty of relearning a skill or adapting to a new machine (Meacham, 1977:152). Once his industrial value was gone, he was "removed from the manufacturing cycle and presented with a broom, shovel and wheelbarrow [Williams, 1915:18]."

Technological change also had an impact on women's work, but not in the manner anticipated. In large cities, technology actually had the effect of increasing work by increasing household production or "homework." For example, in London a variety of factors, such as the high cost of fuel, the distance from necessary raw materials, and the competition for metropolitan land, made large-scale, steam-powered factory production inappropriate. These difficulties were circumvented by the expansion of "sweated trades" in which the pro-duction process was subdivided into its unskilled component parts (Stedman Jones, 1971:107). Although elements of this system of pro-duction had been present early in the century, it became more feasi-ble after technological developments provided the preconditions for a large-scale ready-made clothing industry. The most significant in-ventions were the sewing machine (1846) and the band saw (1858), which allowed articles of clothing to be subcontracted out to women homeworkers, who provided a limitless, flexible, and cheap source of labor—cheap not only because women were in an uncompetitive position in the labor market but also because of the lack of such overhead as rent, fuel, and light (Stedman Jones, 1971:108). Home sewing was one type of work available to older women, as demonstrated by the low rates of retirement of seamstresses (see Table 6.6). Thus, the inability of London to compete with factory production and the invention of the sewing machine combined to strengthen and expand a preindustrial pattern of manufacture based on subcontract and the vertical disintegration of production. The consequence was an expansion of this type of work for women.

Self-employment had advantages that can be documented by com-paring the proportion retired in different occupations. In 1911, the census selected several occupations and reported the proportion of male and female pensioners and retirees according to former occupation. Although the proportion retired was not tabulated by age and included all retirees, some general estimates can be made. As Table 6.5 shows, those males in agriculture, that is, farmers and market gardeners, as well as skilled craftsmen, bootmakers, and tailors, were least likely to be retired—a decided advantage during a period when work was the only guaranteed source of income in old age. Other self-employed workers such as painters and blacksmiths tended to have retirement rates lower than those of white-collar clerks employed by banks and firms. The unskilled occupations of coal miner and domestic servant had the highest percentage retired, as did police and railway officials. The latter were pensioned, whereas the unskilled workers probably retired involuntarily. The expansion of heavy industry was most likely a factor in reducing work for the aged, as demonstrated by the high rate of retirement among coal miners.

Although self-employment was preferable to starvation or the workhouse, many of the self-employed fell into the residual category of scavenger, the bottom of the labor market. Scavengers included bone grubbers, ragpickers, crossing sweepers, messengers, "and a host of other last resort occupations of the old and broken down [Stedman Jones, 1971:63]." Here, old and crippled men, unfit for any other employment, seldom made more than five shillings a week. The most pathetic were the bone grubbers, who, according to Mayhew (1861), were almost exclusively the aged:

> Probably that vacuity of mind that is a distinguishing feature of the class is the mere atomy or emaciation of the mental faculties proceeding from the extreme wretchedness of the class . . . the bone-grubber generally seeks out the narrow back streets, where dust and refuse are cast, or where any dustbins are accessible. . . . Whatever he meets with that he knows is saleable, he puts into the bag at his back. He often finds large lumps of bread which have been thrown out as waste by the servants, and occasionally the housekeeper gives him some bones on which there is a little meat remaining; these constitute the morning meal of most of this class [p. 138].

Self-employed women were also more likely to continue working. As Table 6.6 shows, grocers and innkeepers, who most likely worked in family-owned businesses, had the lowest retirement rates, as did lace makers, who worked in cottage industries at home. Charwomen

TABLE 6.5. *Males Sixty-Five and Older Retired, in Selected Occupations, 1911*

Occupation	Occupied		Retired[a]	
	N	Percentage	N	Percentage
Police	85	1	11,918	99
Railway officials and clerks	630	12	4536	88
Coal miners	6801	28	17,150	72
Domestic indoor servants	851	32	1792	68
Grocers	5187	44	11,710	56
Banking and insurance officials and clerks	2990	44	3786	56
Innkeepers and publicans	4726	45	5879	55
Commercial clerks	5591	48	6094	52
Blacksmiths and strikers	6125	50	6093	50
Cabinetmakers and French polishers	2886	58	2130	42
Commercial travelers	2769	58	2049	42
Painters and decorators	6627	59	4735	41
Tailors	6575	62	4102	38
Farmers and graziers	32,902	64	18,433	36
Bootmakers and shoemakers	12,730	65	6735	35
Nurserymen and market gardeners	16,662	69	7775	31

Source: Census of England and Wales, 1911.

[a] Since the category "retired" included those under 65, the percentage retired will be slightly inflated. However, the number who retired before age 65 is not so large as to make these estimates inaccurate.

The Concept of Retirement

TABLE 6.6. *Females Sixty-Five and Older Retired, in Selected Occupations, 1911*

	Occupied		Retired	
Occupation	N	Percentage	N	Percentage
Teachers	1101	15	6457	85
Commercial clerks	86	26	245	74
Domestic servants	17,130	41	24,893	59
Tailors	2393	60	1603	40
Dressmakers	6697	60	4432	40
Charwomen	11,420	63	6787	37
Hawkers	1477	63	872	37
Seamstresses	5672	67	2789	33
Laundry workers	9819	71	4051	29
Innkeepers	3204	73	1161	27
Lace makers	1400	76	444	24
Grocers	4382	85	758	15

Source: Census of England and Wales, 1911.

and hawkers also continued working, bringing in a small pittance to support themselves and perhaps their children, whereas domestic servants were often cast aside in old age. Again, like older men, the elite among women workers, teachers and commercial clerks, retired at higher rates, perhaps living off pensions or accumulated savings. Some evidence from earlier in the century indicates that annuities were occasionally available as compensation for retired teachers. For example, in 1859 the Governesses' Benevolent Association reported:

On a recent occasion, there were one hundred and twenty candidates for three annuities of twenty pounds each. . . . Of these, ninety-nine were unmarried, and out of this number, fourteen had incomes of, or above, twenty pounds (eleven of which were derived from public institutions or private benevolence, and three from their own savings); twenty-three had incomes varying from one pound to seventeen pounds; and eighty-three ladies had absolutely nothing. It will be recollected that all these ladies are above fifty years of age; and of the utterly destitute, forty-nine were above sixty [quoted in Saville, 1973:330].

Thus, some professional women may have retired with adequate support, but many others doubtless suffered from destitution equivalent to that of their less skilled sisters.

Decline of Agriculture

A second argument states that the change from agriculture to manufacturing as the basic mode of production also reduces work opportunities for the aged. Farming provides a major source of employment for older people, as farming is one of the occupations in which the aged can continue working by adapting the work environment to changing personal requirements (Brennan, Taft, and Schupack, 1967:16; Palmore and Manton, 1974:205). Further, older farmers maintain familial power by controlling inheritance of the land, often forcing sons who cannot wait for their inheritance to emigrate to cities. As agricultural employment declines, work opportunities for the aged are lost, as is power within the household and the community.

The latter half of the nineteenth century was a period of rapid decline for the rural population and the agricultural labor force, as discussed in Chapter 2, and farmers did maintain high rates of labor-force participation. Yet, this romanticized view of the traditional past that centers around the ideal of the family farm is not really the relevant issue. Most farmers were tenant farmers and did not own the land they worked. Although they often passed on the rights to tenancy, their power was subject to the whims of the landowner. Usually it was not the restless farmer's sons, tired of waiting to inherit the land, who moved to urban areas, but rather the underpaid agricultural laborers. Farmer's sons stayed, at least initially, as indicated by an increase in the number of relatives assisting on farms in the last decades of the century (Prothero, 1912:461). If we are to understand the impact of the decline of agriculture on the aged, it is to the agricultural laborer, who made up 12% of the aged labor force, not the farmer, that we must turn.

In order to assess the supply and demand factors that affected the age distribution of agricultural labor, the four counties of East Anglia, which represent the most extreme example of large-scale arable farming in England in the nineteenth century, will be analyzed. This grain-growing region was characterized by the most extensive use of day labor and felt the effects of agricultural decline in the 1870s most severely (Hasbach, 1908:256). In all four East Anglia counties, agricultural employment was universally quite high as late as 1871, ranging from 44% in Essex to 53% in Cambridgeshire. By 1901, Essex, with only 10% employed in agriculture, could no longer be considered agricultural, as the pull of industrial employment decimated agricultural labor. In contrast, the other three counties retained a decidedly rural, nonindustrial character at the turn of the century, as Table 6.7 shows.

Nearly always it was the young who chose or were able to leave, and this out-migration of young adults contributed to the aging of the rural areas.[5] The effects can be seen in population trends. By 1901, there was a significantly higher proportion of older people in the rural

TABLE 6.7. *Working Males Employed in Agriculture in East Anglia, 1871–1901 (percentage)*

County	1871	1901
Essex	44	10
Norfolk	46	33
Suffolk	51	33
Cambridgeshire	53	32

Source: Census of England and Wales, 1871 and 1901.

[5]The aging of rural areas was universal in England. However, the trend was most striking in East Anglia because of the intensive use of labor in arable farming there (Saville, 1957).

districts in each of the four East Anglia counties than in the urban districts, as Table 6.8 shows.

The aging of rural areas meant that the potential pool of available agricultural labor was older. Table 6.9 illustrates the way in which the aged functioned as a reserve labor force, utilized when they were in demand because of a shortage of young men and excluded when other workers were available. In Essex, agricultural labor was in short supply, because industrial jobs that paid higher wages were available. Agricultural employment in Essex declined between 1871 and 1901 for all age categories except the old, where there was a marked increase.

The significance of this becomes clearer when contrasted with the conditions in Norfolk, the county in which large-scale arable farming with its extensive use of day labor was most highly developed. By 1901, industrial development had not occurred to any great extent in Norfolk, so that few alternatives to agricultural employment were available. Although there was an overall shrinkage of agricultural labor, this shrinkage was not evenly distributed among all age categories. The position of men under age 45 remained stable. The decline was experienced most sharply by older men, particularly those over 65, for whom the intercensal change was −29%. Further evidence supporting the argument that the aged served as reserve

TABLE 6.8. *Proportion of the Population Sixty-Five or Older in the Rural and Urban Districts of East Anglia, 1901*

County	Rural		Urban	
	Male	Female	Male	Female
Essex	9	10	4	5
Norfolk	11	12	7	9
Suffolk	11	11	7	8
Cambridgeshire	10	11	7	9

Source: Census of England and Wales, 1901.

The Concept of Retirement

labor can be seen by comparing average agricultural laborer's wages in the four counties. As Table 6.10 shows, wages were the same in all counties as late as 1881. In the next decade, they declined everywhere, but this decline was greater in Essex. Thus, even though the aged made up an increasing proportion of the rural population in the latter half of the nineteenth century, they made up a decreasing

TABLE 6.9. *Distribution of Male Agricultural Laborers by Age in East Anglia, 1871-1901*

County	Age group	Number of Agricultural laborers		Intercensal percentage change
		1871	1901	
Essex	15-24	10,968	7339	-33
	25-44	13,571	9784	-28
	45-64	10,492	7575	-28
	65 and over	4123	5992	+45
Norfolk	15-24	10,095	9284	-08
	25-44	12,182	11,319	-07
	45-64	9734	7679	-21
	65 and over	4337	3077	-29
Suffolk	15-24	9561	7324	-23
	25-44	11,508	9149	-20
	45-64	9342	4940	-47
	65 and over	4144	2694	-35
Cambridgeshire	15-24	5718	4711	-18
	25-44	6790	5143	-24
	45-64	4718	3793	-20
	65 and over	1834	1301	-29

Source: Census of England and Wales, 1871 and 1901.

TABLE 6.10. *Agricultural Laborer's Wages in East Anglia, 1881–1892*

County	1881	1892
Cambridgeshire	12s. 6d.	12s. 0d.
Essex	12s. 6d.	11s. 0d.
Norfolk	12s. 6d.	12s. 0d.
Suffolk	12s. 6d.	12s. 0d.

Source: Hasbach, 1908:323.

proportion of the agricultural labor force, except where it was least desirable.[6]

Although they were an integral part of rural life, these elderly laborers remained on the fringe, generally powerless and deferential. As one newsman described the life of an 80-year-old farm worker:

> His days work was eleven hours of hoeing, or nine hours with allowances for meals. And every winter the old man spends in the workhouse. "And does he find any fault with the workhouse?" I asked of the landlord as we presently jogged along in his light cart. "No, he don't find no fault. He takes it all quiet enough." At threescore years and fifteen or thereabout, I suppose nine hours of hoeing leaves a man little spirit even for grumbling; but here is an object lesson for all the sturdy young fellows from eighteen to twenty-five—11s a week—on piecework—and nine hours of hoeing and the much dreaded workhouse and a pauper's grave at the end of it all [Special Commissioner of the Daily News, 1891:11].

It was common practice for farmers to employ older workers at low wages in the summer. Then these same farmers, who were also often members of boards of guardians, put them in the workhouse in the winter when they applied for relief.

Changing Patterns of Work and Retirement

The nature of retirement changed in the nineteenth century, and its nature varied by social class. For the middle class, it shifted from a

[6] Although a cohort analysis would have been preferable, it was impossible to do because of the lack of county-level figures on migration and death rates.

system of patronage to a privileged few to a gradual withdrawal from the labor force for any businessman with sufficient accumulated assets to allow him to draw upon a rentier income. Middle-class retirement was symbiotic with the needs of an expanding industrial state, since the income-producing assets of the middle-class businessman expanded the amount of capital available for economic growth.

It is no accident, however, that the concept of unemployment appeared around the same time that retirement became a recognized census category, for among the aged poor, retirement and unemployment were synonymous. Although unemployment was initially perceived as a problem of the casual labor force in the cities, its association with old age was gradually recognized. The problem was in determining the cause.

In an examination of retirement patterns for older men, an assessment of selected occupations initially seems to confirm the view that technological change was influential in phasing older workers out of the labor force, since older workers were disproportionately represented in traditional occupations. However, the issue is more complex than just technology, and some care needs to be taken in analyzing several quite different trends. In the newest occupations, those that were truly creations of technological advance, it is correct to infer not that the aged were pushed out but rather that they entered them at rates lower than those of younger workers. Thus, the role of technology was less important than the fact that most older men had already chosen occupations and were unable or unwilling to change jobs. Other occupations, such as general laborer, may have had a disproportionate number of older workers due to the drifting of older men from declining industries or hazardous work where employers feared paying workmen's compensation. On the other hand, technological change may actually have increased work for older women, at least in London, where the need to compete with large-scale factory production expanded the supposedly preindustrial pattern of household production.

Where the impact of technology did have a negative effect on the aged was in traditional occupations, such as weaving, which became mechanized. In this case, older workers who were employed as wage laborers were unable to acquire new skills that would allow them to compete successfully against younger workers, whereas those who were self-employed could not manufacture products as cheaply as those using machines. This situation contrasts with an occupation such as bootmaking, which remained relatively unmechanized. Bootmakers were likely to be highly skilled as well as self-employed, could maintain a monopoly on the market, and were in the relatively favorable position of being able to remain working for as long as they chose.

Older agricultural laborers were among the most marginal of all workers. In the late nineteenth century, when the need for agricultural labor was declining, farmers entrenched their position by using more machinery and employing more kin. Those most vulnerable during this period of transition were unmobile, older agricultural workers who were used as a reserve labor supply, hired at low wages, and employed in the most hazardous and least desirable work. One must be wary of facile conclusions, for a disproportionately aged occupational structure, even in a declining occupation, is not necessarily a sign that older workers are in a disadvantageous position. The degree of mechanization and the extent to which wage labor is used must also be taken into consideration.

There are many indications that rates of retirement among those over 65 were increasing gradually in the latter half of the nineteenth century. Social policy reforms such as the Workmen's Compensation Act made employers hesitant to keep on older workers, who were more likely to be injured on the job. Unions, fearful of jeopardizing newly gained wage guarantees, objected to the practice of employing the aged at lower wages. The proportion of self-employed independent craftsmen, who tended to work longer, declined, and they were replaced by unskilled workers, who retired in greater numbers. The semiskilled and unskilled workers created in massive numbers by heavy industry were wage laborers whose ability to earn cash income was their only resource in old age. For these workers, rates of retirement were high; retirement was involuntary and synonymous with unemployment. Few had alternate sources of income, as indicated by the high rates of pauperization among the aged. Those who did not retire carried on at low-paying, part-time insecure jobs, such as scavenging or charing. Retirement in this transitional period before the pension was characterized by poverty and uncertainty.

Many of the changes that had occurred in the nineteenth century made a pension a more urgent need. However, as we shall see in the next chapter, it was not so much the real needs of the people viewed by sympathetic Victorians imbued with humanitarian instincts that led to the passage of the pension bill. It was rather the growing political power of labor and the middle-class fear of the residuum of casual labor. State socialism increasingly came to be viewed as a necessary response to the failure of Liberalism as a means of taking charge of the incapable and relieving society of a serious danger.

7

The Degradation of Age

In 1895, the Royal Commission on the Aged Poor hesitated to recommend separate living quarters for aged workhouse inmates, fearing an intensification of "the evil association of the old with the old," which "tends to accentuate their defects, to make them more conscious of their infirmities, and to destroy their interest in the future [P.P. XIV, Report, 1895:xl–xli]." At the same time, tales of societal or personal abuse of the elderly abounded, supplementing the more scientific statistical reports of Booth (1891; 1892; 1894; 1899) and the Webbs (1907; 1909; 1910). Shocked Victorians heard of the old man who preferred the workhouse even though his sons were willing to find him a home because "they knocked him about with a poker [Cuttle, 1934:57]." Others pointed to the deplorable but understandable lack of respect for older people, at least among the "lower classes of society [Metcalfe, 1899:21]."

7. The Degradation of Age

Think, for a moment, of the many times you have seen boys or young men, insulting or teasing some old man or woman. . . . The reasons, in my opinion, are that the old man knows and feels his inferior position, and has taken on himself the abject appearance, which but represents his relative condition in life today. And the youths, keenly alive to their position of superiority in every walk of life where they meet the old man (in that they do work which he cannot do, and receive wages which he cannot command), are but exercising their impudence where they feel it is safe to do so, that is, one in an inferior position to theirs [p. 23].

How can this negative view of old age that seemed to permeate Victorian society be explained? Although some might argue that it was a reflection of low status and a degraded standard of living, other interpretations are also possible. In other chapters, we have already seen hints that there were contradictions between what Victorians were saying about the aged and what life was really like. For example, in Chapter 5, many witnesses testifying before the Royal Commission on the Aged Poor emphasized both the destructive effects of poor law policy on working-class family relationships and the dependency of older people, who were often depicted as burdens on their families. Yet in Chapter 3, we saw that throughout the latter half of the century, most older people were living with some relative, that few were in fact abandoned by kin, and that reciprocity, not one-sided dependency, characterized family relations when a minimum standard of living could be maintained.

If older people found sanctuary within the family unit, they did not fare nearly so well in their interactions with the wider society. In both Chapter 3 and Chapter 6, material was presented indicating that it was becoming increasingly difficult for older people to find work. The work that was available was sporadic and low paying. Rates of unemployment were high, and most of the aged among the working class eventually had to request poor relief. Those without kin and no visible means of support were most likely to spend their final days incarcerated in the workhouse. Yet there is no reason to assume that life was measurably or objectively worse than in previous eras. All we know from the evidence presented in previous chapters is that some of the problems of old age were different than they had been in the past.

It was these new problems that were emphasized by those describing what came to be perceived as the degradation of age. From around 1878, when Canon William Blackley first proposed his compulsory insurance scheme, until 1908, when the Old Age Pensions Act was passed, increasing public concern centered around the plight of the aged poor. Booth's (1891; 1892; 1894) statistics and Rowntree's (1901) findings added fuel to reformers' arguments, as various contributory and noncontributory pension plans were brought before the public.

Other writers have attempted to document a decline in the veneration of the aged in the nineteenth century, attributing this shift in attitude to such causes as the perpetuation of the ideals of liberty and equality fostered by the French Revolution (Fischer, 1978) and the movement from romanticism to realism (Achenbaum, 1978).[1] In this chapter, the task will not be to document changes in beliefs about the aged; rather, the focus will be on the meaning of a set of ideas at a given point in time. We shall see that what in retrospect appears to be a degradation of age was actually a theme with political significance, used in different ways by opposing sides to argue for or against the passage of a pension measure.

The Opposing Sides

From the first pension proposal by Canon Blackley in 1878 to the passage of the final bill in 1908, there was a polarization of opinion, with each view supported by a shifting coalition of advocates and opponents. By 1900, the sides had stabilized. The proponents of a pension included Charles Booth, various settlement leaders, the co-operative societies, and most of organized labor.

The ability of labor to organize and support a proposal that would benefit all members of the working class was enhanced by the gains workers had made in regard to political representation. In 1867, they gained urban suffrage. The secret ballot, which allowed workers to

---

[1] See Chapter 1 for an extensive discussion of the literature on attitudes toward old age. It should be noted that Fischer and Achenbaum are almost a century apart in terms of perceiving the turning point in attitudes toward the aged.

vote without fear of reprisals from employers or landlords, was won in 1872, and, finally, in 1884 the rural laborer was enfranchised.

Labor was joined in the fight for a pension by leaders of the settlement movement, which had begun with the opening of Toynbee Hall in 1884 (Mencher, 1967:195). Of middle-class origin, the settlement movement attempted to cement relationships between classes by incorporating the settlement into the community. The policies of the settlement leaders were carefully balanced between a belief in the potential of human nature and a recognition of the power of circumstances over character. "We have not abandoned our old belief in liberty, justice and self-help," asserted Arnold Toynbee, the founder of the first settlement, "but we say that under certain conditions the people cannot help themselves and that then they should be helped by the state representing directly the whole people [quoted in Mencher, 1967:206]." Settlement leaders worked with and encouraged various social movements as a means by which the lower classes could redress the uneven balance of wealth while increasing their own independence and initiative. The pension movement was a natural extension of settlement philosophy.

Lined up in clear and often vociferous opposition were members of the Charity Organization Society, laissez faire Liberals, Conservatives, members of the House of Lords, the staff of the Local Government Board, and the Liberty and Property Defence League. The Charity Organization Society (C.O.S.) was founded in 1869. Its members believed that giving relief to the poor only encouraged the weak and stimulated dependency but that strengthening their character would help them to choose between good and evil. This was made explicit in the second annual report of the C.O.S. with the warning:

> To give material relief, food or money, to everyone who asked for it on the sole conditions of their being what is commonly called deserving and in want, even after the most careful verification of those conditions, would inevitably do more harm than good, though this might not be seen during the first year or two [quoted in Mowat, 1961:25].

Rather, through friendly visiting and moral example the C.O.S. intended to promote "habits of providence and self reliance, and of those social and sanitary principles, the observance of which is essential to the well-being of the poor and of the community at large [quoted in Mowat, 1961:26]." Charity, offered as a "wise gift of an understanding and sympathetic friend," was intended as the "stepping stone to future independence [Bosanquet, 1902:335]." Studies like Booth's (1894) and Rowntree's (1901), which emphasized the contribution of environmental factors to poverty, were criticized by C.O.S. leaders, who argued: "It is not the greater or lesser command of means that makes the material difference in the contentment and efficiency of social life, but the use of means relative to station in life and its possibilities [Loch, 1910:386]." Foresight and self-control, not environmental deprivation, determined one's life chances, and the contribution of the individual was believed to be more central than environmental conditions.

Similar attitudes toward the poor were expressed by members of the Liberty and Property Defence League, which was formed in the 1880s for the purpose of "resisting over-legislation, maintaining freedom of contract, and advocating individualism as opposed to Socialism, entirely irrespective of party politics [quoted in Thompson, 1955:423]." Their opposition to an old age pension was defended in a pamphlet written by Geoffrey Drage (1895) in which he expressed the league's view that "intemperance, want of thrift, and, most of all, want of backbone, are in a majority of cases the cause of destitution in old age [p. 7]." In the ensuing struggle the Victorian tenets of work, thrift, self-help, and respectability were embodied into a moral exemplar against which the character of the aged poor was measured.

The Battle for the Pension

Although the Liberal government has been given credit for passing the Old Age Pensions Act of 1908, the major thrust for this action came from organized labor, which used its growing influence to force a pension on a reluctant Victorian society still imbued with associations of poverty with moral failure. Major departures from laissez faire economics had taken place throughout the nineteenth century,

7. The Degradation of Age

but the pension was significant in that it represented the first symbol of the early welfare state and the first form of income transfer on a national basis outside the jurisdiction of the poor laws.

The idea of a pension was certainly not new to English society. In 1690, Daniel Defoe proposed one to begin at age 50 (Thomas, 1976:240). Guild rules around that time specified that "if any man or woman becomes so feeble through sickness or old age that he can neither work nor trade for himself, he shall be maintained, at the cost of the guild, in such a manner as befits his need [quoted in Wilson and Mackay, 1941:2]." In the eighteenth and early nineteenth centuries, landed gentry and wealthy industrialists retired to country estates, bestowing pensions to those beneath them in the social hierarchy under the prevailing patronage system (Perkin, 1969:49). In the same period, clubs of workingmen proliferated, and legislation was passed encouraging these clubs to use their funds to make special provisions for those members "past their labor [Wilson and Mackay, 1941:4]." Isolated pension schemes such as those for naval warrant officers existed, and some officeholders might bargain with a would-be successor for a pension (Thomas, 1976:242). In 1772, a bill was placed before the House of Commons for voluntary annuities for the aged assisted by the poor rate (Gilbert, 1966:161). Nothing became of this bill, and as the influence of Malthus and Ricardo changed popular attitudes toward the poor, interest in old age pensions on a broader scale declined.

A major source of protection in old age for the working class came from Friendly Societies, organizations of skilled laborers that worked to set up mutual benefit funds. The early Friendly Societies became suspect toward the end of the eighteenth century, as they were perceived as trade unions in disguise. Until 1824, they were banned and forbidden to accumulate funds. When the ban was lifted, Friendly Societies proliferated. They provided protection for the more elite of the working class against sickness and paid death benefits to widows. As the rural exodus to cities and towns proceeded to draw away the younger members, many Friendly Societies collapsed under the burden of supporting increasing numbers of older, ill members.

In 1854, W. E. Gladstone, chancellor of the Exchequer, became concerned with the unstable state of Friendly Societies. He introduced a Government Annuities Bill designed to encourage thrift among the working classes by allowing them to purchase annuities through the Post Office Savings Bank free from "risks of fraud and bankruptcy [Wilson and Mackay, 1941:7]." The funds were to be invested in government securities. Directly attacking the Friendly Societies for their use of paid agents, Gladstone argued that the bill had "grown . . . out of the wholesale error, deception, fraud and swindling which were perpetuated upon the most helpless portion of the community [quoted in Wilson and Mackay, 1941:8]." Gladstone poured scorn on the Friendly Societies for their high cost of management, the vast number of lapses, and the great number of failures, and he emphasized the need for annuities as the safest provision against old age. Against the opposition of the Friendly Societies, whose working-class members were unable to vote, the bill became law. The government was now competing directly with the Friendly Societies for scarce working-class funds.

Despite obstacles such as these, in succeeding decades Friendly Societies continued to grow, eventually approaching a membership of over 4 million largely skilled working-class men (Gilbert, 1966:165). Strictly antisocialist, and manifesting the Victorian ethic of self-help and thrift, Friendly Societies formed a vast network in every middle-size town in England.

From the beginning, Friendly Societies were opposed to state pensions, which they viewed as another attempt to usurp their autonomy. The first recommendations for a contributory old age pension appeared in the early 1870s, when the Royal Commission on Friendly Societies argued for guaranteed pensions paid through a National Friendly Society and managed by the state (Wilson and Mackay, 1941:9). State interference with management was a central threat to the autonomous existence of the Friendly Societies, and they mobilized a concerted and successful opposition to this scheme.

In 1878, Canon William Blackley began a fresh campaign for national insurance on a contributory basis that would provide protection against destitution in old age and protect the thrifty working class against habitual victimization by fraudulent and extortionate insurance offices and Friendly Societies (Wilson and Mackay, 1941:9).

Blackley (1881) argued that his plan was beneficial, not detrimental, to Friendly Societies on the grounds that it would abolish the practice of taxing the thrifty by means of the poor rate "for the support of a large class of wasteful, thriftless, improvident persons [p. 183]." The Friendly Societies, who agreed with Blackley's evaluation of the thriftless, did not accept his plan. Continually fearful of any competition for limited working-class funds that might make private thrift institutions irrelevant to the needs of the nation, they mobilized their resources to defeat this pension plan as well (Treble, 1970:269).

Despite their adherence to the prevailing individualist philosophy, Friendly Societies were also aware of the fact, so aptly demonstrated by Booth (1892, 1894) and later Rowntree (1901), that poverty in old age was not solely the product of character defects but was sometimes the sequel to below-subsistence earnings. Their rejection of a state-aided pension fund was also a rejection of the system of social inequality that reduced the share of income the workers received during their working life. "Let the workers get a larger share of the profits resulting from their own labors," argued Brother J. Prembery, the high chief ranger of the Foresters, "and we venture to think that generally they may be trusted to make all those provisions which a sense of duty requires of them [quoted in Treble, 1970:277]."

By the 1890s, the Friendly Societies began to run into increased actuarial danger. Their tables had been calculated on the assumption that most of their members would die before reaching late middle age and without ever making a claim on their sick benefits. Improvements in life expectancy meant that increasing numbers of their members were living into old age, placing a demand on their sick pay in amounts that their reserve funds had never been calculated to support.[2] The normal assumption that a man worked until he died—the experience of rural England—had been replaced by the dawning recognition that large numbers could not work but did not die. When Charles Booth (1891) suggested a state-financed, universal, noncontributory pension plan, Friendly Societies increasingly recognized that this was the one form of government welfare activity that would

[2] The chances for a male surviving from age 20 to age 65 increased from 53% in 1861 to 61% by 1911 (calculated from Keyfitz and Flieger, 1968).

—178—

be of positive benefit to them. In 1896, three large Friendly Societies passed resolutions in favor of some form of state assistance "provided that the pension is independent of the Poor Law, and does not create any power of Government interference in the general management of the affairs of the Unity [*Bristol Times and Mirror*, May 30, 1896].[3]

In 1890, Sidney Webb stated that no scheme for pensions would be satisfactory if it rested on the payments by the persons who would receive them, that provision should be made by the community as a collective charge. Charles Booth came to a similar conclusion. Joseph Chamberlain, a leading member of the Unionist party, was quick to realize the political significance of the discussion of old age pensions, and in 1891 he linked pensions with good wages, suggesting that the government encourage voluntary savings by paying 5% interest on all deposits accumulated by persons who would save for old age pensions in an officially sponsored system (Sires, 1954:233). A parliamentary committee was formed to study the subject, and it eventually concluded that even a small pension was politically impossible. Thus, the initial pension proposals were middle class in origin. Sustained working-class support, which could only come through working-class organizations, was still not a serious consideration.

The plight of the aged had become sufficiently visible by 1893 for the government to set up a royal commission to study the possibility of a pension. In 1895, the Royal Commission on the Aged Poor reported that the situation of the aged poor was extremely serious, but it could not agree on a single solution. Noncontributory schemes were deemed too expensive, whereas contributory schemes would do nothing for women or the poorest and most sporadically employed members of the working class. Still, Chamberlain urged that some solution be found, for "the foundations of property are made more secure when no real grievance is felt by the poor against the rich [quoted in Wilson and Mackay, 1941:29]."

[3] Considerable Friendly Society opposition to pensions still existed, and the Old-Age State Pension League was formed in 1898 to repudiate the concept of a universal, noncontributory state pension and support only thrift societies (Treble, 1970:280).

7. The Degradation of Age

As witnesses paraded before the Royal Commission, opponents of the pension advanced their own political interests by arguing that the poor suffered in old age because they had failed to pursue the Victorian virtues of ambition, thrift, temperance, and self-reliance. By emphasizing individual responsibility, the Victorians could lay the blame for old age pauperism elsewhere. "Of course they are failures," declared a guardian. "I do not say they have all failed from vice but they have failed from slackness, want of backbone, which prevented them earning their own living [P.P. XIV, Report, 1895:xv]." Pauperism in old age was due to personal moral failure rather than to any conditions inherent in society.

Intemperance was not so much a direct cause of pauperism in old age in and of itself. Rather, it served as an indicator of a lack of strength of character, for "if a man has sufficient grit or backbone, or self-denial to be a teetotaler, that man will not become a pauper [P.P. XIV, Report, 1895:lxviii]." The consequences of deviation even early in life were likely to be reflected in old age:

> I do not think the causes, as so often happens, such as drunkenness, are so easily found at a later stage, because when a person becomes very poor, his capacity for purchasing drink is diminished. . . . And therefore, if you went to the man, unless you had a good deal of evidence about the years that were past, you might think he was in want through no fault of his own [P.P. XIV, Mins. of Ev., 1895:553]."

Thrift, too, was a lifelong habit that could save the deserving from a penurious existence in old age, for it was believed by many that "fear of a destitute old age has contributed more than any other cause to those permanent accumulations of wealth which pass from one generation to another [Mackay, 1899:591]." Thus, when Miss Octavia Hill of the Charity Organization Society was asked if she was familiar with persons "of thrifty and saving habits" who came upon the poor law in old age, she responded, "I was thinking that over pretty carefully and I really could not think of one. . . . I should not like to say there are not such people at all, but I cannot remember one, looking over my old acquaintances among the people [P.P. XIV, Mins. of Ev., 1895:553]."

The Royal Commission concluded by suggesting that another committee, consisting of fewer persons, be appointed to find a solution to the problem. This Committee on Old Age Pensions pursued its inquiry for 2 years. Noncontributory schemes were rejected from consideration on the basis that they would discourage thrift. Forced by the limitations of its philosophical orientation to consider only contributory schemes, which were inacceptable to Friendly Societies, this committee too failed to find any solution (Stead, 1909:34).

Just a few months after the Committee on Old Age Pensions made its report, the British colony of New Zealand passed its own Old Age Pensions Act, a noncontributory scheme that aroused the interest of the nation. Under the combined leadership of F. Herbert Stead, the warden of Browning settlement, Charles Booth, and several prominent labor leaders, a series of conferences were planned to educate the people about the need for a pension.

The pension proposals that had come from middle-class spokesmen initially had no appeal for labor unions, who maintained a skeptical attitude toward the use of governmental power as an instrument of reform. Like Friendly Societies, they feared government competition for funds, and at the Trades Union Congress of 1892 a resolution was passed that any bill to deal with old age pensions "will not be satisfactory unless the superannuation funds of unions are so dealt with as to receive a proportionate amount of subsidy from Parliament [quoted in Sires, 1954:240]."

In contrast to earlier contributory proposals, the movement for a noncontributory pension drew the immediate and sustained support of organized labor, including all the semiskilled and unskilled workers who did not belong to Friendly Societies. There are several reasons why unions changed their views at this time. First, few unions had the resources to pay pensions for any extended period of time. In 1893, 77% of the trade unions had no old age provision, and those that did were reducing rather than extending their benefits (Turner, 1897:5). Unions recognized clearly and quite early that a noncontributory state pension was essential not only for the maintenance of some minimum wage rate but also for their own financial survival. Second, this new proposal was noncontributory and did not compete for unions funds. Finally, as noted in Chapter 6, unions during this period were just beginning to gain some guarantees from industry for minimum wage rates. Older workers were clearly a threat to these wage rates, since they were often willing to work for less just to maintain their jobs. A pension that removed the aged from the labor force would give the working class more control over the work force.

The first conference represented more than a quarter of a million trade unionists, standing for diverse parties and schools of thought. This in itself was remarkable, because a previous International Labor Congress, held just a few months earlier, had broken up in disorder due to serious disagreements between socialist and nonsocialist factions (Stead, 1909:20). The conference ended after a series of speeches by Charles Booth and other pension supporters with unanimous agreement among all those attending to press for a universal pension. Stead (1909) later wrote of this meeting, ''Behold the long desired Labour Party of the future [p. 20].''

So began a battle that was to continue for 8 years. Working through trade unions and trade councils, meetings were planned initially in the working-class, industrial centers in the north, and then spread throughout Great Britain. In 1899, Booth published his *Old Age Pensions and the Aged Poor*, in which he presented for the first time a detailed pension plan. Booth proposed to cut through all the arguments against old age pensions—the discouragement of thrift, the difficulty of discriminating between the deserving and needy and the undeserving, the stigma of pauperism, and the damage to independence of receiving a pension—by granting to everyone a non-contributory pension of five shillings a week at age 65 or 70. A week after the conference the newly formed National Committee of Organized Labor on Old Age Pensions, a coalition of trade unions, trade councils, Friendly Societies, and co-operative societies, including many of the most influential names in the labor movement, met to plan a more concerted strategy. Fredrick Rogers, who later became the first chairman of the Labor Representation Committee, was elected the first secretary (Gilbert, 1966:193).[4]

The strategy of the National Committee initially was to educate

---

[4] See Chapter 2, for a more detailed discussion of the history of organized labor.

the public about their cause. To implement this strategy, they distributed thousands of leaflets, emphasizing the plight of the aged poor, whose only recourse was "the shame of the workhouse or the ignominy of private charity [Stead, 1909:80]." "Hard work for fifty years and more," pleaded Canon Moore Ede (1891), "and then after all the toil and effort to sink down into the submerged tenth at last. There ought to be, there must be, some road out of this corner of darkest England [p. 584]."

Like pension opponents, labor also employed the theme of the degradation of age, but it revised the thrust of the argument. The working class responded to attacks upon their character and their humanity with arguments that attempted to expose conditions within society that might lead to destitution in old age. The cause resided not within themselves but within the new social order created by industrial capitalism. As Frederick Rogers argued in his leaflet entitled "The Worn-Out Workman: What Is to Be Done with Him," "the aged have built up the riches of the nation only to be cast aside [Stead, 1909:103]."

Revising the romantic critique of the machine, labor argued that the introduction of machinery into so many branches of industry had harmed older workers. New technology wrought subtle changes as machine labor replaced human labor. "We have to recognize," testified a union organizer,

> the great increase of machinery, which undoubtedly lessens the opportunity of a man following his employment, especially when he gets old, and secondly, we have to recognize that the increase of machinery destroys to a large extent the skill of the man; it makes him more a machine than a skilled artisan, and that, likewise, has a tendency when he gets out of employment, because he is not a skilled artisan in any sense, he is simply a manual workman [P.P. XIV, Mins. of Ev., 1895:803].

Machines also hastened the aging process, using up human energies more quickly than in the past. "There are tools by which we can work quicker, and we actually do work very much quicker than my father did," stated a skilled worker. "My own family has been in our trade for nearly 100 years, and I find, by comparison, that my father did considerable less work during the week than I do now. . . . We have better tools to work with, but the better tools still involve the quicker work [P.P. XIV, Mins. of Ev., 1895:891]." With increasing insistence, the National Committee on Pensions stressed, "For the worn-out worker, man or woman, who has helped to build the fabric of your national life, demand not charity, but justice [Stead, 1909:197]."

Attacks on one's character are more difficult to refute, and workers searched for moral exemplars who could prove that conditions made it necessary for even hard-working and thrifty men to apply for relief in old age.

> Several years ago an old member of ours—he was the founder of our court in 1857; he was over 70 years of age when he broke down in his health, and he was in receipt of 3s a week from our society—having no other means to live upon, he naturally had to apply to the poor law authorities, and he received another 3s per week, and that, of course, disfranchised the man, and he practically died a pauper. That man was a most intelligent man, a thoughtful man, a reading man, and he felt very acutely that he should have to become a pauper in his old age after, in his opinion, providing for himself in his younger days [P.P. XLV, 1898:39].

Even a thoughtful man, a reading man who adhered to the middle-class virtues of thrift and hard work, could not prevent ultimate pauperization.

The movement among laborers for a pension continued to spread. In 1900, the Trades Union Congress (T.U.C.), the organization of the semiskilled and unskilled mass of workers, passed a resolution at their annual meeting demanding a pension as the right of all citizens, a resolution they continued to pass every subsequent year until the pension's enactment. In 1901, the National Organization of Co-operative Societies passed an identical resolution. A year later the Friendly Societies expressed cautious and tentative support, including in their resolution the stipulation that applicants be "thrifty and deserving." This was firmly and immediately rejected by the T.U.C. and the co-operatives.

The Boer War in South Africa temporarily drew the nation's attention away from the pension issue, and when peace came in 1902 the National Committee on Pensions renewed their efforts vigorously. This time their purpose went beyond education. They intended to request the government to maintain the war taxes to finance the pension, and they embarked on a concerted political effort to support candidates who spoke out decisively on the pension issue.

Their pressure on government to maintain the war taxes failed, but the issue did increase their political awareness of the distinction between middle-class and working-class interests. "How many homes have been broken up," asked a disappointed Stead (1909), "how many an aged toiler has been cast into the dungeon of the workhouse, how many an aged heart has broken, how many multitudes of hoary heads have gone down with sorrow to the grave, how many have slowly starved to death—for want of the pension which might have been theirs in 1903 [p. 170]!" Clearly, it was now class warfare, as the pressing needs of the nation's poor were sacrificed "at the sordid shrine of middle-class and upper-class comfort [p. 170]." The conclusion that the pension supporters drew from their defeat was that their only chance for success was to increase the number of Independent Labour members in the House of Commons.

In 10 years, the Conservatives accomplished little in the way of social reform, and it was natural for people to look to the Liberal party for ameliorative legislation. In 1906, the Liberal party soundly defeated the Conservatives, but the principal programs of the party were political and fiscal rather than social, with the exception of trade union law, education, and the liquor trade. They came to power unpledged as a party to old age pensions (Sires, 1954:244). However, in the same year, for the first time a substantial number of working-class candidates were elected to office, as 29 Independent Labour party members were seated in Parliament. Among them were 11 members of the National Committee on Pensions. For the first time there were representatives in the House of Commons uniformly committed to old age pensions.

The unexpected success of the Labour Representation Committee stunned the Liberals and spurred them to incorporate labor items in their agenda. Almost immediately, Asquith's private secretary began collecting data on pensions and a proposal was put before the Cabinet in 1906 (Hay, 1975:46). More pressure was put on Liberals in 1907 with a loss of seats in two elections in regions that had traditionally been held by old, well-known Liberal families. In an effort to hold the party together, the Liberals turned to social reform, including the labor-oriented Workmen's Compensation Act and the Trades Disputes Bill.[5] Their major concern was to contain labor while satisfying Conservatives that they were not having socialism thrust upon them. As Liberal Prime Minister Campbell-Bannerman wrote in a confidential memo to Asquith, then chancellor of the Exchequer: "If we have sops for Labour, we ought to have some other Bill besides Educ. of general interest to balance them. Otherwise will not the (enemy) or will colour be given to their assertion, which seems to be their main weapon now, that we are in the hands and at the mercy of Labor (which equals socialism) [quoted in Gilbert, 1966:203]." That other bill was the old age pension, which provided a balance to the two labor reform measures. It maintained the reputation of the Liberals as a party of social reform and satisfied the popular interest in supporting an issue that went beyond the interest of the unions.

A victorious labor boasted at the T.U.C. meeting in 1907 that the Trades Disputes Bill was a major victory, because the politicians did not want to enter into battle with organized workers. Now labor wanted old age pensions! It was the first plank incorporated in the T.U.C. platform, asking for universal, noncontributory, and non-discriminatory pensions. In response to concerns about financing the pension, labor leaders argued that a universal pension was an earned right to which "a man who has served the community throughout his working life [was] entitled [Turner, 1897:12]." Labor's value had been usurped, and they should now get a return on what had been appropriated from them. "It was no part of their duty to show how the money could be found," asserted Albert Gill, a member of the Executive Committee of the textile workers:

> That was the function of a Chancellor of the Exchequer. If he would turn his attention to the unearned increment which had accrued to landlords from the land, the mining royalties which in other countries went to the State, but which

[5] The Workmen's Compensation Act was described in Chapter 6. The Trades Disputes Bill (1906) secured to organized workers the right of picketing and freedom from collective responsibility (Beer, 1953:325). It also confirmed the right of peaceful picketing, allowed since 1875 (Thompson, 1965:197).

were here appropriated by the landowner, the large fortunes which were left, and which had been made by the industry of the workers, he would find sources which could be legitimately tapped [*The Times* (London), September 4, 1907].

As a pension became increasingly likely, the opposition made various attempts to modify its noncontributory aspect or stifle it completely. The Local Government Board, with its strong vested interest in the voluntary principle, rejected the idea of a noncontributory scheme and insisted that some test of character to distinguish the deserving from the undeserving be included. The Charitable Organization Society offered particularly vociferous protest, arguing against this progressive collectivism, which would treat the drunkard and wastrel the same as the industrious and provident working man.[6] The C.O.S. had been giving pensions of their own to the "cream of the old working people [quoted in Mowat, 1961:98]." They objected to a pension even to the deserving aged on the grounds that it was

plainly impractical to pension every old man or old woman whose sole qualification is that he or she has never been seen the worse for drink. The whole value and meaning of the plan would be imperiled, and the true interests of the class it is intended to benefit in so far damaged, were not some standard of thrift and uprightness, family duty and the like, steadily maintained [quoted in Mowat, 1961:98].

The Liberty and Property Defence League was opposed to pensions in any form. As Frederick Millar, secretary of the league, wrote, "To contend that persons who simply will not save and invest their savings for their own advantage should have their thriftlessness encouraged at the expense of the community is surely a proposal too unblushing in its effrontery to need further remark [quoted in Stead, 1909:174]."

The growing influence of organized labor combined with a lack of resistance from Friendly Societies forced the hand of the Liberals. As the pension became inevitable, the opposition accepted the noncontributory aspect, seeking instead to narrow the coverage and insert

[6] In 1903, the Charity Organization Society published the *Case against Old Age Pension Schemes*, in which they presented lengthy and detailed arguments against nearly every pension scheme.

stipulations for character and good behavior. After the bill was resoundingly passed in the House of Commons, final arguments against the pension were heard in the House of Lords. Lord Avebury presented a petition against it signed by bankers, merchants, and chairmen of railway companies and insurance companies urging that more study be made of the issue. "The State invites us every day to lean upon it," argued Lord Rosebery in a final and impotent battle cry:

> I seem to hear the wheedling and alluring whisper, sound you may be, we bid you be a cripple. Do you see? Be blind. Do you hear? Be deaf. Do you walk? Be not so venturesome. Here is a crutch for one arm. When you get accustomed to it you will soon want another. . . . Every day the area for initiative is being narrowed. . . . It was self-reliance that built the empire; it is by self-reliance and all that that implies that it must be welded and continued [quoted in Wilson and Mackay, 1941:43].

The final bill was a victory for the National Committee on Pensions and the trade unions, yet it was victory tempered by compromise. As introduced, it provided for a payment of a pension of 5 shillings a week to all British subjects of age 70 whose income did not exceed 26 pounds a year.[7] However, the applicant had to prove that he or she was not a lunatic and was not receiving or had not received poor relief since January 1, 1908. In order to exclude the wastrel, applicants had to prove they had been "habitually" employed in the trade of their choice and had tried to look after themselves and their families. The poor law disqualification was removed within 2 years. The industry test, too, proved to be unworkable and was finally dropped as a requirement in 1919. The pension was not entirely universal, but it had firmly hedged the moralistic Victorian attitude toward the poor. Previously, relief had been granted only from local funds, after application of a test of destitution. Now for the first time payments from national funds were to be granted automatically with no test of destitution (Bruce, 1966:154).

---

[7] The flat cutoff was amended by a sliding scale (Gilbert, 1966:223).

Social Policy and the Degradation of Age

The degraded view of old age that characterized late nineteenth-century England was a social and political force. In a period in which laissez faire individualism was declining and government responsibility expanding, this ideology was useful to middle-class conservatives as a way of reasserting traditional Victorian values and arguing against a pension. Those who did not adhere to the norms of work, thrift, temperance, and self-help were clearly warned, for the consequences of deviation were only too visible in the abject form of the aged pauper. Working-class leaders responded to these attacks on their character by arguing that degradation in old age was not due to personal failure. Rather, the advance of industrial capitalism with its increased reliance on machine technology wore out human energies more rapidly, forcing thrifty and moral individuals to become

Visitor. "SEVENTY-EIGHT, ARE YOU? WELL, KEEP ALIVE TILL THE NEW YEAR, AND YOU'LL GET YOUR PENSION."
Mrs. O'Flanagan. "PINSION, IS IT, ME LADY? AND HWIN WILL I BE GETTING THE EIGHT YEARS BACK-MONEY THE ENGLISH ARE OWIN' ME, THAT'S HWAT I WANT TO KNOW!"

From *Punch, or the London Charivari*, December 23, 1908.

paupers. Labor was the source of wealth, it was argued, and a pension was only a return to the workers of what was rightfully theirs.

Although the pension appears to be a pure confrontation between working-class and middle-class interests, some caution must be used in placing too heavy an emphasis on the revolutionary impact of the pension alone, for it did arise during a period of general Liberal social reform. Between 1906 and 1914, insurance against ill health and unemployment and school meals and medical services for children were introduced. Minimum wages were fixed in certain industries, and some attempt was made to alter the distribution of income in British society (Hay, 1975:11). This case study of one of these movements emphasizes the significance of pressure from below in introducing social reform. Yet the concerted opposition of Friendly Societies must also be taken into account. A more balanced perspective can be maintained by recognizing that the rise of collectivism was not really a change in thought but was rather a compromise between the propertied and the propertyless that led to a more positive role for the state. Rather than taking on the complex task of reforming the financing of the poor law at the local level, Liberal politicians used the old age pension as a means of providing a modest income for the aged outside of the poor law.

The pension bill was passed in the midst of a series of reforms. Historians are still debating why these reforms occurred when they did. It seems apparent that one factor was pressure from organizations of the working class, who had achieved the franchise and were now beginning to assert their political power. However, this does not explain why labor unions and eventually Friendly Societies came to accept the pension after a period of resistance based on fears of state interference in working-class organizations. Clearly, that it was noncontributory played a role, since this meant no competition for working-class funds. However, it may also have been the case that unions saw an opportunity to stabilize wage rates by removing the aged from the labor force. The burden of support of older workers was removed from unions and Friendly Societies and transferred to society as a whole.

8

Lessons from the Past

For many years, sociologists have strived to develop a theory of social change. These attempts have been characterized by a deep conviction that it was possible to order the observable changes in history into a single coherent framework and provide a unified theory of social change (Smith, 1973:1). Many grand theories of social change have been proposed. Cyclical theories such as Khaldun's (1967), Toynbee's (1957), and Sorokin's (1957) perceive time in terms of series of cycles. These theories assert that what may appear to be a linear direction of change is actually only a phase of a cycle that will eventually reverse itself.

In contrast, developmental theories of change that include evolutionary development and dialectical development stress social change as a linear process. Among the evolutionary theorists are Comte (1858), who identified three progressive stages of human development—the theological, the metaphysical, and the Positive—and Spencer (1969), who viewed the natural world as involving a passage "from an indefinite, incoherent homogeneity to a definite coherent heterogeneity." For Spencer, evolution was a process of successive differentiation and integration. Marx and Engels also characterized society in terms of stages, with the distinguishing characteristic being a different mode of production.

One important attribute that these theories share is the common notion that there is a master mechanism operating through long periods of history whose effects are cumulative (Stinchcombe, 1978:8). There are material mechanisms of change, such as Veblen's (1953) view of technology; idealist mechanisms, which give primacy to the role of ideas; interactional mechanisms, which see social interaction, particularly conflict, as the moving force in history; and structural sources of change, including government, status anguish, and generational conflict.

Theories of social change also often share the same basic historical facts to narrate a sequence of events. However, they use the data in different ways to generate concepts that support the larger theory. These concepts, which are a step more abstract than the narrative of the facts, are linked to form causal sequences and thus provide justification for the grand theory. The conflict between the grand theories is in interpreting how the changes occurred, what the master mechanism was.

Structural-Functionalism as a Theory of Social Change

In contrast to theories focusing specifically on social change, structural-functionalism as a more general perspective has emphasized that the study of change must grow out of the prior study of the structure of society (Parsons, 1966). Structural-functionalism views social systems as two or more interacting units, with societies composed of systems of normatively integrated and interrelated parts.

The concept of integration needs elaboration, since it is a crucial aspect of functionalist analysis. Integration is one of the four functional requirements for the survival of a society, with the other three being goal attainment, adaptation, and pattern maintenance (Parsons and Smelser, 1956:18–19). Integration may be one of two kinds, system integration or social integration, although this distinction is not usually recognized by functionalists (Lockwood, 1964). The premise of system integration is that societal institutions must be in harmony. For example, if the economy needs a well-educated labor force, but the educational system is so organized that a great deal of educational talent is wasted, then these two parts of society are malintegrated (Mishra, 1977:47). Social integration involves the reduction of conflict between social groups, like workers and managers. It is concerned with morale, loyalty, and commitment to the collectivity.

The question is, Why should integration be a general necessity, a function essential for the survival of all societies? The answer provided by functionalists is twofold. First, levels of conflict between the component parts of a collectivity must be kept as low as possible to maintain peace. Thus, social control is an implicit component of integration. Second, any society that has the character of a community must have some sentiments of solidarity. Altruism is a normal feature of societies, and individuals have a claim on the community's resources because solidarity suggests that their needs be met. Social change occurs as a means of maintaining integration, keeping harmony, and increasing levels of solidarity.

In response to the criticism that functionalism is a static theory, a doctrine of normative consensus that views change as a deviation from a normal state of equilibrium, Parsons (1964, 1966), Smelser (1959), and other functionalists have explained the way in which social systems change. The most important mechanism in the structural-functionalist approach is structural differentiation—the motor of historical change.

The concept of differentiation was derived from Durkheim (1964), who elevated the division of labor into the central principle of social organization and defined the modernity of recent Western societies largely in terms of the consequences of this type of integration. Durkheim noted that as societies grew in size and complexity, competition invariably increased in proportion to the physical and social density of population. Occupational specialization was the most effective method for regulating the ensuing conflicts of interest, as individuals were integrated by a network of expectations, duties, and rights associated with different roles. Social change occurred through alterations in the nature and structure of roles and norms in a given unit.

Briefly, the functionalist concept of differentiation refers to the notion that development consists of the movement of societies from a simple (undifferentiated) to a complex (highly differentiated) type of social structure. Differentiation is a linear process and is explicitly irreversible, since each component in the system is organically linked to the others. The four functional tasks noted earlier do not change, since they are essentially the same for all human societies. What does change is the nature of institutional arrangements through which the different functions are performed. As the structure becomes more specialized in the course of development, a multifunctional institutional structure, such as the family, splits into several different structures, each with a more specialized function. The differentiation of structures produces imbalances and malintegration that require new forms of integration. This, paradoxically, produces even more specialized structures. In an article on modernization, Smelser (1964) explains this process: "Development proceeds as a contrapuntal interplay between differentiation (which is divisive of established society) and integration (which unites differentiated structures on a new basis [p. 267].'' He goes on to explain the ways in which the change from household production to factory production creates integrative problems:

> How is information concerning employment opportunities to be conveyed to work people? How are the interests of families to be integrated with the interests of firms? How are families to be protected from market fluctuations? Whereas such integrative exigencies were faced by kinsmen, neighbors, and local largesse in pre-modern settings, development gives birth to dozens of institutions and organizations geared to these new integrative problems—labor recruitment agencies and exchanges, labor unions, government regulation of labor allocation, welfare and relief arrangements, co-operation societies, and savings institutions [p. 268].

Although there may be temporary deviations, the universal trend of differentiation will ultimately reassert itself. Further, the universality of the trend, makes it possible to order societies into a hierarchy of types and stages (Parsons, 1960). Thus, the principle of differentiation was expanded by the structural-functionalists to account for not only postrevolutionary Western European industrial societies but also all types of societies. Occupational differentiation became structural differentiation and was applied to all societal institutions, including the polity, the family, the legal system, and systems of belief, rather than being confined solely to the economic sphere.

Modernization theory is derived from functionalism. It is, however, more descriptive than theoretical, for the general approach has been to chart the interrelationship between recent trends and label them "modern." Any society exhibiting certain qualities of social structure and process is thus categorized as a "modern" society. Modernization becomes then merely a system for classifying and ordering societies in a logical fashion from simple to complex (Nisbet, 1969:191). It is a taxonomy, like a museum exhibit. Cultural artifacts are arranged in sequence, representing some constructed history, that is, the history of development.

Since modernization does not ever make the mechanism of social change explicit, does not ever explain how the transition from the "before" to the "after" occurs, we are forced to turn to functionalist explanations of social change, for the same mechanisms are implicit but not formally stated in modernization theory. This is necessary, because it is useless to make statements about the impact of a transition from one type of society to another without any understanding of how that change occurred. Let us now turn to an analysis of the aging and modernization model, using the material presented in this book to examine the adequacy of the concepts of integration and structural differentiation.

Social Change and the Status of the Aged

The theory of aging and modernization that implies a before and after is seriously flawed in two ways. First, the theoretical assumptions behind it are erroneous in terms of the way in which social change is described. Second, it is inadequate in the empirical facts presented. Let us examine how flaws in theory lead by necessity to erroneous interpretations of facts, for it seems obvious that if a general theory of social change and modernization that derives from functionalism is inadequate, then any attempt to attach some singular position to the aged in the before and after is equally flawed. First, we will assess the empirical adequacy of the theory of aging and modernization, and then we will turn to an analysis of its theoretical value.

One premise of modernization theory concerns the impact of the decline of household production on the status of the aged. Under household production, according to modernization theory, the aged hold power and prestige within the family unit. The decline of household production and rise of factory production increases geographical mobility and isolates the aged from close-knit family relationships. The functions that were previously performed by the family are then taken over by other institutions, particularly the state. Clearly a functionalist argument, the underlying theoretical premise here is one of structural differentiation and malintegration, eventually superseded by a new form of integration that is implicitly less satisfactory.

One major flaw in this argument is the romanticization of how household production functioned—the assumption that the aged held power and prestige by their control over the means of production. Although this pattern may have characterized some farm families and some families of master craftsmen, in general, history refutes this view. Peasant farmers, as we saw in Chapter 1, were resented and sometimes abused by children who had to wait to inherit the farm in order to marry. And retirement contracts, the source of protection that they had in the past, were not always enforced.

The case study of household production in Chilvers Coton indicated that older people were most often living in a family setting. In 1851, when the hand-loom ribbon weaving thrived, more than 80% of all aged men and women were living with kin. Yet there are no indications that this household arrangement was based on the power and prestige of the aged. Rather, these were fragile household economies in which family members pooled their resources and combined their labor so that all could survive. Extended family units were not formed by parents moving in with married children. In fact, children married early and established independent households. Extended family units were created in times of crises when widowed or separated children returned to their parents' households.

The decline of domestic production did not destroy the extended family household, but it did alter its composition. By 1901, when the treaty with the French allowing French silks into England had virtually destroyed hand-loom ribbon weaving in Chilvers Coton, still more than 80% of the aged were living with kin. However, the type of household in which older people were found had changed. More older people were living in their own homes with their unmarried children, as a result of such factors as an increase in age at marriage and reduced mortality, and more were living in the homes of married children. Thus, contrary to expectations, industrialization initially decreased the likelihood that older people would be living in the empty nest. This changing household pattern cannot be attributed simply to the decline of household production or, in functionalist terms, to structural differentiation leading to malintegration. Rather, it involved a complex combination of factors, including an increase in the age of marriage, a rise in the standard of living, and changing patterns of work over the life cycle.

Another argument from modernization theory elaborates the consequences of the decline of the extended family. Proceeding from a clearly functionalist framework, the argument contains two circular premises based on the notion of structural differentiation. First, as fewer functions were performed within the family because of the pressures created by industrialization, the state was forced to expand its support for the aged. This, in turn, further weakened the family network, and family members were increasingly forced to rely on the state for economic support.

What can be most readily refuted in this argument is the assumption that nonfamilial support of the aged is somehow unique to postindustrial society. In England from at least the sixteenth century, the poor law was always there as a last resort for the aged poor, and throughout English history vast numbers of older people turned to the state for economic support. Thus, there is little support for the premise that the decline of the extended family network caused an expansion of state support for the aged, for some source of support was always there.

The second argument is that increased state support weakened the family network. Again, the functionalist implications are apparent. Differentiation led to malintegration. However, a case study of the impact of the 1871 "crusade against outrelief" that accompanied the abolition of the Poor Law Board and the shifting of the jurisdiction of poor law responsibility to the expanded Local Government Board allows a different interpretation to be derived.

The 1871 "crusade" reduced poor law support and forced children to contribute to the support of aged parents. Although the official argument supporting the reduction of outrelief was that family members were neglecting their responsibilities to their aged kin, the real issue was the desire of the newly created Local Government Board to expand its political control over rural areas. By forcing local boards of guardians to standardize procedures and implement new means of evaluating outrelief applicants, the central authority decreased local autonomy. The victims were the aged, particularly aged women, who comprised the highest proportion of outrelief applicants.

During the period of the crusade, the number of older women in workhouses increased significantly, as they no longer had any income to contribute to the household economy. Their children simply could not afford to keep them any longer. Further, the pressure placed on relatives to support their aged parents increased family tensions and created additional financial burdens for all family members. The refusal of some children to maintain their aged parents was not a symbol of family breakdown but rather a response to economic hardship caused by the withdrawal of outdoor relief.

The important issue in regard to the impact of the 1871 crusade that accompanied government expansion was not that differentiation lead to malintegration. Rather, it was the power struggle between local government and central authority that was the critical factor. Even more important, and what is totally missed in modernization theory, is that this power struggle was framed within a particular value system, that of laissez faire individualism. Ultimately, it was the repressive nature of the content of the social policy that had the greatest impact on the position of the aged, for the withdrawal of support was accompanied by the assumption that only the "undeserving" aged poor were in need. If an analysis is limited to the modernization framework, the two critical elements of power and values are left unanalyzed.

Another argument from modernization theory associates increased rates of retirement with linear development, as measured by the decline of agriculture, the growth of modern health technology, and the expansion of modern economic technology. The decline of agriculture leads to a loss of independent decision making regarding the timing of retirement; modern health technology increases life expectancy and creates intergenerational competition for jobs; and modern economic technology makes the skills of older workers obsolete.

The analysis of retirement presented in Chapter 6 indicated that the introduction of technology did put older workers at a disadvantage. Competition with machine-made objects led to a decline in wages, and when an older worker could no longer keep pace with the machine, unemployment resulted. Wage laborers with no skills were the most vulnerable and had the highest rates of retirement. To the extent, then, that industrialization increased the proportion of wage laborers and reduced opportunities for skilled, self-employed work, it did contribute to a loss of work for the aged. However, even this simple relationship is attenuated by the fact that industrialization also multiplied the numbers of home workers in urban areas.

The linear view of development implicit in the association of retirement with modern economic technology, modern health technology, and agricultural decline also ignores the extensive evidence of peasant retirement. Although supportive arguments for the causal link between these variables and retirement have been developed through cross-cultural comparisons, historical evidence negates the comparative conclusions. Retirement in "modern" society is unique only to the degree that it is associated with massive intergenerational income redistribution through a state bureaucracy. Retirement, itself, is not new.

Increased retirement could, however, have led to the passage of a pension bill, and within this framework the pension could be viewed as another example of structural differentiation arising from a societal need for integration because of the loss of work for the aged. However, equally plausible alternative explanations for the pension are that it was a conflict between working- and middle-class interests over income distribution, that it was desirable for propertied interests as a means of coopting the growing power of labor, and that industrial capitalists had a need for a more efficient and well-regulated labor force that would exclude marginal, aged labor.

The issue of the meaning of work in old age has also been ignored in the modernization literature. The focus on relationships between linear variables has led us away from the human aspects of the issue. In Chapter 6 we saw that much of the work done by older men and women was harsh, low-paying, irregular, and degrading. Given the positive attitude of most older people toward the guaranteed state pension, it seems difficult to evaluate the trend toward state support as a negative one. The question, then, is, Why has increased retirement combined with economic support for the aged through intergenerational income transfers been associated with low status? What, then, does the concept of status mean?

All of the variables discussed earlier—numbers retired, percentage living with kin, proportion receiving state support—have been used by sociologists as indicators of status. In contrast, historians have tended to define status as veneration or respect. According to their arguments, in the "before," the aged were venerated, and then there was a turning point in age relations that led to a degraded view of old age.

If the linear variables seem to be weak or even erroneous measures of status, then the question arises as to whether it is more accurate to assess status in terms of the rhetoric of age. The case study of the pension movement that was presented in Chapter 7 illustrated that the degraded view of old age expressed in late nineteenth-century England was a political weapon, not linked in any direct manner to the material conditions of the aged. It was used by conservative opponents of a pension to argue that destitution in old age was an individual responsibility, the inevitable result of thriftlessness, intemperance, and lack of ambition. Pension advocates responded by arguing that degradation in old age was not due to personal failure.

Rather, society had failed to live up to its responsibilities to its workers, as the advance of industrial capitalism with its increased reliance on machine technology wore out human energies more rapidly and forced thrifty and moral individuals to become paupers. These arguments arose because the problems of old age became increasingly visible toward the end of the century, as the working class gained a voice in government and had the political power to implement some of their programs through organized labor.

That the theme of a degraded old age had some "use" value should make us wary of assuming that any set of ideas about the aged is linked directly to their material conditions and hesitant to use beliefs or ideologies alone as indicators of status. Further, even if the rhetoric of age does have some tangible meaning that directly reflects the status of the aged (a term that is becoming increasingly opaque), then we must finally ask, To whom would this apply? Certainly not to the masses of aged poor who have been propertyless and powerless throughout history. If the elderly in Western society ever had high status solely on the basis of age, then we must assume that this perquisite was reserved for a wealthy elite and not for the typical older worker who was likely to spend his or her final years dependent on the parish or incarcerated in the workhouse.

It should be apparent from the preceding discussion that there are many empirical flaws in the aging and modernization model. Other studies have also pointed to the empirical inadequacies of the model, but discussions have generally ignored the problems in the underlying theoretical rationale. Upon closer inspection, we can see that the empirical flaws occur partly because of the theoretical inadequacies of integration and structural differentiation as mechanisms of social change. Turning first to the concept of integration, we see clearly that in nineteenth-century England the mechanism of social change was conflict, not a striving for consensus. It was conflict between classes that ultimately led to vast changes in the economy, the polity, and social structure.

This leads to a second point, that it is not only conflict that caused social change but power differentials as well. The shift from a regulated society to one in which theories of laissez faire predominated to a gradual acceptance of limited state socialism was the result of shifting political power. Thus, it is a specific type of conflict that was a prime mover in social change in nineteenth-century England: political conflict based on social class differences. Modernization theory with its emphasis on integration has almost entirely ignored the issue of the impact of changes in public policy and the underlying cause of those shifts.

Finally, it is important to recognize that it is often coercion and cooptation rather than integration that maintain what may be the appearance of harmony. The 1871 circular on poor law policy, which was analyzed in Chapter 5, demonstrates quite clearly that an effective way of reducing "system malintegration" is to coerce those who are relatively powerless into compliance. Further, as shown in Chapter 7, when coercion of the working class became ineffectual because of its increased political power, cooptation became the means for achieving "integration." The result was not integration but the maintenance of a system that maximized the protection of property interests.

Structural differentiation is equally inadequate in explaining social change. Certainly, there was increasing specialization in the nineteenth century. Specialization occurred in the poor law, in public health, in municipal government, and in numerous other bodies representing state authority. Specialization also occurred in the economy, as occupational diversity proliferated. However, the general trend toward increasing specialization ignores many other changes that were occurring in British society, as well as the nature of these changes.

If increased specialization is regarded as a multiplication of roles and organizations, then differentiation cannot account for changes in substance. Nothing is contained in the emphasis on specialization that might account for changes in values and beliefs, in income and status power differentials of various social groups as well as the life chances of individuals. For example, there were substantial changes in poor law policy in the nineteenth century, as we saw in Chapters 4 and 5. Certainly one trend was toward increasing specialization of function, as the multipurpose relieving officer of the parish was gradually· replaced by a multiplicity of government bureaucrats. However, to view bureaucratic growth per se as the significant aspect of poor law change misses entirely an equally important aspect, that of the nature of the policy itself and the manner in which it was implemented. Given the harshness with which the 1871 circular was implemented and its negative impact on older people and their families, it would be difficult to interpret this example as one geared toward solving an integrative problem. Rather, it caused tension and put tremendous pressure on families already under economic strain. What is missing in the modernization view is a focus on substance.

A second problem with the emphasis on differentiation in social change is that it becomes impossible to regard change as the result of human action. In the view of change as simply adaptation, a reflex action on the part of the social organism, the human processes involved in the differentiation of structures and their subsequent reintegration are lost. Thus, a functionalist explanation might see as inevitable the rise of organized labor, but this explanation in no way accounts for the struggles, the values, and the conflicts entailed, and, as described in Chapter 2, these struggles were substantial and in many ways unique for organized labor in late nineteenth-century England. Similarly, the movement for the pension, which expanded the state bureaucracy, could be viewed as a natural process of structural differentiation, but this misses entirely the meaning of the arguments that gave birth to that form of income transfer.

When we do proceed to an analysis at the individual level, we see that human beings do, in fact, act to determine their own life chances, not only in major struggles, such as those of labor against political economy, but also on a much smaller scale. In Chilvers Coton, individuals worked within their households to create family stability despite market fluctuations that drastically altered the state of the local economy. These families were integrated not by differentiation but by decisions of individuals on a daily basis. The organic analogy that is inherent in functionalism and implicitly a part of modernization theory ignores the fact that societies are composed of individuals.

Finally, there are many problems in a model that implies linear development and assumes that change continually moves in the direction of increasing societal complexity. One problem with this view is that empirical evidence indicates that elements or parts of a system associated with a traditional society, such as household production, may reappear in a somewhat modified form in a more developed society. We saw, for example, in Chapter 2 that industrialization, under certain conditions, led to deindustrialization and the vertical disintegration of the mode of production. Another problem is that development may be uneven, so that there is no necessary relationship between economic growth, political change, and family structure. Thus, the expected causal relationships simply do not materialize. In Chapter 3, for example, economic change (the decline of household production) that was stimulated by political change (the demand for free trade) did not have the expected effect of increasing the proportion of nuclear family households. Rather, the opposite occurred. Similarly, in Chapter 6, the rise of technology was associated with a decrease in work for older men but an apparent increase in available work for older women.

If a linear model of development proves inadequate under even limited circumstances when the predicted causal sequences are carefully analyzed, then it should be immediately apparent that this model could not serve as a universal theory for all societies. The question, then, is, What implications has this for the study of aging and social change?

The key variable in most studies of aging and social change has been that of status, and it seems clear that one of the first tasks must be to redefine the meaning of status. What, after all, do we mean when we speak of the status of the aged? Is it meaningful to describe status as a combination of variables, such as percentage in labor force, percentage living alone, and percentage receiving support from the state? I would argue that none of these criteria is an indicator of status. They are simply readily measurable variables that can easily accommodate a linear model of development. Further, the linear modernization model has falsely led to the assumption that the status relationships that arise in age-graded societies are qualitatively similar to those identified in societies with complex class structures. Rather, we must redefine status in broader terms and then ask what maintains the existing power structure and under what conditions is power likely to be associated with age.

A broader and more adequate definition of status should transcend the empirical level and include theoretical concepts that subsume all concrete indicators. Recent definitions have described status in terms of three universal goals toward which all old people everywhere will strive. These goals include "physical and emotional security, the respect of other members of the community, and an assurance that they are playing a useful part in the life of the family and society [Amoss and Harrell, 1981:5]." When these goals are met, the status of the aged is high; when they are not, the status of the aged is low. In this abstract sense, then, the status of the aged in a given society can be assessed by examining the relative success old people have in achieving their goals. The task can then be expanded to include an analysis of the factors that determine the ability of the aged to achieve these goals. According to Amoss and Harrell (1981:5), the key factors are the balance between the cost old people represent to the group and the contributions they make and the degree of control old people maintain over resources necessary for the fulfillment of needs of the younger members of the group. Dowd (1980) has added to this a stress on the impact of social class.

This definition is free of the false assumptions inherent in modernization theory, because it is not associated with any particular societal type or any particular empirical indicators. Further, it does not assume that all aspects of status are linked together in some linear fashion. Thus, it becomes possible to recognize that one indicator of high status may be satisfied although another is not, and this is consistent with both comparative and historical data that demonstrate that there is no necessary link between the various elements of status. For example, peasant farmers could guarantee their own physical security through their control over the inheritance of their land, but this did not guarantee them the respect of their children. Similarly, pensions provide a degree of physical and emotional security that is not necessarily accompanied by any guarantee of a useful role in the family or community.

Defining status in terms of universal goals does not imply that a given type of society—that is, traditional—necessarily satisfies these goals. This, too, is consistent with available data that demonstrate that there is no universal societal type defined as traditional or preindustrial that provides automatic high status for the aged. Rather, there is tremendous cross-cultural and historical diversity. The belief that low status is associated with modernization has arisen from a developmental model that assumes that a gerontocracy is the universal pattern of all preindustrial communities and that societal development erodes the structural determinants of gerontocracies.

In the final analysis, a theory is merely a constructed view of the world that is superimposed on a body of facts. A theory cannot be defined in terms of those facts but must appear at a higher level of abstraction, so that it is capable of subsuming the relevant empirical indicators under a variety of conditions. The model of aging and modernization does not satisfy the requirements of theory, since it is derived from a limited accumulation of facts. Further, the predicted causal relationships are not consistent with the theory, even in this one rather limited case study. It should be apparent that there is no "before" and "after" in age relations and no simple turning point in history. If sociologists and historians continue to address the issue of how social change affects the status of the aged, they must redefine status in more abstract terms and then analyze how change affects such factors as costs, contributions, and their ability to control resources.

The Economics of Age in the
Twentieth Century

Between 1901 and 1947, the numbers of persons in Britain who were aged 65 and over grew from less than 2 million to more than 5 million, yet after the passage of the Old Age Pension Act of 1908, there was a dearth of information focusing on the problems of the aged.[1] They had disappeared as a focus of public concern (Townsend and Wedderburn, 1965:10). During the 1940s, national attention again was directed to age-related issues,[2] and in 1941 the government set up a Committee of Inquiry chaired by Sir William Beveridge to examine the social security system. The outcome of the inquiry, the

[1] In 1925, a contributory pension scheme was introduced and the qualifying age was lowered from 70 to 65.

[2] In 1940 women became entitled to pensions at age 60 on the grounds that wives are usually younger than their husbands.

Beveridge Report, recommended that the elderly as well as other groups be covered by an insurance scheme and that an assistance board should be established to provide for those not covered. Contributions were to be compulsory and benefits universal and not means tested. The state's responsibility was to provide a minimum, while voluntary action by individuals to supplement this minimum was encouraged. Monetary benefits were only a part of what was termed a "comprehensive policy of social progress" that was to include the provision of better services in health, education, and housing.[3]

The Beveridge Report was accepted with one important exception. The concept of a national minimum standard of benefits that would have meant regular cost of living increases was rejected. Rather, benefits were to be fixed and reviewed at intervals. National insurance became compulsory for everyone of working age except married women, with pensions to be paid at retirement (65 for men and 60 for women).

In 1948, the National Assistance Act set up the National Assistance Board to aid those without resources, including those who were not insured or those whose insurance benefits were inadequate. Among its provisions was the termination of the existing poor law as a source of assistance for the needy (Tinker, 1981:42). After hundreds of years, the poor law finally ceased to exist.

Two years later, Seebohm Rowntree, the social scientist who had conducted the original survey of the causes of poverty in York in 1899, chaired a committee to evaluate the problems of aging. Among the main conclusions of the Rowntree committee were that acute poverty among the aged had been largely abolished, that state pensions were adequate, and that the National Assistance Board was reasonably successful in adjusting benefits to need in a reasonable manner (Tinker, 1981:44).

In 1966, the National Insurance Act changed the underlying premise of a basic minimum embodied in the original insurance con-

[3] A vast network of social and personal services for the aged was created, some under the jurisdiction of the National Health Service and others through independent local bodies. For detailed descriptions of services for the aged in Britain, see Tinker, 1981, and Hobman, 1981.

cept by introducing a graduated pension scheme. Higher pensions were to be paid to those who had put in higher contributions due to higher earnings.

Further alterations in the social security system were introduced in the 1970s. The National Insurance Act of 1970 provided cash benefits for people aged 80 and over who were too old to come into the National Insurance Scheme when it began in 1948. The Social Security Act of 1973 "provided for all employed people to be covered by a second, earnings related pension on top of the basic state provision [Tinker, 1981:43]." In 1975, the Social Security Pensions Act statutorily linked pensions to the rise in prices or earnings, whichever was greater, and finally in 1978 the former graduated pension scheme was replaced by one that protected the pension rights of those who were absent from work for reasons of child care or to look after the old or the sick (Tinker, 1981:43).

In 1968–1969, Peter Townsend conducted a national survey to "determine the extend of poverty in the United Kingdom and give some explanation for its existence [Townsend, 1979:17]." He came to some rather startling conclusions that contradicted the earlier findings of the Rowntree committee and that are reminiscent of some conditions that existed in the nineteenth century prior to any extensive state intervention in the welfare of the elderly.

Townsend (1979:285) discovered that 32% of all those classified as living in poverty were aged 65 or over and that as many as 51.6% of men and 59.7% of women aged 65 and over were living in households in poverty or on the margins of poverty. The figures are remarkably similar to those of Charles Booth nearly a century earlier despite the implementation of the massive bureaucratic income transfer programs that had occurred in the intervening years. Townsend (1979: 287) attributed the extent of old age poverty to the fact that economic deprivation is still associated with the life cycle and that economic growth benefited some age groups more than others. Old age poverty had been transferred from the individual to the state, with the state now maintaining large numbers of older people below the poverty level. Clearly the problem of poverty in old age has not been alleviated because the related problems of low levels of resources and restricted access to resources still exist.

Many of the older people in the Townsend survey were eligible to receive supplementary benefits, and yet like their nineteenth-century ancestors who hesitated to apply for relief, they, too, through pride, feelings of independence, or simply ignorance did not apply for supplementary benefits. For example, one elderly disabled couple (aged 81 and 70) believed that "poverty was people's own fault" and even though their income fell below the state poverty line were described as "too independent to apply for supplementary benefit [Townsend, 1979:329]."

Other nineteenth-century parallels can also be found in the Townsend report. In 1970, social class was still a major determinant of poverty in old age. Those who had higher salaries during their working years enjoyed more opportunities to save and acquire property as well as greater access to occupational pension schemes. Thus resource acquisition was tied to social class that in turn was associated with income levels in old age. For example, over 60% of those older people with present or prior occupations classified as skilled manual, semiskilled, or unskilled manual labor had net disposable household incomes below or on the margins of the poverty standard as opposed to only 41.7% of those in nonmanual occupations (Townsend, 1979:801). Although the incidence of poverty was highly correlated with class position, Townsend noted that even when class was held constant, more of the old than the young were in poverty. This he attributed to the fact that "the protective mechanisms and resources . . . are diminished in old age by the different processes of exclusion from employment, falling value of certain resources . . . in relation both to rising real incomes of the community at large and inflation, and lack of protection for women . . . [Townsend, 1979:802]." Thus, whatever their class origins the elderly share the social status of an "underclass."

Before World War II, the state financed old age pensions rather than retirement. Since the retirement rule came into operation as a condition for receipt of a pension, employment among the elderly has been considerably reduced. On reaching pensionable age, older people are faced with the choice of retiring or continuing to work without a pension. After retirement, the earnings rule reduces the incentive to engage in part-time work and encourages employers to offer low wages (Townsend, 1979:805). Those who continue to work experience poor working conditions. In the Townsend survey, "Many worked outside. Relatively more were subject to short notice. Two thirds of (older) men spend *all* their working time standing or walking about [1979:80]." These working conditions seem comparable in many ways to the degraded labor performed by older people in the nineteenth century—low wages, reduced amounts of relief for those who continue working, and undesirable jobs.

The general trend in research on older people has been to study them in isolation, independent of the economy, the polity, and the general structure of society. A central theme in the literature has been adjustment to old age or changing social roles in later life, the expectation being that adjustment should vary according to residence, gender, race, or some other exogenous factors. The one exception to the lack of attention to wider societal institutions has been the focus on the ways in which the growth of the state bureaucracy has contributed to the decline of the extended family. Yet there is no concrete research evidence that the extension of support to the aged through a bureaucratic structure is inherently harmful in its effects on family relationships and no reason to assume that intrafamilial economic support is inherently superior to intergenerational income transfer programs. The ability of the family to maintain its aged members is always dependent on its economic stability, and throughout English history, the family always turned to the state in times of trouble. What is apparent is that the problem of old age poverty has not been significantly alleviated by the implementation of social security pensions. The economic and social institutions created by industrial capitalism have remained largely untouched, and these are the sources of inequality. The problem of old age poverty will only be solved when opportunities for access to resources are reorganized.

References

Primary Sources

Census

1851 Census of England and Wales
1861 Census of England and Wales
1871 Census of England and Wales
1881 Census of England and Wales
1891 Census of England and Wales
1901 Census of England and Wales
1911 Census of England and Wales

Parliamentary Papers

1834 XXXVII Commission for Inquiring into the Poor Laws, Reports of Assistant Commissioners.
1839 XX Special Report of the Poor Law Commissioners on the Further Amendment of the Poor Law.

References

1895 XIV Royal Commission on the Aged Poor, Report.
1895 XIV Royal Commission on the Aged Poor, Minutes of Evidence.
1898 XLV Treasury Committee on Old Age Pensions, Report.
1909 XXXVII Royal Commission on the Poor Laws, Report.

Manuscript Sources

Cambridge Group for the History of Population and Social Structure

Census Papers, Population Returns for 1851 and 1901, Chilvers Coton, Enumerator's Schedules.

Cambridgeshire Record Office

Minute Book of the Board of Guardians, 1869-1889, Vol. 24-35. G/C/A.
Settlement Papers, 1894. G/C/A.S.10.
Union Letter Book, 1883. G/C/AC9.

Contemporary Newspaper and Periodical Literature

The Clarion, September, 1892.
Cambridge Independent Press, April, 1883.
Bristol Times and Mirror, May, 1896
The Times, London, September, 1907.

House of Commons

Letter to the Board of Guardians, Barnsley Union, October 26, 1852, No. 111 of 1852-53, p. 17.

Books and Articles

Achenbaum, W. Andrew
  1978   *Old Age in the New Land.* Baltimore: Johns Hopkins University Press.
Amoss, Pamela T., and Stevan Harrell
  1981   *Other Ways of Growing Old.* Stanford, Calif.: Stanford University Press.

References

Anderson, Michael
  1971 *Family Structure in Nineteenth Century Lancashire.* London: Cambridge University Press.
  1972 "Household structure and the Industrial Revolution: Mid-nineteenth century Preston in comparative perspective." Pp. 215–235 in Peter Laslett (ed.), *Household and Family in Past Time.* Cambridge: Cambridge University Press.
  1977 "The impact on the family relationships of the elderly of changes since Victorian times in governmental income-maintenance." Pp. 36–59 in Ethel Shanas and Marvin Sussman (eds.), *Family, Bureaucracy and the Elderly.* Durham, N.C.: Duke University Press.
Ashforth, David
  1976 "The urban poor law." Pp. 128–148 in Derek Fraser (ed.), *The New Poor Law in the Nineteenth Century.* London: Macmillan.
Beer, Max
  1953 *A History of British Socialism.* London: George Allen and Unwin.
  (1919)
Bell, Richard
  1903 "The reign of Labour." *National Review* 42: 188–197.
Bengston, Vern, James Dowd, David H. Smith, and Alex Inkeles
  1975 "Modernization, modernity and perceptions of aging: A cross-cultural study." *Journal of Gerontology* 30: 688–695.
Benson, John
  1980 *British Coalminers in the Nineteenth Century.* New York: Holmes and Meier.
Bentham, Jeremy
  1952 *Jeremy Bentham's Economic Writings,* ed. W. Stark. New York: Burt Franklin.
  1970 *An Introduction to the Principles of Morals and Legislation,.* ed. J. H. Burns and H. L. A. Hart. University of London: Athlone Press.
Berkner, Lutz
  1972 "The stem family and the developmental cycle of the peasant household: An eighteenth century Austrian example." *American Historical Review* 77: 398–418.
Blackley, W. L.
  1878 "National insurance: A cheap, practical and popular means of abolishing poor rates." *Nineteenth Century,* 4: 851–853.
  1881 "The effect of national insurance on sound Friendly Societies." *The Quarterly Magazine of the Independent Order of Odd Fellows* (July): 182–185.
Blaug, Mark
  1963 "The myth of the Old Poor Law and the making of the New." *Journal of Economic History* 23: 151–184.
  1964 "The poor law report reexamined." *Journal of Economic History* 24: 229–245.

References

Booth, Charles
  1891   "Enumeration and classification of paupers and state pensions for the aged." *Journal of the Statistical Society* 54: 600–643.
  1892   *Pauperism, a Picture and Endowment of Old Age, and Argument.* London: Macmillan.
  1894   *The Aged Poor in England and Wales.* London: Macmillan.
  1899   *Old Age Pensions and the Aged Poor.* London: Macmillan.
Bosanquet, Helen
  1902   *The Strength of the People.* New York: Macmillan.
Bowley, Arthur L.
  1937   *Wages and Income in the United Kingdom since 1860.* Cambridge: Cambridge University Press.
Braun, Rudolf
  1966   "The impact of cottage industry." Pp. 53–64 in David S. Landes (ed.), *The Rise of Capitalism.* New York: Macmillan.
Brennan, Michael, Philip Taft, and Mark Schupack.
  1967   *The Economics of Age.* New York: W. W. Norton.
Bruce, Maurice
  1966   *The Coming of the Welfare State.* New York: Schocken.
Brundage, Anthony
  1972   "The landed interest and the New Poor Law: A reappraisal of the revolution in government." *English Historical Review* 87: 27–48.
  1975   "The landed interest and the New Poor Law: A reply. *English Historical Review* 90: 347–351.
  1978   *The Making of the New Poor Law.* New Brunswick, N.J.: Rutgers University Press.
Burgess, Ernest
  1960   *Aging in Western Societies.* Chicago: University of Chicago Press.
  1962   *Social Welfare of the Aging.* New York: International Association of Gerontology.
Burns, John
  1893   *The Unemployed.* Fabian Tract No. 47. London: The Fabian Society.
Butler, Christina
  1919   *Domestic Service: An Inquiry by the Women's Industrial Council.* London: G. Bell and Sons.
Bythell, Duncan
  1969   *The Handloom Weavers.* Cambridge: Cambridge University Press.
Chambers, Jonathan D., and Gordon E. Mingay
  1966   *The Agricultural Revolution, 1750–1880.* London: B. T. Batsford.
Charity Organization Society
  1903   *The Case against Old Age Pension Schemes: A Collection of Short Papers.* London: Macmillan.

Checkland, S. G.
1964   *The Rise of Industrial Society in Britain, 1815–1885.* London: Longmans,
         Green.
Cherry, Ralph, and Scott Magnuson-Martin
1979   "Modernization and the staus of the aged in China: Decline or equaliza-
         tion?" *Sociological Quarterly* 22: 253–261.
Chudacoff, Howard, and Tamara Hareven
1978   "Family transitions into old age." Pp. 217–243 in Tamara Hareven
         (ed.), *Transitions, the Family and the Life Course in Historical Perspective.* New
         York: Academic Press.
1979   "From the empty nest to family dissolution: Life course transitions into
         old age." *Journal of Family History* 4: 69–83.
Clapham, John H.
1932   *An Economic History of Modern Britain.* Vols. 2, 3. Cambridge: Cambridge
         University Press.
Cohn, Richard M.
1980   "Economic development and the status of the aged." Paper presented to
         the American Sociological Association, New York, August.
Collins, Doreen
1965   "The introduction of old age pensions in Great Britain." *Historical Journal*
         8: 246–259.
Comte, Auguste
1958   *The Positive Philosophy,* trans. Harriet Martineau. New York: Calvin
         Blanchard.
Cowgill, Donald
1974a   "The aging of populations and societies." *Annals of the American Academy of
         Political and Social Science* 415: 1–18.
1974b   "Aging and modernization: A revision of the theory." Pp. 123–146 in J.
         Gubrium (ed.), *Late Life: Communities and Environmental Policy.* Spring-
         field, Ill.: Charles C. Thomas.
Cowgill, Donald, and Lowell D. Holmes
1972   *Aging and Modernization.* New York: Appleton-Century-Crofts.
Cuttle, George
1934   *The Legacy of the Rural Guardians.* Cambridge: W. Heffer & Sons.
Dawes, Frank
1973   *Not in Front of the Servants: Domestic Service in England, 1850–1939.* London:
         Wayland Publishers.
Deane, Phyllis
1965   *The First Industrial Revolution.* Cambridge: Cambridge University Press.
Deane, Phyllis, and W. A. Cole
1964   *British Economic Growth, 1688–1959.* Cambridge: Cambridge University
         Press.

References

Demos, John
  1970   *A Little Commonwealth: Family Life in Plymouth Colony*. New York: Oxford
          University Press.
  1978   "Old age in early New England." *American Journal of Sociology* 84:
          248-287.
Digby, Anne
  1976   "The rural poor law." Pp. 149-170 in Derek Fraser (ed.), *The New Poor
          Law in the Nineteenth Century*. London: Macmillan.
  1978   *Pauper Palaces*. London: Routledge and Kegan Paul.
Dobb, Maurice
  1926   *Capitalist Enterprise and Social Progress*. London: George Routledge and
          Sons.
Dowd, James J.
  1980   *Stratification among the Aged*. Monterey, Calif.: Brooks/Cole.
Drage, Geoffrey
  1895   *Old Age Pensions*. London: Liberty and Property Defence League.
Drake, Michael
  1969   *Population and Society in Norway, 1735-1865*. Cambridge: Cambridge
          University Press.
Dunkley, Peter
  1973   "The landed interest and the New Poor Law: A critical note." *English
          Historical Review* 88: 836-841.
Durkheim, Emile
  1964   *The Division of Labor in Society*. New York: Free Press.
  (1893)
Ede, W. More
  1891   "National pensions: One way out of darkest England." *Contemporary
          Review* (April): 580-596.
Eliot, George
  1858   *Scenes of Clerical Life*. Edinburgh: William Blackwood and Sons.
Evans, George Ewart
  1957   *Ask the Fellows Who Cut the Hay*. London: Faber and Faber.
Fischer, David Hackett
  1978   *Growing Old in America*. New York: Oxford University Press.
Foner, Anne, and David Kertzer
  1978   "Age stratification and the changing family." *American Journal of Sociology*
          84: 340-365.
Fraser, Derek
  1973   *The Evolution of the British Welfare State*. London: Macmillan.
  1976   *The New Poor Law in the Nineteenth Century*. London: Macmillan.
Friedmann, Eugene A., and Harold Orbach.
  1974   "Adjustment to retirement." Pp. 609-645 in Silvano Arieti (ed.),
          American Handbook of Psychiatry. Vol. 1. New York: Basic Books.

References

Gaunt, David
  1979   "The retired farmer: His property and his family relations since the Middle Ages: Northern and Central Europe." Paper presented to the Cambridge Group for the History of Population and Social Structure.
Gilbert, Bentley B.
  1964-   "The decay of nineteenth-century provident institutions and the coming
  1965   of old age pensions in Great Britain." *Economic History Review* 17: 551-563.
  1966   *The Evolution of National Insurance in Great Britain: The Origins of the Welfare State.* London: Michael Joseph.
Grant, Margaret
  1939   *Old Age Security, Social and Financial Trends.* Washington, D.C.: Social Science Research Council.
Greenwood, M.
  1936   "English death rates, past, present and future." *Journal of the Royal Statistical Society* 99: 674-707.
Greven, Philip J.
  1970   *Four Generations: Population, Land, and Family in Colonial Andover, Massachusetts.* Ithaca, N.Y.: Cornell University Press.
Gusfield, Joseph.
  1967   "Tradition and modernity: Misplaced polarities in the study of social change." *American Journal of Sociology* 72: 351-362.
Gutchen, Robert M.
  1961   "Local improvements and centralization in nineteenth century England." *Historical Journal* 4: 85-96.
Gutteridge, Joseph
  1969   *The Autobiography of Joseph Gutteridge.* London: Evelyn, Adams and Mackay.
Haines, Michael R.
  1977   "Fertility, nuptiality, and occupation: A study of coal mining populations and regions in England and Wales in the mid-nineteenth century." *Journal of Interdisciplinary History* 8: 245-280.
Hall, P. G.
  1962   "The East London footwear industry, an industrial quarter in decline." *East London Papers* 5 (April): 3-21.
Halper, Thomas
  1978   "Paternalism and the elderly." Pp. 321-339 in Stuart F. Spicker, Kathleen M. Woodward, and David D. Van Tassel (eds.), *Aging and the Elderly; Humanistic Perspectives in Gerontology.* Atlantic Highlands, N.J.: Humanities Press.
Hamilton, Lord George
  1910-   "A statistical survey of the problems of pauperism." *Journal of the Statisti-
  1911   cal Society* 74 (December): 1-34.

References

Hasbach, W.
 1908   *A History of the English Agricultural Laborer.* London: P. S. King and Son.
Hauser, Philip M.
 1965   "Observations on the urban-folk and urban-rural dichotomies as forms
         of Western ethnocentrism." Pp. 503-518 in Philip M. Hauser and Leo
         Schnore (eds.), *The Study of Urbanization.* New York: Wiley.
Hay, J. R.
 1975   *The Origins of the Liberal Welfare Reforms, 1906-1914.* London: Macmillan.
 1978   *The Development of the British Welfare State, 1880-1975.* London: Edward
         Arnold.
Heath, Richard
 1893   *The English Peasant.* London.
Hewitt, Margaret
 1958   *Wives and Mothers in Victorian Industry.* Westport, Conn.: Greenwood
         Press.
Hobman, David
 1981   *The Impact of Aging, Strategies for Care.* New York: St. Martin's Press.
Hobsbawm, E. J.
 1964   *Laboring Men.* London: Weidenfeld and Nicolson.
 1968   *Industry and Empire.* London: Weidenfeld and Nicolson.
Homans, George C.
 1940   *English Villagers of the Thirteenth Century.* Cambridge, Mass.: Harvard
         University Press.
Horn, Pamela
 1975   *The Rise and Fall of the Victorian Servant.* New York: St. Martin's Press.
Howell, Cicely
 1976   "Peasant inheritance customs in the Midlands, 1280-1700." Pp.
         112-155 in Jack Goody, Joan Thirsk, and E. P. Thompson (eds.), *Family
         and Inheritance.* Cambridge: Cambridge University Press.
Hughes, Jonathan R. T.
 1960   *Fluctuations in Trade, Industry and Finance.* Oxford: Clarendon Press.
Jones, E. L.
 1964   "The agricultural labor market in England, 1793-1822." *Economic
         History Review* 17: 322-338.
Keyfitz, Nathan, and Wilhelm Flieger
 1968   *World Population: An Analysis of Vital Data.* Chicago: University of Chicago
         Press.
Khaldun, Ibn
 1967   *The Muqaddimah: An Introduction to History,* trans. Franz Rosenthal and ed.
         N. J. Dawood. Princeton, N.J.: Princeton University Press.
Kitteringham, Jennie
 1975   "Country work girls in nineteenth century England." Pp. 75-138 in
         Raphael Samuel (ed.), *Village Life and Labor.* London: Routledge and
         Kegan Paul.

References

Knodel, John, and Etienne van de Walle
  1979 "Lessons from the past: Policy implications of historical fertility studies." *Population Development Review* 5 (June): 217–246.
Kreps, Juanita M.
  1977 "Intergenerational transfers and the bureaucracy." Pp. 21–35 in Ethel Shanas and Marvin Sussman (eds.) *Family, Bureaucracy and the Elderly.* Durham, N.C.: Duke University Press.
Laslett, Peter
  1976 "Societal development and aging." Pp. 87–116 in Robert Binstock and Ethel Shanas (eds.), *Handbook of Aging and the Social Sciences.* New York: Van Nostrand Reinhold.
Leggett, William F.
  1949 *The Story of Silk.* New York: J. J. Little.
Levine, David
  1977 *Family Formation in an Age of Nascent Capitalism.* New York: Academic Press.
Litchfield, R. Burr
  1978 "The family and the mill: Cotton mill work, family work patterns, and fertility in mid-Victorian Stockport." Pp. 180–196 in Anthony S. Wohl (ed.), *The Victorian Family.* London: Croon Helm.
Loch, Charles S.
  1910 *Charity and Social Life.* London: Macmillan.
Lockwood, David
  1964 "Social integration and social change." In George K. Zollschan and Walter Hirsch (eds.), *Explorations in Social Change.* London: Routledge and Kegan Paul.
Lubenow, William C.
  1971 *The Politics of Government Growth, Early Victorian Attitudes toward State Intervention, 1833–1848.* Newton Abbot: David and Charles.
Lyons, John S.
  1979 "Family response to economic decline: English cotton handloom weavers in the nineteenth century." Paper presented to the Conference of Europeanists, Washington, D.C., March.
McBride, Theresa M.
  1976 *The Domestic Revolution: the Modernisation of Household Service in England and France, 1820–1920.* New York: Holmes and Meier.
MacDonagh, Oliver
  1958 "The nineteenth century revolution in government: A reappraisal." *Historical Journal* 1: 52–67.
Macfarlane, Alan
  1978 *The Origins of English Individualism.* Oxford: Basil Blackwell.
McGregor, Oliver R.
  1957 "Social research and social policy in the nineteenth century." *British Journal of Sociology* 8 (June): 146–157.

References

Mackay, Thomas
  1899   *A History of the English Poor Law.* London: P. S. King and Son.
McKeown, J., and R. C. Record
  1962   "Reasons for the decline of mortality in England and Wales during the nineteenth century." *Population Studies* 16 (November): 94–122.
March, Lucien
  1912   "Some researches concerning the factors of mortality." *Journal of the Statistical Society* 75: 505–538.
Martin, Ernest W.
  1972   "From parish to union: Poor law administration, 1601–1865." Pp. 25–56 in Ernest W. Martin (ed.), *Comparative Development in Social Welfare.* London: George Allen and Unwin.
Marvel, Howard P.
  1977   "Factory regulation: A reinterpretation of early English experience." *Journal of Law and Economics* 20: 379–402.
Mayhew, Henry
  1861   *London Labor and the London Poor.* London: Dover.
Meacham, Standish
  1977   *A Life Apart: The English Working Class, 1890–1914.* London: Thames and Hudson.
Mencher, Samuel
  1967   *Poor Law to Poverty Program.* Pittsburgh: University of Pittsburgh Press.
Metcalfe, John
  1899   *The Case for Universal Old Age Pensions.* London: Simpkin, Marshall, Hamilton, Kent and Co.
Midwinter, Eric C.
  1972   "Victorian social provision: Central and local administration." Pp. 191–219 in E. W. Martin (ed.), *Comparative Development in Social Welfare.* London: George Allen and Unwin.
Mill, John Stuart
  1902   *Principles of Political Economy.* New York: D. Appleton.
  (1884)
Mingay, Gordon E.
  1979   *Rural Life in Victorian England.* London: Futura.
Mishra, Ramesh
  1977   *Society and Social Welfare: Theoretical Perspectives on Welfare.* London: Macmillan.
Mitchison, Rosalind
  1977   *British Population Change since 1860.* London: Macmillan.
Morgan, David H.
  1975   "The place of harvesters in nineteenth century village life." Pp. 29–72 in Raphael Samuel (ed.), *Village Life and Labor.* London: Routledge and Kegan Paul.

References

Morris, R. J.
1979   "The middle class and the property cycle during the Industrial Revolution." In T. Christopher Smout (ed.), *The Search for Wealth and Stability: Essays in Economic and Social History Presented to M. W. Flinn.* London: Macmillan.

Morrison, G. B.
1911   "Age and unemployment." *Journal of the Statistical Society* (July): 863–868.

Mowat, Charles Loch
1961   *The Charity Organization Society, 1869–1913.* London: Methuen.

Munnichs, Joep M. A.
1977   "Linkages of old people with their families and bureaucracy in a welfare state: The Netherlands." Pp. 92–116 in Ethel Shanas and Marvin Sussman (eds.), *Family Bureaucracy and the Elderly.* Durham, N. C.: Duke University Press.

Nef, John
1954   "The progress of technology and the growth of large scale industry in Great Britain, 1540-1640." Pp. 88-107 in Eleanora M. Carus-Wilson (ed.), *Essays in Economic History.* London: E. Arnold.

Newby, Howard
1977   *The Deferential Worker.* New York: Penguin.

Nisbet, Robert A.
1969   *Social Change and History: Aspects of the Western Theory of Development.* New York: Oxford University Press.

Oxley, Geoffrey
1974   *Poor Relief in England and Wales, 1601-1834.* London: David and Charles.

Page, William (ed.)
1908   *The Victoria History of the Counties of England: Warwickshire.* Vol. 2. London: Dawsons.

Paillat, Paul
1977   "Bureaucratization of old age: Determinants of the process. Possible safeguards and reorientation." Pp. 60-74 in Ethel Shanas and Marvin B. Sussman (eds.), *Family, Bureaucracy and the Elderly.* Durham, N.C.: Duke University Press.

Palmore, Erdman
1975   *The Honorable Elders: A Cross-Cultural Analysis of Aging in Japan.* Durham, N.C.: Duke University Press.

Palmore, Erdman B., and Kenneth Manton
1974   "Modernization and the status of the aged: International correlations." *Journal of Gerontology* 29: 205-210.

Parris, Henry
1960   "The nineteenth-century revolution in government: A reappraisal reappraised." *Historical Journal* 3: 17-37.

References

Parsons, Talcott
  1960   *Structure and Process in Modern Societies.* Chicago: Free Press.
  1964   "Evolutionary universals." *American Sociological Review* 29: 339–357.
  1966   *Societies: Evolutionary and Comparative Perspectives.* Englewood Cliffs, N.J.:
         Prentice-Hall.
Parsons, Talcott, and Neil J. Smelser
  1956   *Economy and Society.* London: Routledge and Kegan Paul.
Perkin, Harold
  1969   *The Origins of Modern English Society.* London: Routledge and Kegan Paul.
Perry, J. J.
  1977   *British Farming in the Great Depression.* Newton Abbot: David and Charles.
Pinchbeck, Ivy
  1930   *Women Workers and the Industrial Revolution, 1750–1850.* London: George
         Routledge and Sons.
Pollard, Sidney
  1959   *A History of Labor in Sheffield.* Liverpool: Liverpool University Press.
Prest, John
  1960   *The Industrial Revolution in Coventry.* London: Oxford University Press.
Prothero, Rowland E.
  1912   *English Farming, Past and Present.* London: Longmans, Green.
Rheinstein, Max
  1965   "Motivation of intergenerational behavior by norms of law." Pp.
         241–266 in Ethel Shanas & Gordon Streib (eds.), *Social Structure and the
         Family.* Englewood Cliffs, N.J.: Prentice-Hall.
Ricardo, David
  1908   *Principles of Political Economy and Taxation,* ed. E. K. Gonner. London: G.
         Bell.
Roberts, David
  1959   "Jeremy Bentham and the Victorian administrative state." *Victorian
         Studies* 2: 193–210.
Rose, Michael E.
  1971   *The English Poor Law, 1780–1930.* Newton Abbot: David and Charles.
  1972   *The Relief of Poverty, 1834–1914.* London: Macmillan.
  1976   "Settlement, removal and the New Poor Law." Pp. 25–44 in Derek
         Fraser (ed.), *The New Poor Law in the Nineteenth Century.* London: Mac-
         millan.
Rostow, W. W.
  1960   *The Stages of Economic Growth.* Cambridge: Cambridge University Press.
Rothstein, Theodore
  1929   *From Chartism to Laborism: Historical Sketches of the English Working Class
         Movement.* New York: International Publishers.
Rowntree, B. S.
  1901   *Poverty: A Study of Town Life.* New York: Howard Fertig.

References

Sabean, David
  1976   "Aspects of kinship behavior and property in rural western Europe before 1800." Pp. 96–111 in Jack Goody, Joan Thirsk, and E. P. Thompson (eds.), *Family and Inheritance.* . Cambridge: Cambridge University Press.

Salzman, Louis F. (ed.)
  1947   *The Victoria History of the Counties of England: Warwick,* Vol. 4. London: Oxford University Press.

Samuel, Raphael
  1975   "Village labor." Pp. 3–26 in Raphael Samuel (ed.), *Village Life and Labor.* London: Routledge and Kegan Paul.

Saul, S. B.
  1969   *The Myth of the Great Depression.* London: Macmillan Press.

Saville, John
  1957   *Rural Depopulation in England and Wales, 1851–1951.* London: Routledge and Kegan Paul.
  1960   "Trade unions and free labor: The background to the Taff Vale decision." Pp. 317–350 in Asa Briggs and John Saville (eds.), *Essays in Labor History.* London: Macmillan.
  1973   *Working Conditions in the Victorian Age.* Westmead, England: Gregg International Publishers.

Sellars, Edith
  1908   "Old age pensions and the 'belongingless' poor: A workhouse census." *Contemporary Review* 93: 147–157.

Shanas, Ethel
  1962   *The Health of Older People: A Social Survey.* Cambridge, Mass.: Harvard University Press.

Shanas, Ethel, Peter Townsend, Dorothy Wedderburn, Henning Friis, Poul Milhoj, and Jan Stehouwer
  1968   *Old People in Three Industrial Societies.* London: Routledge and Kegan Paul.

Shorter, Edward
  1975   *The Making of the Modern Family.* New York: Basic Books.

Sires, R. V.
  1954   "The beginning of british legislation for old age pensions." *Journal of Economic History* 14: 229–253.

Smelser, Neil
  1959   *Social Change in the Industrial Revolution.* Chicago: University of Chicago Press.
  1964   "Toward a theory of modernization." Pp. 258–274 in Amitai Etzioni and Eva Etzioni (eds.), *Social Change.* New York: Basic Books.

Smith, Adam
  1937   *An Inquiry into the Nature and Causes of the Wealth of Nations.* New York:
  (1776) Modern Library.

References

Smith, Anthony D.
  1973   *The Concept of Social Change: A Critique of the Functionalist Theory of Social Change.* London: Routledge and Kegan Paul.
Smith, Daniel Scott
  1979   "Historical change in the household structure of the elderly." Workshop on the Elderly of the Future, Committee on Aging, National Research Council. Annapolis, Maryland.
Sorley, William R.
  1973   *A History of British Philosophy to 1900.* Westport, Conn.: Greenwood Press.
Sorokin, Pitirim
  1957   *Social and Cultural Dynamics.* Boston: Porter Sargent.
Sorokin, Pitirim, and Carle Zimmerman
  1929   *Principles of Rural-Urban Sociology.* New York: Henry Bolt.
Spencer, Herbert
  1969   *Principles of Sociology,* ed. Stanislav Andreski. London: Macmillan.
Special Commissioner of the Daily News
  1891   *Life in Our Villages.* London: Cassell.
Stannard, David E.
  1978   "Growing up and growing old: Dilemmas of aging in bureaucratic America." Pp. 9-20 in Stuart F. Spicker, Kathleen M. Woodward, and David D. Van Tassel (eds.), *Aging and the Elderly: Humanistic Perspectives in Gerontology.* Atlantic Highlands, N.J.: Humanities Press.
Stead, Francis Herbert
  1909   *How Old Age Pensions Began to Be.* London: Methuen.
Stearns, Peter
  1977   *Old Age in European Society.* London: Croom Helm.
Stedman Jones, Gareth
  1971   *Outcast London: A Study in the Relationship between Classes in Victorian Society.* Oxford: Clarendon Press.
Stinchcombe, Arthur L.
  1978   *Theoretical Methods in Social History.* New York: Academic Press.
Streib, Gordon, and Wayne Thompson
  1960   "The older person in a family context." Pp. 447-475 in Clark Tibbetts (ed.), *Handbook of Social Gerontology.*. Chicago: University of Chicago Press.
Sussman, Herbert L.
  1968   *Victorians and the Machine.* Cambridge, Mass.: Harvard University Press.
Taylor, Arthur J.
  1968   "The coal industry." Pp. 37-70 in Derek H. Aldcroft (ed.), *The Development of British Industry and Competition, 1875-1914.* Toronto: University of Toronto Press.
  1972   *Laissez-Faire and State Intervention in Nineteenth Century Britain.* London: Macmillan.

References

Thomas, Keith
1976   "Age and authority in early modern England." *Proceedings of the British Academy,* 62: 205-248.
Thompson, E. P.
1955   *William Morris, Romantic to Revolutionary.* London: Lawrence and Wishart.
1965   *The Making of the English Working Class.* London: Victor Gollancz.
Thomson, David
1950   *England in the Nineteenth Century.* Middlesex, England: Penguin.
Tilly, Charles
1981a   "Protoindustrialization, deindustrialization, and just plain industrialization in European capitalism." Center for Research on Social Organization Working Paper No. 235. University of Michigan: Ann Arbor, Michigan.
1981b   "Britain creates the social movement." Center for Research on Social Organization Working Paper No. 232. University of Michigan: Ann Arbor, Michigan.
Tilly, Louise, and Joan Scott
1978   *Women, Work and Family.* New York: Holt, Rinehart and Winston.
Tinker, Anthea
1981   *The Elderly in Modern Society.* New York: Longman.
Tonnies, Ferdinand
1957   *Gemeinschaft und Gesellschaft.* New York: Harper.
Townsend, Peter
1957   *The Family Life of Old People.* London: Routledge and Kegan Paul.
1979   *Poverty in the United Kingdom.* Berkeley: University of California Press.
Townsend, Peter and Dorothy Wedderburn
1965   *The Aged in the Welfare State.* London: G. Bell and Sons.
Toynbee, Arnold
1957   *A Study of History.* Vols. 6-10, ed. D. C. Somerwell. New York: Oxford University Press.
Treble, James H.
1970   "The attitudes of Friendly Societies toward the movement in Great Britain for state pensions, 1878-1908." *International Review of Social History* 15: 266-299.
Treveylan, George M.
1956   *British History in the Nineteenth Century and After (1782-1919).* London: Longmans, Green.
Turner, George
1897   *The Case for State Pensions in Old Age.* Fabian Tract No. 73. London: The Fabian Society.
Uhlenberg, Peter
1978   "Changing configurations of the life course." Pp. 65-98 in Tamara Hareven (ed.), *Transitions, the Family and the Life Course in Historical Perspective.* New York: Academic Press.

References

Veblen, Thorstein
  1953   *The Theory of the Leisure Class.* New York: Mentor Books.
  (1899)
Wall, Richard
  1977   ''The responsibilities of kin.'' *Local Population Studies* 19 (Autumn): 58–60.
Warner, Frank
  1921   *The Silk Industry of the United Kingdom—Its Origin and Development.* London: Drane's.
Webb, Sidney
  1907   *Paupers and Old Age Pensions.* Fabian Tract No. 135. London: The Fabian Society.
Webb, Sidney, and Beatrice Webb
  1909   *The Break-Up of the Poor Law: Being Part One of the Minority Report of the Poor Law Commission.* London: Longmans, Green and Co.
  1910   *English Poor Law Policy.* London: Longmans, Green.
Weber, A. F.
  1967   *The Growth of Cities in the Nineteenth Century.* Ithaca, N.Y.: Cornell University Press.
Weber, Max
  1968   *Economy and Society.* New York: Bedminster Press.
Williams, Alfred
  1915   *Life in a Railway Factory.* London: Duckworth.
Williams, Raymond
  1973   *The Country and the City.* London: Chatto and Windus.
Wilson, Arnold, and G. S. Mackay
  1941   *Old Age Pensions: An Historical and Critical Study.* London: Oxford University Press.
Wrigley, E. A.
  1969   *Population and History.* New York: McGraw Hill.
  1977   ''Reflections on the history of the family.'' *Daedalus* 106 (Spring): 71–85.

Index

Index

Beveridge Report, 207
Blackley, William, 110, 173, 177–178
Boer War, 184
Booth, Charles, 58, 92–93, 106, 111,
    113, 123, 171, 173, 175, 178–179,
    181–182
British Socialist Party, 51
Burgess, Ernest, 4, 61

C

Chamberlain, Joseph, 179
Charity Organization Society, 174–175,
    180, 187
Chartism, 49
Chudacoff, Howard, 17, 21
Circular on Outdoor Relief
    implementation of, 125–136
    provisions of, 101, 121, 123, 124, 136
Coal miners, 71, 81, 82, 84, 87, 88
Coal Mining
    in Chilvers Coton, 65–66, 69, 75–76,
    83
    expansion of, 42
Cohn, Richard, 6
Combination Acts, 46
Committee on Old Age Pensions, 181
Comte, Auguste, 191
Corn Law, 47, 54
Cottage industry, see Domestic
    production
Cowgill, Donald, 4–5, 8

D

Demos, John, 21
Denaby Main, 51
Domestic production
    continuation of, 40–42
    decline of, 38–40, 61–62, 64, 77
    functioning of, 62, 70–71
    transition from factory to, 27
Domestic service, 77, 145–148
Dowd, James, 6, 205
Durkheim, Emile, 2–3, 193

E

Eliot, George, 65
Elizabethan Poor Law, see Poor law
Empty nest, 81, 83
Engels, Friedrich, 192
Equality Index, 6

F

Fabian Society, 59, 113
Factory Act, of 1833, 55
Factory production, 38–39, 41, 44, 196
Family
    breakdown, 18–20, 61, 122, 137
    impact of industrialization on, 4, 13,
    63–64, 196–197
    living arrangements of, 80–89,
    196–197
    patterns of work in, 62–63, 64
    wage economy, 62–63, 83–88
Fertility
    decline in, 31–32
    social class differentials in, 31
Fischer, David Hackett, 9–10, 173
Friendly Societies
    attitudes toward pension, 177–179,
    181–182, 184, 187, 190
    history of, 176–177

G

Gaunt, David, 14, 63
Gilbert's Act, 96
Gladstone, W. E., 176–177
Government Annuities Bill, 177
Grandparents, 64, 84–85, 87, 88, 89
Green, T. H., 57

H

Hareven, Tamara, 17, 21
Harrell, Stevan, 8, 205
Holmes, Lowell, 4, 8
Household composition
    impact of life expectancy on, 13, 81
    patterns of, 13–14, 15, 64, 77–80,
    84–88, 196–197

Index

Household production, *see* Domestic production

I

Industrialization
  decline in growth, 44–45
  expansion of, 36–38
  growth of heavy industry, 42–44
  impact on aged, 4, 10, 20, 24, 197
  impact on family, 4, 13, 63–64, 89
  impact on household composition, 16–17
  impact on retirement, 154–162
Industrial Revolution, *see* Industrialization
Inkeles, Alex, 6
Institutionalization, of aged, 18, 99, 103, 107–110, 129–132
International Labor Congress, 90, 182

K

Khaldun, Ibn, 191

L

Labor
  aristocracy, 49, 50
  casual, 155
  unions, 49–51, 103, 140–141, 157, 173, 176, 181–188
  unskilled, 43, 50
  wage, 37, 157
Labour party, 52, 103, 113, 182, 185
Labour Representation Committee, 51–52, 182, 185
Laissez faire, 53–58, 97, 201
Laslett, Peter, 8, 13, 24
Liberal party, 51, 174, 185, 187, 190
Liberty and Property Defence League, 174–175, 187
Life cycle
  impact of demographic change on, 17
  patterns of work over, 21–22, 63, 143–148
  of poverty, 112–113, 209

Life expectancy
  aged, 83
  improvements in, 4, 17
Local Government Board, 57, 101, 111, 112, 124, 126, 127, 130, 174, 187, 198

M

Manton, Kenneth, 5–6, 20
Marriage, age at, 82
Marshall, Alfred, 58
Marx, Karl, 192
Mercantilism, 52
Mill, John Stuart, 57
Modernization
  criticism of, 7–8, 9, 22–23, 195–206
  theory of, 3–7, 195–197
Mortality
  decline of, 17, 28–30, 83
  medical contribution to, 29
  by occupation, 30
  variation by social class, 29–30
Municipal Corporations Act, of 1835, 48

N

National Assistance Act, 207
National Assistance Board, 207
National Committee of Organized Labor on Old Age Pensions, 182, 184, 188
National Insurance Act, of 1966, 207
National Insurance Act, of 1970, 208

O

Occupation(s)
  changes in, 75–76, 139–143
  for men, 71, 77–79, 139–143, 155–158, 164–167, 200, 204
  for women, 21–22, 63, 70–74, 77, 143–148, 158–162, 200, 204
Old Age Pensions Act
  impact of, 19, 124, 138, 206
  impact of labor on, 175
  passage of, 138, 173
  provisions of, 113, 115

Index

Older men
  family relationships of, 14–15, 16–17,
    64, 80–81, 84–88, 104–105, 107,
    134–135
  work for, 71, 77–79, 139–143,
    155–158, 164–167, 200, 204
Older women
  family relations of, 14, 16–17, 64,
    80–81, 84–88, 104, 107, 117,
    128–130, 132, 134–136
  work for, 63, 71–73, 143–148,
    158–162, 200, 204

P

Palmore, Erdman, 5–6, 20
Parish Councils Act, 121
Parliamentary Reform Movement, 47
Parsons, Talcott, 192–193
Pauperism
  among aged, 91–93, 99–100, 101–111,
    117–118, 122–123, 128–132
  causes of, 180
  history of, 94–98
  relationship to unemployment,
    149–150
Pension
  Booth's plan, 182
  history of, 110–115, 137, 173–188
  impact of labor on, 173–174, 181–186
  opposition to, 174–175, 180–181
  as patronage, 46, 176
  proponents of, 173–174, 181–186
  provisions of, 113–114, 188
  reasons for, 170, 199, 200
  relationship to poor law, 115, 137,
    176, 179, 190
Political power
  distribution of, 45–52
  in pension struggle, 173–188
  centralization of, 115, 118–121,
    132–133, 137
  history of, 94–103, 118–121
  policy toward aged, 19, 99–100,
    101–102, 103–110, 111–112,
    117–118, 122–124, 128–132, 137
  relief under, 93, 103–110
Poor Law Board, 100, 101, 121, 198
Poor Law Commission, 100, 119, 110

Poverty, *see also* Pauperism
  causes of, 112–114, 207
  in old age, 10, 91–92, 101–102, 115,
    117, 123, 208–209, 210
  rates of, 93, 115
Power loom, 39, 70, 157
Public Health Act, 56

R

Reform Bill, of 1832, 48, 49, 55
Retirement
  causes of, 4–5, 10, 20–22, 154–166,
    167–168, 199, 209
  contracts, 14–15, 63
  middle class, 151
  rates of, 151, 159–161
  recognition of, 151
  relationship to unemployment, 150,
    167
Ribbon weavers
  employment of, 69
  household composition of, 77–88,
    196–197
  out-migration of, 76
  history of, 65–68
Rogers, Fredrick, 182–183
Rowntree, Seebohm, 112–113, 175, 178,
    207, 208
Royal Commission on the Aged Poor
  formation of, 103
  recommendations of, 111, 123–124,
    179
  testimony from, 104–110, 122,
    133–136, 140, 180
Royal Commission on Friendly Societies,
  177
Royal Commission on the Poor Laws,
  124

S

Scott, Joan, 62–63, 82–83
Select Committee on the Aged
  Deserving Poor, 111
Settlement movement, 174
Smelser, Neil, 193–194
Smith, Adam, 2, 53